REPUTATIONS

THOMAS MORE

John Guy

Professor of Modern History,
University of St Andrews

A member of the Hodder Headline Group
LONDON
Co-published in the United States of America by
Oxford University Press Inc., New York

First published in Great Britain in 2000 by
Arnold, a member of the Hodder Headline Group,
338 Euston Road, London NW1 3BH

http://www.arnoldpublishers.com

Co-published in the United States of America by
Oxford University Press Inc.,
198 Madison Avenue, New York, NY10016

British Library Cataloguing in Publication Data
A catalogue record for this book is available from the British Library

Library of Congress Cataloging-in-Publication Data
A catalog record for this book is available from the Library of Congress

ISBN 0 340 73138 9 (hb)
ISBN 0 340 73139 7 (pb)

1 2 3 4 5 6 7 8 9 10

Production Editor: Julie Delf
Production Controller: Fiona Byrne
Cover Design: Terry Griffiths

Typeset in 10 on 12 pt Sabon by Phoenix Photosetting, Chatham, Kent
Printed and bound in Great Britain by MPG Books, Bodmin, Cornwall

What do you think about this book? Or any other Arnold title?
Please send your comments to feedback.arnold@hodder.co.uk

Contents

General editorial preface

Hero or villain? Charlatan or true prophet? Sinner or saint? The volumes in the Reputations series examine the reputations of some of history's most conspicuous, powerful and influential individuals, considering a range of representations, some of striking incompatibility. The aim is not merely to demonstrate that history is indeed, in Pieter Geyl's phrase, 'argument without end' but that the study even of contradictory conceptions can be fruitful: that the jettisoning of one thesis or presentation leaves behind something of value.

In Iago's self-serving denunciation of it, reputation is 'an idle and most false imposition; oft got without merit, and lost without deserving', but a more generous definition would allow its use as one of the principal currencies of historical understanding. In seeking to analyse the cultivation, creation, and deconstruction of reputation we can understand better the well-springs of action, the workings out of competing claims to power, the different purposes of rival ideologies – in short, see more clearly ways in which the past becomes History.

There is a commitment in each volume to showing how understanding of an individual develops (sometimes in uneven and divergent ways), whether in response to fresh evidence, the emergence or waning of dominant ideologies, changing attitudes and preoccupations of the age in which an author writes, or the creation of new historical paradigms. Will Hitler ever seem *quite* the same after the evidence of a recent study revealing the extent of his Jewish connections during the Vienna years? Reassessment of Lenin and Stalin has been given fresh impetus by the collapse of the Soviet Union and the opening of many of its archives; and the end of the Cold War and of its attendant assumptions must alter our views of Eisenhower and Kennedy. How will our

perceptions of Elizabeth I change in the presence of a new aware-
ness of 'gendered history'?

There is more to the series than illumination of ways in which
recent discoveries or trends have refashioned identities or given
actions new meaning – though that is an important part. The
corresponding aim is to provide readers with a strong sense of the
channels and course of debate from the outset: not a Cook's Tour
of the historiography, but identification of the key interpretative
issues and guidance as to how commentators of different eras
and persuasions have tackled them.

Preface

'A man for all seasons'? Thomas More is certainly a man for all purposes. Canonized as a saint of the Roman Catholic Church by Pope Pius XI in May 1935, he is also a hero of the former Soviet Union, where an obelisk was sculptured on Lenin's orders after the Revolution and unveiled in Moscow's Alexandrovsky Gardens. Inscribed on it are some 18 names, including those of Marx, Engels and (in Cyrillic script) 'T. More'. When the 500th anniversary of More's birth was celebrated in 1978, *The Times* leader announced, 'If the English people were to be set a test to justify their history and civilization by the example of one man, then it is Sir Thomas More whom they would perhaps choose'. Most spectacularly, More played the role of moral paragon at the outset of the impeachment trial of President Clinton on 14 January 1999.

Is there an historical Thomas More? Which of the many characterizations that have attached to his name, some blatantly incompatible, are upheld by the sources? When I began this book, I thought it would be fairly straightforward to separate 'fact' from 'fiction'. I was entirely wrong! Reassessing More presents an extraordinary challenge. In the first place, he is not, and will never be, primarily an historical figure. His role as an alleged 'persecutor' of the Protestant reformers and of those who distributed William Tyndale's translation of the *New Testament* is especially difficult to judge (see Chapter 6). So emotive is the subject of Thomas More, I soon realized that his iconic status obscures, rather than illuminates, his historical significance.

By far the severest challenge faced by those who have attempted to write the biography of Thomas More is posed by the huge gaps in the sources. We know relatively little about him before he entered Henry VIII's service and was sworn as a King's councillor at the age of 40. As a councillor, King's Secretary, Chancellor of the Duchy of Lancaster and (finally) Lord Chancellor, his name regularly appears in the official archives. Yet even then, it is his 'public' and not his 'private' life that is represented in these documents. Scholars have to rely on the legacy of the sixteenth-century biographers, notably William Roper, Nicholas Harpsfield and Thomas Stapleton, for so many of the missing 'facts'. These 'facts' are then cited indiscriminately, even though the earliest 'Lives' sometimes report 'facts' that are demonstrably incorrect or mutually incompatible. Other 'facts' are uncorroborated: they represent the recollections of former members of More's household or the 'stories' circulating among the recusant community in England and the Netherlands in the 1560s.

In such circumstances, modern biographers have usually opted out. They have either privileged one set of disputed 'facts' over their alternatives for fear of contradicting a shibboleth, or else they have preferred one particular version of the 'story' because it suits their own purposes. The result is that conjectures masquerading as 'facts' are asserted or recycled concerning More's education, his relationship with his father, his alleged monastic or priestly 'vocation', his sexual proclivities and attitude to women, his supposed 'loathing' of politics and Court life, his alleged inactivity in his 'retirement' after his resignation as Lord Chancellor, and the reputed domestic idyll of his household at Chelsea. Interpretations are constructed (or attacked) on the basis of a pinhead by iconoclastic 'revisionists' just as much as by their hagiographical or 'mainstream' predecessors. No one has yet been willing to confront the unwelcome 'truth' that the earliest 'Lives' were selective and subjective. They were informed by religious typologies. They were scarcely attempting to deal in what today would be called 'facts'. Most of all, they were constructing or projecting an image. 'Image-makers' and 'spin doctors' are not novel to the present day nor are they the sole creation of modern political parties. Their equivalents were at work in the sixteenth century, refracting or distorting what historians later took to be the 'primary sources' for the life and career of Thomas More.

This book seeks to reconsider key themes in More's life in conjunction with the divergent portrayals that have arisen to explain or condemn or exculpate. It shows that many of the earliest sources for his biography were contrived or manipulated by those who had one eye at the very least on his posthumous fame and reputation. As well as considering his life and reputation, I will seek to show the ways in which 'image-makers' were at work in his lifetime or shortly after his death. More was himself adept in the art of public relations. In his epitaph which he composed himself, in his letters written in 1534 from Chelsea to Thomas Cromwell, and in those sent to his favourite daughter, Margaret, after his imprisonment in the Tower, he was putting his own 'version' of the 'facts' on record. His letters to Margaret justified his conduct and his 'scruple of conscience', even though she had obtained permission to visit her father in the Tower. The very existence of these letters to his daughter is significant. Scholars have begun to realize that the letters, especially those preserved by Mary Bassett, Margaret's daughter, had more than one audience (see Chapter 9). We ourselves are one audience, since More was writing at least partly for posterity.

Now that I have finished this book, I no longer believe that a truly historical biography of Thomas More can be written. The sources are too problematic. Historians cannot legitimately 'invent' what amounts to a relatively high proportion of their facts, while undue conjecture irritates the reader. The task is to excavate, and thereby to expose, the substructure of evidence on which scholars must construct their interpretations. We need to see with greater clarity not only the different portrayals that have arisen to debate Thomas More, but to recognize the limits of what we can and cannot know about him, laying bare those points of transition between the sustainable and the conjectural. In this book I will seek to use this approach to help reevaluate such topics as More's entry into royal service, his family and domestic life, his intellectual aspirations, his role in politics and the early Reformation, his beliefs on Henry VIII's kingship and the royal supremacy as expressed in the Tower and at his trial, and his beliefs on the power of the papacy and of the General Council of the Roman Catholic Church. To the questions 'Who was Thomas More and for what did he so "silently" die?', I have sought to give better informed, if doubtless no less controversial, answers.

For persuading me to write this book, I am grateful to Christopher Wheeler, Director of Humanities Publishing and commissioning editor at Arnold. He never seemed to doubt that I would produce the typescript on time. I wish to thank him for his advice and support. I am especially grateful to Julia and

Emma, who must feel that they lost an entire summer to this project but who never complained. I acknowledge the generous support of the Leverhulme Trustees, who awarded me a year's Research Fellowship in 1997–8. Although this book was not itself my project in that year, the synopsis was planned then. I am also grateful to the Research Leave Committee of the University of St Andrews for a semester's leave in 1999, when the bulk of the book was written.

John Guy
16 November 1999

Acknowledgements

The author would like to express his warmest thanks and obligation to Clarence H. Miller, Executive Editor, and to the co-editors of the Yale Edition of the Complete Works of St Thomas More (15 vols, 1963–) for what has become the indispensable contribution to More studies. The other essential works are E.F. Rogers, ed., *The Correspondence of Sir Thomas More* (Princeton, NJ, 1947) and Rogers, ed., *St Thomas More: Selected Letters* (New Haven, CT, 1961). I gratefully acknowledge the assistance of the staff of the British Library and Public Record Office over the last 25 years.

Abbreviations

BL	British Library
CSPS	*Calendar of State Papers, Spanish* (13 vols, London, 1862–1954)
CW	Yale Edition of the Complete Works of St Thomas More (15 vols, New Haven, CT, 1963–)
CWE	Collected Works of Erasmus (59 vols, Toronto, 1974–)
EW	*The English Works of Sir Thomas More* eds W.E. Campbell and A.W. Reed (London, 1931)
Harpsfield	Nicholas Harpsfield, *The life and death of Sir Thomas Moore, knight, sometymes Lord high Chancellor of England, written in the tyme of Queene Marie* ed. E.V. Hitchcock (Early English Text Society, Original Series no. 186, London, 1932)
Logan, Adams and Miller	*More: Utopia. Latin Text and English Translation* eds G.M. Logan, R.M. Adams and C.H. Miller (Cambridge, 1995)
LP	*Letters and Papers, Foreign and Domestic, of the Reign of Henry VIII* eds J.S. Brewer, J. Gairdner, and R.H. Brodie, 21 vols in 32 parts, and Addenda (London, 1862–1932)
Opus Epistolarum	*Opus Epistolarum Des. Erasmi Roterodami* ed. P.S. Allen (12 vols, Oxford, 1906–58)
PRO	Public Record Office
Rogers, ed., Correspondence	*The Correspondence of Sir Thomas More* ed. E.F. Rogers (Princeton, NJ, 1947)
Rogers, ed., Selected Letters	*St Thomas More: Selected Letters* ed. E.F. Rogers (New Haven, CT, 1961)

Roper	*Two Early Tudor Lives: the Life and Death of Cardinal Wolsey by George Cavendish; The Life of Sir Thomas More by William Roper* eds R.S. Sylvester and D.P. Harding (New Haven, CT, 1962)
Stapleton	*The Life and Illustrious Martyrdom of Sir Thomas More* trans. P.E. Hallett (London, 1928)
STC²	*A Short-Title Catalogue of Books Printed in England, Scotland and Ireland, and of English Books Printed Abroad* eds W.A. Jackson, F.S. Ferguson and K.F. Pantzer, 2nd edn (3 vols, London, 1976–91)
Trapp and Herbrüggen	J.B. Trapp and H. Schulte Herbrüggen, *'The King's Good Servant': Sir Thomas More 1477/8–1535* (London, 1977)

Manuscripts preserved at the PRO are quoted by the call number in use there. The descriptions of the classes referred to are as follows:

C 1	Chancery, Early Chancery Proceedings
C 54	Chancery, Close Rolls
C 65	Chancery, Parliament Rolls
C 78	Chancery, Decree Rolls
C 82	Chancery, Warrants for the Great Seal, Series II
C 193	Chancery, Miscellaneous Books
C 263	Chancery, Files, Legal Miscellanea (Injunctions)
E 36	Exchequer, Treasury of the Receipt, Miscellaneous Books
OBS	PRO, Obsolete Lists and Indexes
SP 1	State Papers, Henry VIII, General Series
SP 2	State Papers, Henry VIII, Folio Volumes
STAC 2	Star Chamber Proceedings, Henry VIII

Note on the earliest biographies

A key to the three earliest 'Lives' of Thomas More most frequently referred to in this book may be helpful (for the editions of these 'Lives' which are cited in the notes, see the Abbreviations and Further reading).

Roper   The *Life of Sir Thomas More* by William Roper, More's son-in-law, written in or shortly after 1557. Roper implied that it was merely a compilation of notes for an 'official history' of More by Harpsfield (see below), but it is by far the most authoritative of the earliest 'Lives'. It remained in manuscript until first published at St Omer under the title, the *Life, Arraignment and Death of that Mirror of All True Honour and Virtue, Sir Thomas More* (1626). Reprinted in 1716 by the antiquarian, Thomas Hearne. Later editions or reissues appeared in 1729, 1731, 1765, 1817, and frequently thereafter. Roper's declared aim was to show that 'in his days', his father-in-law had been 'accompted' a man 'worthy perpetual famous memory'. He was a man of 'singular virtue'. A man 'of a clear, unspotted conscience . . . more pure and white than the whitest snow'.

Harpsfield   The *Life and Death of Sir Thomas More* by Nicholas Harpsfield, Archdeacon of Canterbury in Mary Tudor's reign, was commissioned by the surviving More family members in or shortly after 1557. The work depicted Henry VIII as a tyrant: the English Reformation was precipitated by his 'lusts'. More was 'a man of virtue', who preferred to die rather than to tell an untruth or take an oath in vain. His martyrdom, Harpsfield concluded, was for a cause which 'toucheth religion and the whole faith'. Completed in manuscript by the end of 1558 or the beginning of 1559, and presented to William Roper as a New Year's gift. Publication was prevented by the accession of Elizabeth I. The 'Life' remained in manuscript until 1932, when first published by the Early English Text Society.

Stapleton
The *Life of Thomas More* by Thomas Stapleton, Professor of Theology at Louvain and Douai, was written in Latin and published at Douai in 1588 as the final part of the trilogy, *Tres Thomae, seu de S. Thomae Apostoli rebus gestis, de S. Thoma Archiepiscopo Cantuariensi et Martyre, D. Thomae Mori Angliae quondam Cancellarii Vita.* Later editions appeared at Cologne and Graz in 1612 and 1689. Versions were included in collected editions of More's *Latin Works* which appeared after 1620, including Stapleton's own. It was widely circulated and served as an inspiration for the English recusant tradition until Catholic Emancipation in 1829. The earlier parts of the trilogy were the 'Lives' of St Thomas the Apostle and St Thomas Becket. Stapleton organized the work thematically not chronologically. He availed himself of the European literature on More, and drew extensively on the stories and reminiscences which circulated among the Catholic exiles in the 1560s.

Members of the More family relevant to the text

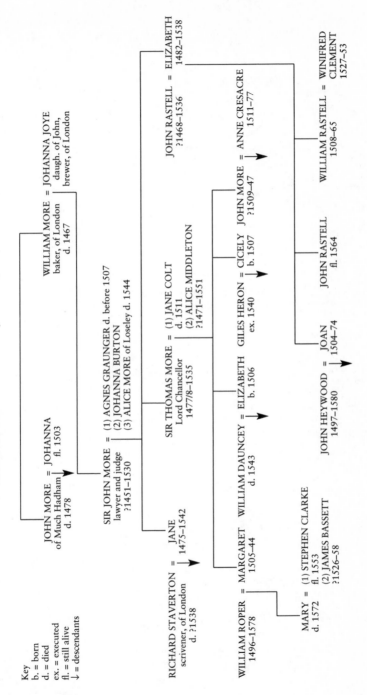

Key
b. = born
d. = died
ex. = executed
fl. = still alive
↓ = descendants

JOHN MORE = JOHANNA
of Much Hadham   fl. 1503
d. 1478

WILLIAM MORE = JOHANNA JOYE
baker, of London   daugh. of John,
d. 1467   brewer, of London

SIR JOHN MORE = (1) AGNES GRAUNGER d. before 1507
lawyer and judge   (2) JOHANNA BURTON
?1451–1530   (3) ALICE MORE of Loseley d. 1544

JOHN RASTELL = ELIZABETH
?1468–1536   1482–1538

SIR THOMAS MORE = (1) JANE COLT
Lord Chancellor   d. 1511
1477/8–1535   (2) ALICE MIDDLETON
    ?1471–1551

RICHARD STAVERTON = JANE
scrivener, of London   1475–1542
d. ?1538

WILLIAM DAUNCEY = ELIZABETH
d. 1543   b. 1506

GILES HERON = CICELY   JOHN MORE = ANNE CRESACRE
ex. 1540   b. 1507   ?1509–47   1511–77

WILLIAM ROPER = MARGARET
1496–1578   1505–44

JOHN HEYWOOD = JOAN
1497–1580   1504–74

WILLIAM RASTELL = WINIFRED
1508–65   CLEMENT
    1527–53

MARY = (1) STEPHEN CLARKE
d. 1572   fl. 1553
    (2) JAMES BASSETT
    ?1526–58

JOHN RASTELL
fl. 1564

|1|

An historical Thomas More?

'Sir Thomas More, the most brilliant lawyer of his generation, a scholar with an international reputation, the centre of a warm and affectionate family life which he cherished, went to his death rather than take an oath in vain.' These words could have been spoken at almost any time between More's execution on 6 July 1535 and the present. They were, in fact, delivered in the United States' Senate on 14 January 1999. The speaker was Congressman Henry Hyde, the Chairman of the Judiciary Committee of the House of Representatives: the occasion was the opening of the impeachment trial of President William Jefferson Clinton. The speech was transmitted live across the world, shown on hundreds of television stations in America alone and broadcast on both the radio and live on the internet. Most of the next day's newspapers, notably those in the English-speaking world, highlighted the references to More. Even in Scotland, where the national Parliament was about to be restored and a degree of autonomy from England secured, the headline of the country's leading newspaper crowed: 'TV Nation raised on Oprah Winfrey watches bemused as Sir Thomas More takes the stand.'[1]

Quoting Robert Bolt's play *A Man for All Seasons* (1960), Mr Hyde informed the senators: 'As [More] told his daughter, Margaret, "When a man takes an oath, Meg, he's holding his own self in his own hands. Like water and if he opens his fingers *then* – he needn't hope to find himself again ..." '.[2] In other words More is the most exemplary case that even the American constitutional system of government can imagine of a man whose 'word is his bond'. As Congressman James Sensenbrenner, who spoke next after Hyde, put it: 'the truth is the truth and a lie is a lie'.

We think we know who More is. He was the author of *Utopia* (1516), the most avant-garde work of humanist moral philosophy north of the Alps and one of the crowning achievements of the Renaissance. He was a man of 'singular virtue'. A man 'of a clear, unspotted conscience . . . more pure and white than the whitest snow'.[3] As a legal advocate, he was 'a man of an angel's wit and singular learning'.[4] As a writer, his name is inscribed 'in the ledgers of Minerva'.[5] His family life at Chelsea was a domestic idyll. As a King's councillor and Lord Chancellor, he was 'that worthy and uncorrupt magistrate'.[6] Later, he won international fame as the *refusenik* who challenged the tyranny of Henry VIII. Faced with the King's demands to swear an oath to the Act of Succession and to affirm the validity of the King's title as Supreme Head of the Church of England, he defended the cause of 'conscience' against the State. R.W. Chambers concluded his classic biography in 1935 by comparing him to Socrates and Abraham Lincoln.[7]

For the majority of people, More's stand against the King is most clearly defined in the film of *A Man for All Seasons* (1966). Directed by the veteran Oscar-winner Fred Zinnemann, who also made *From Here to Eternity*, Paul Scofield played Thomas More, with Robert Shaw as Henry VIII, Orson Welles as Cardinal Wolsey, Wendy Hiller as Alice More and Susannah York as Margaret Roper. The film won six Academy Awards. According to *Variety*, the trade journal of the American film and entertainment industry, the pundits described it as primarily for 'the class audience'.[8] They were proved wrong. Cinemas were packed. The picture retained its top position until the release of the James Bond thriller *Casino Royale*. *Variety* cited this as 'proof' that a film 'without sex, violence or songs' could be a box-office hit.[9]

We know what More looked like. Several contemporary versions of the paintings and drawings of More and his family by Hans Holbein the Younger have survived (see Chapter 4). They were first popularized in 1890, when a hugely successful Exhibition on the Royal House of Tudor in London inaugurated the tradition of large-scale special exhibitions based on temporary loans. Some 15 paintings or drawings of More and his family were shown. Since the total number of exhibits exceeded 1500, these items could have been eclipsed. But reviewers noted that they were among the star attractions, notably the half-length portrait of More as Chancellor of the Duchy of Lancaster, a detail from which appears on the cover of this book. Almost as popular were the black and coloured chalk drawings of More's domestic circle from the Royal Collection at Windsor that were preparatory to the family group portrait. Although frequently exhibited since, they had rarely been seen in public before 1890.[10]

We also know what More wrote. Since 1963, the Yale Edition of the Complete Works of St Thomas More has published fully annotated editions of every single one of his literary works. He wrote around 30 major titles (the exact tally depends on how the Latin and English poems and a number of other shorter pieces are counted). Whereas previously his writings other than *Utopia* and the *Dialogue of Comfort against Tribulation* were relatively inaccessible, they are now available in every leading library. It is a task which involved dozens of co-editors and editorial assistants over a period of almost 40 years. Completed to a consistently high standard, the project is a model of its type. Amounting to 15 volumes in 21 large parts, it rivals the most opulent of the editorial projects of the Victorian age, the indispensable *Letters and Papers, Foreign and Domestic, of the Reign of Henry VIII*.

What is it about More that people so admire? One of the best and most concise summaries comes at the end of Thomas Stapleton's *Life of Thomas More*, which was written in 1588 and served as an inspiration for the English recusant tradition until Catholic Emancipation in 1829. More had followed his 'conscience' to the death, but had always remained 'a man of honour'. He was not a 'rebel'. He did not resist Henry VIII. He was the victim of a law which he had violated 'neither by word or deed'.[11] 'This law, moreover, concerned religion and not the policy of the State'. Although he refused to bend, he had not challenged the law or criticized anyone who had accepted it. He had simply 'kept silence'.

He was a man of 'learning, virtue and integrity'. He was 'brilliant in wit, so kind and gentle, dear to all and harmful to none'. He had rendered great services to the King. Although he had 'loathed' Court life and would have preferred the 'contemplative' vocation of his youth, he had never shirked his public duty. He had served as a King's councillor, the King's secretary, and finally Lord Chancellor. He knew the King better than anyone. He could have exploited this intimacy to win fame, honours and worldly wealth but his motives were pure and unselfish.

When the King's suit for the annulment of his marriage to Catherine of Aragon arose in 1527 and More was consulted, he had replied 'so openly, candidly, and sincerely' that Henry was not (initially) offended.[12] Of all the King's councillors, More alone was willing to speak the truth. 'He would not flatter nor deceive his prince'.[13]

But when the King's character began to change and 'lust' ruled in place of virtue, More resigned. When Henry demanded More's conformity in his 'retirement' to the King's divorce and re-marriage, and the Act of Succession threatened him with the oath, 'he neither said nor did anything'. He 'might certainly have spoken' and embarrassed both the King and the realm. But he did not. He condemned neither the oath nor (later) the Act of Supremacy: 'he merely kept silence for conscience' sake'.[14] Attainted for refusing the oath of succession and later tried for treason, he 'bore patiently' the loss of worldly fortune and honours, the company of his family, 'and finally life itself'.

This is the legend of More's reputation. How much of it is true? The historian's task is to adjudicate. As the divergent interpretations cited in this book illustrate, this is not easy. Writing about More presents an extraordinary challenge. He is not simply an historical figure, he is a saint and martyr of the Roman Catholic Church. In December 1886, he was beatified by Pope Leo XIII, the step preceding canonization. In May 1935, he was canonized as a saint by Pope Pius XI. His sainthood obscures, rather than illuminates, his historical significance. Attention focuses on his death rather than his life; his heroic stand against Henry VIII rather than the choices that impelled him to take that stand. One of the priorities of this book will be to give as much weight to the shibboleths which circumscribe the earlier phases of More's life as it gives to those which surround his political and legal career and his imprisonment, interroga-tions and trial.

A related and even greater challenge is that many of the earliest sources for More's life and career have been partly contrived or manipulated by those who believed that his martyrdom would bring him, and the cause for which he died, an inextinguishable fame and reputation. As well as considering the more recent literature of praise, blame or exculpation, this book will focus on the ways in which 'image-makers' and 'spin doctors' were at work either in More's own lifetime or shortly after his death, influencing or distorting what historians now suppose to be the 'primary sources'. Unless this fundamental point is addressed, it is impossible to make sense of the later interpretations. It should be stressed that 'image-making' was not merely the concern of More's earliest biographers. It will be argued that Erasmus' repeatedly-cited vignette of More to Ulrich von Hutten (1519) takes an idealized view (see Chapters 2–4). More himself, particularly in his later letters and in Margaret Roper's so-called 'letter' to Alice Alington, was putting his own version of the facts on record for the benefit of posterity (see Chapters 8–10).

More's family and domestic life is one notable area where an image of the private foundations of More's virtuous public personality have been laid down on somewhat doubtful assumptions. The dilemma is that the scale of distortion is unknown (see Chapter 4). The most vivid images of More's domestic life at Chelsea come not from historical documents, but are extrapolated from Erasmus' vignette and Holbein's iconography. Erasmus sought to publicize throughout Europe what he considered to be the ideal of a Christian humanist life. He attributes to More the virtues immortalized by Cicero's *De officiis*, the 'golden text' of Italian and northern European humanism. This has to be taken into account. His description of More's domestic scene is also read anachronistically today. It actually describes what Erasmus said he remembered from visits to More's household before 1511. When he wrote to Hutten, he had not met More's family for almost a decade. And he never set foot in Chelsea: More did not buy his estate there until 1524.

In a similar way, Holbein's family group portrait, of which the best surviving copy is at Nostell Priory, Yorkshire, constructs an image of More's household as a centre of culture, piety and domestic bliss. It creates the entirely false impression that More's establishment was a tightly-knit circle of around a dozen (see Chapter 4). Two notes on the pen and ink drawing which was Holbein's original sketch for the *mise-en-scène* give stage directions for the rearrangement of artefacts and state that Alice, More's second wife, should sit instead of kneel. The proposed changes are thought to represent More's intervention.[15] If so, he was keenly interested in the way his family life was depicted. All of Holbein's images of More and his domestic circle are connected to the family group portrait, for which the *mise-en-scène* was set by More himself.

The most straightforward example of the manipulation of facts for posterity is More's account of his 'retirement' (see

Chapters 8–9). He followed the advice of the Roman rhetoricians that we should present ourselves to the world as we wish to be perceived by others, allying 'expediency' with 'honesty' in order to secure the reputation which we maintain is properly ours. He donned the mask of self-fashioning to protect himself from rumours that he had resigned after a dispute with the King. His resignation had been spectacular. Edward Foxe, one of the King's innermost advisers and propagandists in the divorce suit, and a man in a position to know everything which passed at Court, was agog. He wrote within hours: 'News here be none other but that Sir Thomas More hath resigned the office of the Chancellor and the Parliament is prorogued until the 5th day of November'.[16]

In his epitaph, which he wrote himself and immediately had cut in stone, More claimed that he had resigned to have 'some years of his life free, in which he little and little withdrawing himself from the business of this life, might continually remember the immortality of the life to come'.[17] This echoed the words he had used to the King when surrendering the Great Seal. Such a stance was politically 'prudent'. It was also true – but it was not the whole truth. To ensure maximum publicity, More sent a transcript of his epitaph to Erasmus in a letter that he knew would be printed and circulated in Europe. He told him:

> Some chatterboxes around here began to spread the rumour that I had resigned my office unwillingly and that I had kept that detail a secret. So, after making arrangements for the construction of my tomb, I did not hesitate to make, on my Epitaph, a public declaration of the actual facts, to allow anyone a chance to refute them, if he could.[18]

When his critics spotted the epitaph cut in stone, they had accused More of being 'boastful'. This, he informed Erasmus, was splendid, because it meant that they could not 'deny its truth'.[19] By ensuring that his version of these events was sent to Erasmus, who would see that it received the maximum publicity, More was protecting his reputation. He was shaping an image, and doing so at the very same moment that he published his *Apology*, the book in which he re-entered the public sphere in order to defend his actions as Lord Chancellor and in particular his role as an inquisitor in cases of suspected heresy (see Chapters 6, 9).

If 'image-making' was in progress during More's own lifetime, what is the status of the earliest biographies? How and in what circumstances were they compiled? What exactly did they seek to achieve? The three most important of these 'Lives' were written by Roper, Harpsfield and Stapleton between 1557 and 1588. Two further composite biographies appeared between 1599 and 1620. These works (especially the first three) are frequently cited by historians as if they are unimpeachable 'primary sources', yet it has never been disputed that their authors had their sights set on More's recognition as a martyr and saint. The lobbying began in earnest in Mary Tudor's reign (1553–8), when a Catholic queen restored allegiance to Rome. William Roper, More's son-in-law, wrote his *Life of Sir Thomas More*, and Nicholas Harpsfield, Archdeacon of Canterbury, began the *Life and Death of Sir Thomas More*.

Roper's *Life* is linked to William Rastell's folio edition of More's *English Works* (1557). Rastell was More's nephew and publisher. He had printed almost all of More's English works that were issued during his lifetime. He had also obtained copies of the unpublished works, including the Tower writings and many of More's letters. Copies possibly came from Margaret Roper, More's favourite daughter, or more likely from her own daughter, Mary Bassett, since Margaret died in 1544. Roper refers directly to Rastell's transcripts of More's letters. His *Life* either closely followed on from the *English Works*, or else he had access to the manuscript. Rastell was strongly in favour of a biography of his uncle. He had started one himself in exile during Edward VI's reign (1547–53), but only three fragments of it have survived.[20] Roper circulated his own *Life* with a disclaimer. He implied that it was merely a compilation of notes. Modern scholarship disagrees. Richard Sylvester says that this 'so-called "artlessness" is as fictional as the role in which he [Roper] casts himself'.[21] Roper is the most authoritative of the earliest biographers. He cannot be challenged with impunity. This is demonstrated by his accounts of the case of the Pope's ship, and of More's entry into royal service in the spring of 1518, where revisionist historians who doubted his version of events have come unstuck (see Chapter 3). But he admitted that he had refreshed his memory from More's Tower letters when describing earlier events. He also put words into More's mouth. His accounts of the perjury of Sir Richard Rich and of More's 'endorsement' of the papal supremacy at his trial are particularly suspect, since neither incident is corroborated by the other contemporary reports of the trial, and Roper himself had not been present (see Chapter 10).

Roper wrote to show that 'in his days', More had been 'accompted' a man 'worthy perpetual famous memory'.[22] This phrase is telling. The agenda of More's champions in the 1550s was directed against the slur that his 'silence' in the Tower (see Chapter 9), and reluctance to affirm the papal plentitude of power (see Chapter 10), put him in a lower division of martyrs to John Fisher, who had unequivocally denied the royal supremacy and affirmed that of the Pope, for which he had been executed by Henry VIII a fortnight or so before More. The slur was in the official sermon at the burning of Archbishop Cranmer at Oxford in 1556, when Dr Henry Cole preached that 'it seemed meet, according to the law of equality, that as the death of the Duke of Northumberland of late made even with Thomas More Chancellor ... so there should be one that should make even with Fisher of Rochester'.[23] The deaths of Bishops Ridley, Hooper and Ferrar 'were not able to make even' with Fisher. It 'seemed meet' that Cranmer should be joined to them 'to fill up their part of equality'.[24] (The account of the sermon is from a Catholic eye-witness and not from John Foxe's *Acts and Monuments*. There is no reason to doubt what was said.) In other words, the spokesman for Mary's regime claimed that Fisher's martyrdom was worth four times as much as More's. It was to redress this imbalance that Roper began compiling the *Life*.[25]

Roper showed his manuscript to Nicholas Harpsfield, who knew Rastell in exile under Edward VI, and who was restored to preferment in 1554.[26] Harpsfield began the *Life and Death of Sir Thomas More* immediately. His biography was commissioned. It was meant to be the 'official history' of Thomas More.[27] Longer and more ambitious than Roper's, it ransacked the writings of More and Erasmus and drew on the recollections of More's family. It also used the reports of the trial that circulated in Europe. The gist is that More's career was subverted by the corrupt desires of Henry VIII. At the core was the *Treatise on the Pretended Divorce of King Henry VIII from Catherine of Aragon*, which was planned as an appendix, but which soon asserted itself as an independent work.[28] Harpsfield's *Life of More* argued that Henry VIII was a tyrant. The Reformation was precipitated by his 'lusts'. More's refusal to conform was based on his refusal to lose his status as 'a man of virtue'. His heroic death was exemplary. It has universal meaning. Harpsfield concluded that More had been martyred for a cause which 'toucheth religion and the whole faith'.[29] It was a nobler cause than those for which earlier English saints who shared his forename had suffered. He was a worthier candidate for canonization than Thomas Becket.[30]

From the viewpoint of posterity, Harpsfield was the right man at the wrong time. When Elizabeth I inherited the throne in November 1558, the tables were turned. Protestantism became England's official religion. Harpsfield was deprived of his archdeaconry and sent to the Fleet prison, where he remained until 1574.[31] His *Life* was completed by 1558 or the beginning of 1559, and presented to Roper as a New Year's gift; but it was never published. It did not become the 'official history'. It remained in manuscript until 1932, when it was edited by the Early English Text Society.

Many of More's surviving family and their descendants now joined the recusant community in exile. They went mainly to Douai and Louvain in the Netherlands, where they cherished More's memory and ensured that copies of Roper's and Harpsfield's 'Lives' were kept in circulation. These manuscripts had suddenly become clandestine works. Copies were made for reintroduction into England, where they were passed from hand to hand in a similar way to the samizdat literature in the former socialist republics of Eastern Europe.[32] Sometimes they fell into the wrong hands. The manuscript of Harpsfield's *Life* now at Emmanuel College, Cambridge, is liberally defaced with iconoclastic marginalia and puritan attacks on the 'practices' of 'popery'.[33]

Meanwhile, progress was slow in securing papal recognition of Fisher and More. In 1579, Pope Gregory XIII sponsored an unsuccessful invasion of Ireland by James Fitzmaurice.[34] Queen Elizabeth was denounced as a tyrant. And in an effort to rally Catholic resistance at home, the Pope recognized the cause of the English martyrs who had died under Henry VIII.[35] Fisher had the pre-eminent claim, but More was next on the list. By a special decree, the Pope allowed their relics to be used in the consecration of altars, provided no more ancient relics were available.[36] When a complete cycle of frescoes of the Holy Martyrs was commissioned for the Church of St Stephen in Rome, the Pope permitted frescoes of the English martyrs, including More, to be placed in the English College. These had faded or been vandalized by the end of the eighteenth century, but their likeness is known because 36 copper-plate engravings were published in *Ecclesiae Anglicanae Trophaea* (1584), a work

which is the foundation of the devotional tradition of the iconography of More.[37]

Stapleton began his *Life of Thomas More* once the *Trophaea*
had revived the cause of More's canonization. The work was
finished as the Spanish Armada sailed up the Channel, most
likely a coincidence, since the author's gaze was on Rome. An
exile who was Professor of Theology at Louvain and Douai, his
book was in Latin and published at Douai. Later editions
appeared at Cologne and Graz in 1612 and 1689. Versions were
also included in the collected editions of More's *Latin Works*
which appeared after 1620, including Stapleton's own.[38] The
result was that the work had a wide circulation.

The *Life* was the final part of a trilogy in which the other
saints' lives were those of St Thomas the Apostle and St Thomas
Becket. Its polemical force lay in this juxtaposition. As an interpretation, it was guided by Harpsfield, except that Stapleton
wrote thematically, not chronologically. He incorporated the
European literature on More and the Reformation into the work,
drawing on the reminiscences which had circulated among the
exiles in the 1560s and on the anecdotes of the surviving More
circle. Nothing could overcome the fact that Stapleton had not
known More. He was not born until the month in which More
himself was executed and he did not write the *Life* until he was
in his fifties, when his memory of what he had learned in the
1560s had dimmed.[39] Unlike his predecessors, Stapleton wrote
allusively. His arguments were coloured rhetorically. His work is
invaluable, but can be difficult to interpret, notably in those
passages which describe More's early vocation and entry into
politics (see Chapters 2–4).

Stapleton failed in his main aim. When Elizabeth survived in
the long war against Philip II and the Protestant James VI of
Scotland succeeded to the English throne in 1603, the Pope lost
interest in More and the English martyrs. Their cause was
forgotten at Rome until the baton was taken up by Cardinal
Wiseman and Cardinal Manning after the Catholic revival of the
1850s. What remained of the exile tradition reflected a recognition by those in the Netherlands that their hero was destined
for obscurity and their own exile was likely to be permanent.[40]

A composite *Life of Sir Thomas More* by a writer known only
as Ro. Ba. was completed around 1599. It adds little to the
earlier narratives except for anecdotes of dubious provenance.[41]
Eight manuscripts are extant, but the reception of the work is

impossible to judge, and no printed edition appeared until 1950. Lastly, More's great-grandson, Cresacre More, wrote a *Life* by a similar process of accretion.[42] A single arresting statement appears in this work. Cresacre remarks that More 'lived four years amongst the Carthusians, dwelling *near* the Charterhouse' rather than actually *in* the Charterhouse (see Chapter 2).[43] This raises intriguing possibilities. Otherwise, the *Life* is derivative. It has little to commend it to the historian, although it lays claim to be the best general biography until the Victorian T.E. Bridgett's *Blessed Thomas More* (1891).[44]

As in More's later letters, his epitaph or Holbein's iconography, the earliest biographers were putting their version of the 'facts' on record. They were lobbying to secure More's recognition by the Catholic Church as a martyr and saint. They were deliberately constructing an image. Their views are 'opinions' rather than 'facts'. Roper's *Life* is the least polemical, but even his 'artlessness' is feigned. Rhetorical games are being played, especially when the 'sayings' of More are reported. In the course of these games, 'image' and 'reflection' become confused, but they nourish and reinforce one another. These writers did not create 'primary sources' in the same sense as the State Papers, or the records of the Courts of Chancery or King's Bench – and even these records can be treacherous. Their 'Lives' are hagiographical. Harpsfield's is thickly polemical. They blur the lines between 'history' and 'story', blending truth, fiction and 'miracles' in ways that are unimaginable today.[45] This is not to deny that as sources they are essential: we cannot discuss More's life and reputation without them. But they reflect a point of view. They are 'authentic', but deceptively so: they represent the 'More' whom these authors have chosen to depict. They are also prone to skirt or omit an unpleasant truth. It has long been known that Rastell entirely omitted one of More's letters and altered the wording of another in the transcripts in his *English Works*, because the originals would have created the wrong impression in Mary's reign.[46] Again, Stapleton suppressed More's admission that he had never placed the Pope's authority above that of the General Council of the Church, a statement which at Rome would have been inconvenient, if not tantamount to heresy, after the Council of Trent.[47]

How did More emerge from relative obscurity? How was his 'rehabilitation' achieved in Protestant England? The key lies in the leitmotif of the earliest biographies, that More did not resist

Henry VIII.[48] He would suffer death rather than tell an untruth or take an oath in vain. But he would not 'oppose' the King, nor would he criticize anyone who had taken the oath and conformed. 'He merely kept silence for conscience' sake'. This 'story' is intrinsic to the process whereby More would be rediscovered as a Protestant (as well as a Catholic) hero. Stapleton wrote in the ideological crisis years of the 1580s. He was sensitive to the Protestant link between Catholic 'conscience' and treason after the papal excommunication of Elizabeth by the bull *Regnans in Excelsis* in 1570. He represented the values that would later be fundamental to political consciousness in the aftermath of the Civil Wars of the seventeenth century. His narrative mapped 'silence' and 'non-resistance' onto More's stand against the King. He rejected the appeals of those Jesuit seminarians, led by William Allen and Robert Parsons, who in his own lifetime had counselled rebellion and the overthrow of the 'heretical' Elizabethan State.[49]

Stapleton is a crucial intermediary here. The idea that he was unknown in seventeenth-century England because he wrote in Latin must be rejected. The shapers of opinion, whether clergy or laity, were fluent in Latin and bought books from the Continent. Political theorists and historians of the Reformation, in particular, required the European literature for their libraries. Harpsfield's biography was not published until 1932. Roper's was out of print between 1626 and 1716, whereas Stapleton's was disseminated as a separate title and as a companion to More's *Latin Works*. A relatively cursory survey of the inventories of the libraries of the Cambridge colleges shows that Stapleton was a stock author whose work was widely available and perhaps widely read by students of the Reformation and Counter-Reformation.

The watershed was the Revolution of 1688. Both Stapleton's and Roper's narratives could make it appear as if More after his resignation as Lord Chancellor had adopted a stance of 'passive resistance' against Henry VIII's oath of succession (see Chapter 9). R.W. Chambers used exactly that suggestive phrase in his 1935 biography.[50] More's actions, read this way in the different political context of the 1680s and 1690s, put him in a comparable position to those Anglican Nonjurors who had refused the new oath of allegiance to William III and Mary in 1689. It followed that his 'treason' could be morally, if not legally, assimilated to the Anglican consensus. Whatever else More may have been in the eyes of the Anglican establishment of the later seventeenth century, he was not among those Catholics (or Protestants) 'who turn religion into rebellion, and faith into faction'.[51] After the oath of allegiance of 1689, his stand against Henry VIII became comprehensible to conformists when set into the context of a 'legitimist' reading of Anglican political theology.

The one inescapable obstacle to the 'rehabilitation' of More was John Foxe's *Acts and Monuments* (1563 and innumerable later editions and reprints), the definitive work of Protestant history and martyrology. This multi-volume classic was read in cathedrals, universities, parish churches, schools, and ordinary domestic households. It castigated More as a 'papist' and an inquisitor. He had been 'accounted' in his day 'a man both witty and learned'. But he was 'a bitter persecutor . . . of good men, and a wretched enemy against the truth of the Gospel'. He bore a 'blind devotion . . . to the pope-holy see of Rome, and so wilfully stood in the pope's quarrel against his own prince, that he would not give over till he had brought the scaffold of the Tower-hill, with axe and all, upon his own neck'.[52]

Foxe had compiled a dossier of 'credible witnesses' to the effect that More was a heresy hunter. He had interrogated suspected heretics at his house at Chelsea. He had also resorted to violence. He had flogged at least three suspects in his garden. One had been tortured with ropes until 'the blood started out of his eyes'.[53] Others had been imprisoned in the stocks which More conveniently kept at home (see Chapter 6). Foxe himself later conceded that a number of these charges were false. Several were withdrawn in the second edition of the *Acts and Monuments* in 1570. But his interpretation was standard none the less. It was reiterated in 1758 by the Reverend Ferdinando Warner in the *Memoirs of the Life of Sir Thomas More*. Warner observed: 'But amidst all the Encomiums which I think are due to the Memory of Sir Thomas More . . . I must not conceal from the Readers, what was a great Allay to all his Virtues, his furious and cruel Zeal in the Persecution of Hereticks.'[54]

In mid-Victorian England this paradigm could still be etched in a virtually unaltered design into the opening volumes of J.A. Froude's *History of England from the Fall of Wolsey to the Defeat of the Spanish Armada*, which appeared in 1856 and supposedly marked the first 'professional' history of the reign of Henry VIII. Most recently, it has reappeared unchanged in Jasper Ridley's *Thomas Wolsey and Thomas More: the Statesman and the Fanatic* (1982).[55] According to Ridley, if More had lived in the twentieth century, he would have justified the 'liquidation of millions of human beings as a regrettable but necessary measure', or else approved 'the extermination of three-quarters of the world's population by nuclear weapons' (see Chapter 6).[56]

On the other side of the ledger, More's status in Protestant eyes was enhanced by the circulation of Ralph Robinson's translation of *Utopia*, which first appeared in 1551. Previously, *Utopia* was only available in Latin editions printed on the Continent. Whereas the Latin versions were read by a minority of the élite, Robinson's translation was accessible. A colloquial and literalist translation that lacked the ambiguity and nuances of the original, it was dedicated to Sir William Cecil, later Lord Burghley, privy councillor to Edward VI and chief minister to Elizabeth, who offered the sure guarantee of respectability (see Chapter 5).[57]

More claimed in *Utopia* that the most urgent duty of moral philosophy was to discover the root causes of injustice and poverty. In the Latin editions, his argument is abstract and can scarcely be approached by anyone lacking a prior knowledge of the writings of Plato and Cicero. Robinson not only popularized the book, he gave it a literalist slant and made it directly relevant to the debate on the humanist educational curriculum and the Protestant reform of the 'commonwealth'. Five separate editions of his translation appeared between 1551 and 1639.[58] Thereafter, new editions followed regularly if intermittently, culminating in those of the nineteenth century, by which time More was a household name.

More's 'rehabilitation' in Protestant England was not swift. It was not until the mid-eighteenth century that opinion swung decisively in his favour. It was the anti-sacerdotalism of the leading historian Gilbert Burnet, Bishop of Salisbury, which most effectively transformed More into a conformist polemical asset. In 1684, Burnet produced a new translation of *Utopia*. In volume three of the *History of the Reformation* (1679–1714), he developed an argument which would make an indelible mark on the historiography.[59] With breathtaking audacity, Burnet argued that More had been a Protestant reformer *avant la lettre* when he wrote *Utopia* (see Chapters 5–6). It was precisely because the Roman Catholic Church claimed him as its martyr that his comments were so invaluable.[60] When More wrote *Utopia*, he had expressed his 'first and coolest thoughts'. If he had died at that time, he would have been reckoned among those who, although they had accepted the authority of Rome, saw clearly

'the errors and corruptions of that body'. He numbered among
those who lacked the 'opportunities of declaring themselves more
openly for a Reformation'.[61]

Burnet subordinated More's social radicalism to his alleged
religious 'radicalism', making his reputation congenial to the
Anglican establishment. At a stroke, the *History of the
Reformation* became the source of what is (now) the well-worn
interpretation that More was a 'reformer' in 1516 who recanted
his ideas as Lord Chancellor. As Burnet framed the case:

> It is not easy to account for the great change that we find
> afterwards [More] was wrought up to: he not only set him-
> self to oppose the Reformation in many treatises, that, put
> together, make a great volume: but when he was raised up
> to the chief post in the ministry, he became a persecutor
> even to blood; and defiled those hands, which were never
> polluted by bribes . . . .[62]

It was More's role as an inquisitor, set forth in the *Acts and
Monuments*, that remained the stumbling-block. The schizophrenia created by this tension has persisted to the present day. It
is the main theme of Peter Ackroyd's *Life of Thomas More*
(1998), which seeks to reconcile More's humanist philosophy
with his uncompromising traditionalism and conservatism.
Richard Marius, whose *Thomas More* (1984) represents the
most distinguished modern biography, admits that More 'seduces
biographers. We all end up by liking him'.[63] But he judges More's
role as an inquisitor severely.[64] Only Chambers argued that More
could be fully exonerated from the charges levelled by Foxe. As
he disarmingly (if evasively) wrote, More's 'patience and courtesy
towards heretics' is 'revealed only to the careful student of his
private life'.[65] Such debates can never be finally resolved. It is not
simply that the sources are defective or deceptive; the schizophrenia is too deeply embedded. The argument will continue to
evolve.

The idea that More was a Protestant reformer *avant la lettre*
inaugurated the tradition that culminated in *A Man for All
Seasons*, whereby his reputation becomes almost a transferable
skill. His name is invoked in national assemblies, the law courts
or the media less to help us understand things about the past than
to win arguments or prove points about religious faith or the rule
of law in the present. As at the Clinton impeachment trial, his
example is a mantra for those who wish to name and shame. It

correlates to whatever 'truths' will exploit his reputation as a man of virtue. The 'More' who is known to the world is some-times the historical More, but usually it is not. It will in almost every case be the 'More' whom we have chosen to imagine. His true personality, his beliefs, even what he actually said or wrote, are less important than fitting the pieces of the jigsaw to suit our own heroic image.

The result is that thousands of books and articles have been written about More, and hundreds of churches, hospitals and schools named after him. He is the focus of a flourishing inter-national association, the *Amici Thomae Mori* (the 'Friends of Thomas More'), based in Angers, France, with branches in the United States, England, Germany, Italy and Japan. An entire journal, *Moreana*, is dedicated to his life and influence. A search of the combined databases of the British Library and the major European research libraries throws up 2687 separate entries. Most of these items are hagiographical or inconsequential. (They cover everything from More's use of patristics to his role in American folk humour, from his ecclesiology to his view of Utopian egg incubation.)

Although it is only those works which I believe to have made a genuine contribution to the historical debate of Thomas More's life and career which I will seek to consider in this book, it is worth pausing briefly to consider one or two examples of the ephemera. Robert Southey's *Sir Thomas More: or Colloquies on Progress and Prospects of Society* (1829) is one. The most reactionary of the Romantic poets, Southey liked to stage 'conversations' with exemplary historical figures, and in 1829 it was More's turn. His two volumes form an extended dialogue in which Montesinos (the fictional equivalent of Raphael Hythlodaeus in *Utopia*), conducts a debate with More's ghost. The agenda covers everything from war, steam, population, social improvement and the manufacturing system to religion, atheism, trade, America, the colonies and Ireland. Superficially open to argument, the work is a rant against Catholic Emancipation, the lack of social and religious discipline among the working classes, and the threat to English identity through the mismanagement of the Tory government.[66] 'More' condemns all the 'evils' that Southey himself abhorred. Thus, Catholic Emancipation was a surrender to Irish terrorism, which had 'subverted' the English constitution.[67] Urbanization and com-mercialization had eroded public morality.[68] The Acts of Union had flooded the House of Commons with Scots and Irish MPs.[69] 'More' even predicted Civil War in America on the grounds that 'the principle of religious obedience' did not exist there. Without the bond of religion, the Federal State could only be maintained by force.[70]

If this seems bizarre, things were only a little better by the 500th anniversary of More's birth. As the editor of *The Times* announced, 'If the English people were to be set a test to justify their history and civilization by the example of one man, then it is Sir Thomas More whom they would perhaps choose'. The claims of King Alfred, Elizabeth I, Shakespeare, Gladstone and Sir Winston Churchill were fleetingly considered, but the laurels went to More.[71] Feature articles followed on his 'lasting inspiration'.[72] The Anglican Dean of Westminster had obviously dashed for his copy of Chambers' biography of More. In his stand against the King, he wrote, More 'links himself up with Socrates'. He had also seen *A Man for All Seasons*, since he claimed that More was 'asserting the final right of the individual conscience to authenticate itself', which is Bolt's interpretation but not More's (see Chapter 10). Like Burnet, the Dean claimed that More was a Protestant reformer *avant la lettre*. Had More had his way, the papacy would have been 'purged' and the Church 'drastically' reformed. More's legacy is that 'the Reformation was not a gigantic mistake from which we need to be rescued'.

The Catholic columnist writing on the same day was equally keen on 'relevance'. He maintained that More's life and career were better appreciated since the Second Vatican Council (1962–5). The Council had acknowledged the autonomy and value of the laity. More's political service reflected this approach. If he had troubled heretics, this at least proved his commitment to the laity's role in the Church. His view of the papacy and of authority in the Church was moderate. He was not unswerving in his commitment to tradition. He was 'harshly critical of clerical abuse, superstitious practices and papal corruption'. But he remained a loyal Catholic, whose vision of Christian unity was ecumenical. Like the Vatican Council, he realized that 'change was of the essence of the Church'.

The historian should not be tempted to mock. Both these 1978 articles were thoroughly misleading, but each had a grain of truth. And nothing is likely to change. At his speech at the inauguration of the More Memorial Exhibition in Chelsea

in 1929, G.K. Chesterton acclaimed More as 'the greatest
Englishman, or, at least, the greatest historical character in
English history'.[73] He argued that his reputation was higher than
at any time since his death, but not as high as it would be in
2029. This prediction is almost certain to be proved right. The
trajectory is established, since in the celebrations to mark the
year 2000, More featured in special exhibitions at the Tower of
London, the British Museum and Lambeth Palace, was a central
figure of the Millennium Map in London, and was the subject of
a BBC programme on New Year's Eve. Whatever it is that draws
people of all nationalities and religious denominations (or none)
to him, his fascination seems to be inexhaustible.

Notes

1 *The Scotsman*, 15 January 1999 (news report by Tim Cornwell).
2 R. Bolt, *A Man for All Seasons* (London, 1960), p. 83.
3 Roper, p. 197.
4 Trapp and Herbrüggen, p. 134.
5 Logan, Adams and Miller, p. 19.
6 R.W. Chambers, *Thomas More* (London, 1935), pp. 16–19, 267–74,
   351–6.
7 Chambers, *Thomas More*, pp. 398–400.
8 J.R. Nicholl, 'More Captivates America: the Popular Success of *A
   Man for All Seasons*', *Moreana* 13 (1976), pp. 139–44.
9 Nicholl, 'More Captivates America', p. 143.
10 Catalogue to the *Exhibition of the Royal House of Tudor, The New
   Gallery, Regent Street, 1890* (London, 1890).
11 Stapleton, p. 226.
12 Stapleton, pp. 226–7.
13 Stapleton, p. 227.
14 Stapleton, p. 227.
15 Trapp and Herbrüggen, p. 86.
16 PRO, SP 1/70, fo. 41 (*LP* V, no. 1025).
17 Trapp and Herbrüggen, p. 140; Rogers, ed., *Selected Letters*, p. 182.
18 Rogers, ed., *Selected Letters*, p. 179.
19 Rogers, ed., *Selected Letters*, p. 178.
20 Harpsfield, pp. 219–52.
21 Roper, p. xvi.
22 Roper, p. 197.
23 D. MacCulloch, *Thomas Cranmer: A Life* (London, 1996), pp. 554–
   605.
24 Cranmer's burning was highly controversial, since he had recanted.
   When condemned to the stake, he had not relapsed. According to
   canon law, he was not an 'obstinate' heretic. More, whose antipathy
   to heresy was implacable but who adhered strictly to the canon and
   common law (see Chapter 6), would in such circumstances have

freed the prisoner after penance had been performed. A special argument was needed to justify the breach of canon law. MacCulloch, *Cranmer*, pp. 600–1.

25 J. Ridley, *The Statesman and the Fanatic: Thomas Wolsey and Thomas More* (London, 1982), p. 287.

26 Harpsfield, pp. clxxv–ccxiv.

27 T. Betteridge, *Tudor Histories of the English Reformations, 1530–83* (Aldershot, 1999), pp. 130–6.

28 Harpsfield, p. cciv.

29 Harpsfield, p. 214.

30 Harpsfield, p. 214.

31 Chambers, *Thomas More*, p. 31.

32 C. Hulse, 'Dead Man's Treasure: the Cult of Thomas More', in D.L. Miller, S. O'Dair and H. Weber, eds, *The Production of Renaissance Culture* (Ithaca, NY, 1994), p. 217.

33 Harpsfield, pp. xiv–xv.

34 S.G. Ellis, *Tudor Ireland* (London, 1985), pp. 278–80.

35 T.E. Bridgett, *Life and Writings of Blessed Thomas More* (London, 1924), p. xxix.

36 Bridgett, *Blessed Thomas More*, p. xxx.

37 N. Circinianus, *Ecclesiae Anglicanae Trophaea, per Io. Bap. de Cavalleriis Aeneis Typis Repraesentatae* (Rome, 1584). There are copies in the University Library and Trinity College, Cambridge.

38 The *Life* was not translated into English until 1928. This was done by P.E. Hallett, then Vice-Postulator for the Cause of Canonization of Blessed John Fisher and Blessed Thomas More. The timing was evidently critical. A declaration certified that Stapleton's uses of the words 'saint' and 'miracle' were 'in a purely human sense, and all intention of anticipating the judgement of the Church is utterly disclaimed'. More was canonized seven years later. Stapleton, p. iv.

39 Trapp and Herbrüggen, p. 136.

40 Hulse, 'Dead Man's Treasure', p. 217.

41 Ro. Ba., *The lyfe of Syr Thomas More, sometymes Lord Chancellor of England* ed. E.V. Hitchcock and P.E. Hallett (Early English Text Society, Original Series no. 222, London, 1950).

42 Cresacre More, *The Life of Sir Thomas More* (London, 1828).

43 Cresacre More, *The Life of Sir Thomas More* (London, 1828), p. 25 (my italics).

44 Cresacre wrote between 1615 and 1620. His *Life* was published at Douai in or about 1631. It was reissued in 1726, and a new edition by the Reverend Joseph Hunter appeared in 1828. The same generation undertook the printing of Roper's *Life*, which appeared at St Omer in 1626 under the title the *Life, Arraignment and Death of that Mirror of All True Honour and Virtue, Sir Thomas More*. There was no reprint or reissue until 1716, when an edition was published by the antiquarian, Thomas Hearne. A new edition from a better manuscript was prepared by the Reverend John Lewis in 1729. Reissues appeared in 1731, 1765 and 1817, the last of which was re-edited by S.W. Singer who had also edited More's *History of King Richard III* in 1821.

45 For a valuable summary, see P. Collinson, 'Truth, Lies and Fiction in Sixteenth-Century Protestant Historiography', in D.R. Kelley and D.H. Sacks, eds, *The Historical Imagination in Early Modern England* (Cambridge, 1997), pp. 37–68.

46 Rogers, ed., *Selected Letters*, pp. 193–202, and p. 202 n. 5.

47 Rogers, ed., *Selected Letters*, p. 214.

48 Stapleton, p. 227.

49 Stapleton, p. 228.

50 Chambers, *Thomas More*, p. 294.

51 J.C.D. Clark, *The Language of Liberty, 1660–1832* (Cambridge, 1994), p. 156.

52 G. Townsend, ed., *The Acts and Monuments of John Foxe* (8 vols, London, 1843–9) 5, p. 99.

53 Townsend, ed., *Acts and Monuments* 4, p. 689.

54 F. Warner, *Memoirs of the Life of Sir Thomas More* (London, 1758), pp. 67–8.

55 J. Ridley, *The Statesman and the Fanatic: Thomas Wolsey and Thomas More* (London, 1982).

56 Ridley, *The Statesman and the Fanatic*, pp. 292–3.

57 S. Alford, *The Early Elizabethan Polity: William Cecil and the British Succession Crisis, 1558–1569* (Cambridge, 1998), pp. 14–28.

58 These editions were published in 1551, 1556, 1597, 1624 and 1639.

59 G. Burnet, *History of the Reformation of the Church of England* (6 vols, London, 1820) 3, pp. 42–7.

60 Burnet, *History of the Reformation* 5, p. 42.

61 Burnet, *History of the Reformation* 5, pp. 45–6.

62 Burnet, *History of the Reformation* 5, p. 46.

63 R. Marius, *Thomas More* (New York, 1984), p. xxiv.

64 Marius, *Thomas More*, pp. 386–406.

65 Chambers, *Thomas More*, p. 86.

66 R. Southey, *Sir Thomas More: or Colloquies on Progress and Prospects of Society* (2 vols, London, 1829). For relevant background, see P. Harling, 'Robert Southey and the Language of Social Discipline', *Albion* 30 (1998), pp. 630–55.

67 Southey, *Sir Thomas More* 1, passim.

68 Southey, *Sir Thomas More* 1, pp. 113–99; 2, p. 212.

69 Southey, *Sir Thomas More* 2, p. 209.

70 Southey, *Sir Thomas More* 2, pp. 198–9.

71 *The Times*, leader (7 February 1978). An irate correspondent protested that no scientist had been nominated, but did not suggest More's demotion; *The Times* (11 February 1978), letter to the editor by Mr G.L. Wilde.

72 *The Times* (7 February 1978).

73 Ridley, *Thomas More*, p. 290.

|2|

Action or contemplation?

Who was Thomas More? And what made him tick? Erasmus in the prefatory letter to the *Praise of Folly* called him 'A Man for All Seasons', the accolade popularized by Robert Whittinton in his *Vulgaria* (1520) and most familiar today as the title of Robert Bolt's play. One suspects that More himself wanted to be remembered not for *Utopia* or his achievements as Lord Chancellor, but for his stand against Henry VIII.[1] The Paris Newsletter, which circulated in French on the Continent within a fortnight of his execution, says that he protested on the scaffold that he died 'the King's good servant but God's first' (see Chapter 11). His earliest biographers believed that their 'Lives' would bring him, and the cause for which he died, an immortal fame on earth. More had been Henry VIII's intimate councillor and secretary. Later, he was appointed Lord Chancellor. But in 1532 he resigned, and by the spring of 1534 his face was set against the King on a matter of conscience. It was a moral scruple which at the time even his own family could not understand and one which only a very small minority of the English bishops and clergy appeared to share.

No satisfactory account of More's early life has been written. Too much remains unknown. We must rely on the earliest biographers, none of whom knew More as a young man. William Roper, his son-in-law, whose *Life of Sir Thomas More* was written about 1557, probably entered his service in or around 1518, when he was in his early twenties and More was forty. Nicholas Harpsfield, whose *Life and Death of Sir Thomas More* was meant to be the 'official history' of Thomas More, wrote shortly after Roper, but was only sixteen when More died. He had the benefit of information from More's dependents, but none of those family members who survived into Mary's reign could have witnessed anything at first hand before 1514. Thomas Stapleton, whose *Life of Thomas More* drew extensively on the reminiscences of the Catholic exiles in the Netherlands in the 1560s, did not write until 1588, and he himself was not born until the month in which More was executed.

This chapter will introduce Thomas More. It will provide some biographical background and discuss the education in law and philosophy which he received, before turning to the first significant debate about his life: his residence in his early twenties for some three or four years in or about the London Charterhouse. Although few facts are know about this period, the 'Lives' of Harpsfield and Stapleton have encouraged claims by revisionist historians that More was a 'failed' candidate for the priesthood 'tormented' by his sexuality. According to this view, More entered the Charterhouse because he wished to become a priest or monk, but sexual arousal got the better of him. He found that a life of celibacy was impossible, even though he wore a hair shirt and whipped himself to subdue desire. He was forced to abandon his ambition, and was haunted by 'failure' for the rest of his life. His sense of guilt was finally assuaged by his stand against Henry VIII. Only as a prisoner in the Tower could he find peace of mind.

We know only the bare facts of More's life before the age of thirty or so. He was born in London; the date was probably Friday, 6 February 1478.[2] He was the second child and eldest son of John More, then a junior barrister living in Milk Street, Cripplegate. His mother was Agnes Graunger, who had married John More in 1474 and was the daughter of one 'Thomas Graunger' whose identity has been disputed. Perhaps this 'Thomas Graunger' was the wealthy merchant and Stapler (i.e. wool exporter) who was elected an alderman of London in 1503 and was later appointed Master of the Skinners' Company. Possibly he was an older and less affluent citizen of the same name, who was involved in minor lawsuits and was mentioned as a Warden of the Tallow Chandlers' Company in 1467. The precise identification hardly matters, since in either case the family was anchored in the City of London. John More was the son and heir of William More, a London citizen and guildsman free of the Bakers' Company, and on his mother's side was descended from Johanna Leycester, daughter and heir of a prosperous London gentleman and royal servant, John Leycester.

John More was a successful advocate and (later) judge. He had entered Lincoln's Inn in 1475, when he was about twenty-four years of age. Although promotion eluded him at first, he steadily built up his legal practice and by 1495 had been elected a double reader. He was created a serjeant-at-law in 1503, and crowned his career as a judge in the Courts of Common Pleas (1518) and King's Bench (1520). His most important private client as a young practitioner was Edward Stafford, 3rd Duke of Buckingham, by whom he was handsomely rewarded.[3]

Thomas More was taught the rudiments of Latin grammar at St Anthony's School in Threadneedle Street, and then placed as a page in the household of Cardinal Morton. Roper, who in 1521 married More's eldest daughter, Margaret, claimed that Morton often told his guests, 'This child here waiting at the table, whosoever shall live to see it, will prove a marvellous man'.[4] Roper sought to highlight More's virtuosity as well as his virtue.[5] More's talent was exceptional, which is why Morton took responsibility for his education. Morton was Henry VII's intimate councillor, Archbishop of Canterbury and Lord Chancellor. He held the post of Chancellor of Oxford University and was one of the most influential patrons of the age. He had been imprisoned by Richard III and was closely connected with Henry VII's succession to the throne in 1485. In Richard III's reign he had been linked to the unsuccessful revolt led by the 3rd Duke of Buckingham's father, which is how John More may have come to know him. More later expressed his admiration for Morton by casting him in the role of a philosopher-prince in his *History of King Richard III* and Book I of *Utopia*.

When More was aged fourteen or fifteen, Morton sent him to Oxford to pursue his studies, either at St Mary's Hall or Canterbury College, or possibly both in succession. John More must have consented to this, but remained adamant that his son should shortly enter the legal profession. For all his innate good humour and love of practical joking, the elder More was a man of inflexible opinions. Hence, about the year 1494, Thomas was recalled to London to begin his study of common law. He successfully mastered the rudiments at New Inn and was admitted to Lincoln's Inn at the age of eighteen in February 1496. Within five years or so, he had completed all his legal training and was called to the bar as a junior barrister.[6]

From the outset, More's commitment to a legal education, and to the career expectations and values it implied, was precarious.

Under Morton's patronage, Oxford was becoming a centre for the cycle of learning known as the *studia humanitatis*. The scholasticism of St Thomas Aquinas and Duns Scotus, for which the university had previously been renowned, was being replaced by a humanist curriculum with grammar and rhetoric at its core. The new priorities were classical and biblical languages, for which More showed an immediate flair. Little can be discovered about his exact programme of studies beyond the fact that humanist scholars such as William Grocyn, who gravitated between Oxford and London, were among those who inspired him and drew him with an almost magnetic force towards a life of letters. Under their tutelage, More discovered a passion for the study of classical texts, which he further indulged as a law student and which threatened to crowd out his legal studies, at least in the view of his father. Until 1501 or thereabouts, More was still reading Greek literature in the Latin translations that had been handed down from the Middle Ages, which is hardly surprising. The practice was standard in Europe outside of Italy. Almost no one in England apart from Grocyn read Greek texts in the original language until Thomas Linacre returned from Padua and Venice in 1499.[7] The leap forward in Greek studies occurred between 1500 and 1520. It would be More himself who, in one of his earliest letters as a King's councillor, criticized those 'Trojan' or reactionary elements at Oxford who continued to prefer Latin to Greek studies and who had called the students of Greek 'heretics'.[8]

The philosophy to which More was exposed by his humanist education is the crux of his early life and career. In the age of Lorenzo Valla (1406–57), the focus had been on law and philology, but by 1500 it had shifted towards the moral and political philosophy of the canonical authors, notably Plato, Aristotle, Cicero, Quintilian and Seneca. In the Greek texts, the emphasis was on virtue, social justice and the perfection of a *respublica* or 'commonwealth'. In the Latin literature, it was on the merits of public life as this was represented by the *vir civilis*, the 'active citizen' who knew how to plead for justice and how to advocate wise and honourable policies in the councils or assemblies of the commonwealth and who, in this respect, resembled the Roman model of the 'perfect orator'.[9]

The dichotomy between Greek and Latin literature should not be exaggerated. It was not a straight choice between philosophy and public life. The connection between the two had first been established in Aristotle's *Rhetoric*, where rhetoric was said to be a combination of the science of logic and of the ethical branch of politics.[10] Following Aristotle's lead, Cicero had argued for a close relationship between 'rhetoric' and 'reason'. One of his principal aims was to harmonize politics and philosophy in Roman literature, following their division by the commentators into separate and competing disciplines. But despite these efforts, a tension still existed between Greek and Roman attitudes. Although the Roman rhetoricians shared the moral and educational values of Greek philosophy, they doubted whether 'reason' or wisdom alone could win people round to the cause of justice and truth. They held that the persuasive power of 'perfect' oratory, or what amounted to political skills, would be essential if people were to be induced to support the cause of virtue and abandon that of vice.

It is easy to see how 'eloquence' in these circumstances could become the end rather than the means. Erasmus was troubled by the question at the time of his translation of the Greek *New Testament* (1516). A dilemma for the humanists was to probe the purpose of moral argument and the mission to which they believed themselves called. A potential conflict was seen to exist between 'expediency' and 'honesty', or what was successful and what was right. In a classical context, this took the form of a clash between *negotium* or 'action' (a 'practical philosophy' of public duty and political participation), and *otium* or 'contemplation' (an 'idealist philosophy' of moral absolutism).[11] In a Christian context, the tension was expressed as a clash between 'Martha' and 'Mary', or between the lay and monastic lives. In the eyes of the Church, the 'contemplative' or religious life was traditionally held to be superior to the 'active' or lay life. The case for this priority had been established by St Augustine and St Gregory in their *Sermons*, and by their successors.

The clash between 'action' and 'contemplation', relatively stereotyped in Italian humanist thought by 1500, was still latent in England when More was at Oxford, but it had become overt by the time that Linacre returned from Italy. It underpins the arguments of Hythlodaeus and 'Thomas Morus' in Book I of *Utopia* (see Chapter 5). In its simplest form, the case for moral absolutism and the contemplative life can be put thus: 'Truth does not dwell in the courts of princes, only lies, spiteful criticism and fawning flattery, men pretending to be what they are not and pretending not to be what they are'. This standpoint was influenced by Plato and the Florentine humanist Marsilio Ficino, and the aim of those who advocated it was to defend spiritual and intellectual values in an age regarded by the sceptical as commercial and corrupt. The case for the active life is expressed in the dictum: 'It is insufficient to take pleasure in private study and the bare contemplation and knowledge of things set apart from public affairs, since the one is the end of the other'. Such a position was derived from Aristotle's *Politics* and Cicero's *De officiis*, in particular from Cicero, whom the humanists believed to have written the classic defence of civic duty and the merits of the 'politick life'.

It was at Lincoln's Inn that More began to cultivate his sense of moral purpose and to reformulate the classical and Renaissance debates between 'rhetoric' and 'reason', 'action' and 'contemplation'. He started to write poetry and prose: the conventional means whereby intellectuals from Dante and Petrarch onwards sought self-knowledge and expressed their divided impulses at times of political and religious upheaval, or analysed the condition of the world and themselves. More's genius was always his ability to debate both sides of a question (a technique still known to classicists as rhetoric *in utramque partem*) and to dramatize the internal conflicts of his mind, preferably by using literary devices such as paradoxes, dialogues, or other open-ended forms to facilitate debate without a closure.

About the year 1497, More contributed the introductory and concluding verses for John Holt's *Milk for Children*, a Latin grammar dedicated to Cardinal Morton and intended for the use of his pages at Lambeth palace, where Holt had been appointed schoolmaster.[12] Already More had acquired a sophisticated sense of Latin style, but his most exhilarating experience as a law student occurred in the summer of 1499, when he obtained an introduction to the rising star of northern European humanism, Erasmus of Rotterdam. The meeting was arranged by Lord Mountjoy, briefly Erasmus' pupil in Paris, who was familiar with the More family. In the company of Edward Arnold, another law student, who later practised in the Court of Chancery while More was Lord Chancellor, More and Erasmus visited the royal schoolroom at Eltham palace, where they were presented to Prince Henry, Henry VII's younger son. This was the first encounter with the future Henry VIII, who was then eight years old. Within twenty years More would become the King's trusted councillor and secretary, attending on him daily at Court and stimulating his intellectual interests while reading his mind more acutely even than Cardinal Wolsey. But about this initial meeting we know almost nothing beyond the fact that More mischievously upstaged Erasmus by presenting a set of complimentary Latin verses to Henry, and Erasmus was so embarrassed at having no gift to offer that within three days he had composed a Latin poem of 150 lines in honour of the Prince.[13]

More's quest for self-knowledge quickly led him into fields remote from the 'erudition' of the common lawyers and caused something of a breach with John More. Erasmus later said that More 'was treated almost as if disinherited because he was thought to be deserting his father's profession'.[14] For four years after his call to the bar, he frustrated his father's wishes. He joked in November 1501 that he had 'shelved' his Latin books, but only because he had started to learn Greek.[15] He had gained admission to the humanist circle of Linacre, Grocyn and John Colet, a triumvirate under whose auspices an intellectual transformation was achieved. Linacre is said to have been the only Englishman before the 1520s to have attained a level of classical erudition comparable to that of his Italian contemporaries.[16] In Venice, he had helped to prepare the first edition of the works of Aristotle in the original Greek. On his return to England, he was appointed tutor to Prince Arthur, Henry VII's elder son, who died suddenly from a virulent form of influenza in 1502. On Henry VIII's accession in 1509, Linacre was appointed royal physician on the grounds of his unrivalled medical knowledge.

With Linacre and Grocyn as his humanist mentors, More was introduced to the classical Greek authors in their original versions. With Colet as his spiritual mentor, he probed in depth the writings of the early Church Fathers, especially the great Latin Fathers, St Augustine and St Jerome. At the same time he was perfecting his linguistic skills by translating Greek epigrams into Latin verse under the guidance of the grammarian, William Lily, and by composing vernacular poems with such pithy titles as *A Merry Jest how a Serjeant would learn to be a Friar*. According to Richard Pace, another protégé of Linacre who had studied in Italy and served Cardinal Bainbridge in Rome before becoming Henry VIII's secretary in 1515, More did not follow the traditional literalist method of studying a language, learning letters first, then syllables, then words and phrases, and finally complete sentences. Instead he employed an inductive method, reading whole passages at sight and divining and defining the meanings of words from their contexts. He could do this because he was 'the possessor of a talent more than human'.[17]

Why More threw himself into these classical and patristic studies must remain a matter of conjecture. His initial purpose may only have been to acquire the techniques of a fully-fledged rhetorician. Yet his choice of mentors is suggestive. If Linacre was England's most accomplished classical scholar, Colet and Grocyn were the champions of the view that 'reason', and in particular Christian wisdom as expressed in the New Testament, should always take precedence over 'eloquence'. It was Colet and Grocyn who were most likely to set the clash between 'action' and 'contemplation' into the Christian context of a dialogue between 'Martha' and 'Mary'. Colet is the indicative figure. He was not the most distinguished humanist. He had cabbalistic and occult views that were old-fashioned even for the sixteenth century, and did not know Greek until later taught by John Clement, whom More appointed as tutor to his own children in or about 1514. But it was Colet who first warned Erasmus of the perils of 'eloquence' simply for its own sake. His goal was to restore theology and philosophy to their positions as queens of the human sciences. He had studied briefly in Italy. Returning about 1496, he took Oxford by storm with his lectures on the Epistles of St Paul. Erasmus visited Oxford in the autumn of 1499 and was thrilled that Colet lectured 'wholesale not retail'.[18] When interpreting the Old Testament story of Cain and Abel informally over dinner, Colet became 'intoxicated with a sort of holy frenzy'. The pitch of his voice altered, his eyes lit up, and his countenance became suffused.[19] 'When I listen to Colet', exclaimed Erasmus, 'it seems to me that I am listening to Plato.'[20] And this must have been More's experience in or about 1502.

While continuing his intellectual pursuits, More earned his living by part-time lecturing to law students at Furnivall's Inn. He was discovering his own identity, and chose not to reside at Milk Street or Lincoln's Inn. He lodged instead in or close to the Charterhouse at East Smithfield. It was there that the Carthusian Order in London was established, and space was provided for outsiders seeking spiritual direction or confession to a priest.[21] With its solemn liturgies, silence and austerity, the Charterhouse had long provided a source of religious inspiration for Londoners. The question is, why exactly did More lodge there? Was it to test his vocation for the religious life? Or did he always intend to remain a layman? Was his decision to leave the cloister the result of his inability to accept a life of celibacy? Was he a 'failed' candidate for the priesthood?

This is the first of a string of shibboleths about More which historians cannot ignore and which are considered in this book. The legend holds that he wanted to be a priest or monk, but sex got in the way. After testing his vocation, he realized that 'he would not be able to conquer the temptations of the flesh that come to a man in the vigour and ardour of his youth'.[22] He therefore left the Charterhouse in order to marry. In the twentieth century, both non-confessional writers such as R.W. Chambers and Peter Ackroyd, and Catholics such as Anthony Kenny and E.E. Reynolds, have treated More's sexuality delicately.[23] This was not true of the nineteenth century, when his 'decision' to 'reject' the cloister was the target of outright Protestant versus Catholic polemic on the merits of monasticism and clerical celibacy.[24] Most recently, the controversy has been reignited, but from a different angle. More's alleged 'failure' to become a priest or monk has been made a leitmotif by revisionist historians, who have argued that he spent the rest of his career trying to compensate for this 'failure' and to make his peace with God and himself.

In encouraging radically divergent accounts of the same meagre assortment of facts, the Charterhouse debate is typical of the ways in which interpretations of More's life are constructed. The sources are defective and deceptive. They are also inconsistent. Roper noted that More 'gave himself to devotion and prayer in the Charterhouse of London, religiously living there without vow about four years'.[25] He said nothing about More's vocation or his 'desire' to be a priest. He also said nothing about More's sexuality or hair shirt in this context. The 'story' began with Harpsfield, who built on Roper's *Life*, which he amplified with the anecdotes of More's surviving family, none of whom had known him in his early life. 'It seemeth by some apparent conjectures', said Harpsfield, that in the Charterhouse More was 'inclined either to be a priest, or to take some monastical and solitary life'. This was because he continued 'four years and more full virtuously and religiously in great devotion and prayer' with the Carthusians, but 'without any manner of profession or vow'.[26] Stapleton went even further. He claimed that More 'debated with himself and his friend Lily the question of becoming a priest'. He had 'an ardent desire' for the religious life, 'and thought for a time of becoming a Franciscan'.[27]

This is the 'story', but it grew by accretion from Roper's statement that More lived 'religiously ... without vow' in the Charterhouse. Cresacre More, a direct descendant of Thomas More, dissented from Harpsfield when he wrote that his great-grandfather 'lived four years amongst the Carthusians, dwelling near the Charterhouse, frequenting daily their spiritual exercises, but without any vow'.[28] This is an intriguing formulation. It looks as if Cresacre chose his words with precision. The question must be asked: did More live in the Charterhouse itself, or merely 'near' it? If the latter is true, Harpsfield's 'apparent conjectures' may tell us more about his own priorities than More's.

Harpsfield was among those clergy who held the lay life to be inferior. His purpose was to explain why More 'did not pursue the life contemplative at the Charterhouse ... [which] he had for certain years so graciously commenced'.[29] His narrative reflects his clerical bias. On the same evidence, it can equally well be argued that More lodged in or about the Charterhouse because it was the pre-eminent centre of lay piety for Londoners, and because it had a nationally renowned library which included such devotional works as the *Cloud of Unknowing*, Walter Hilton's *Scale of Perfection* and the *Imitation of Christ* by Thomas à Kempis (More thought the author of the *Imitation* was the Parisian conciliarist, Jean Gerson, but this is neither here nor there).[30] The Catholic historian, T.E. Bridgett, writing shortly after More's beatification in 1886, struck a distinctly judicious note. He anticipated the standpoint of the Second Vatican Council when he acknowledged the autonomy and value of the laity. He stressed that More's choice of the layman's life was a calm one 'guided by perfect humility'.[31] After three or four years' study, More knew that he was 'called' to the active life, whereupon, in or about January 1505, he married Jane Colt. Slightly different emphases have been provided by different biographers, but generally this interpretation was standard until challenged in the late 1970s at a series of international conferences to mark the quincentenary of More's birth.

According to these critiques, More's decision to leave the Charterhouse in favour of marriage was 'sudden' and 'unexpected', a line of argument that is deployed to support the inference that he was a 'failed' candidate for the priesthood 'tormented' by his sexuality. The proponents of this thesis, Sir Geoffrey Elton and Richard Marius, seek to inscribe More's life and public career within a paradigm of sin and redemption.

Although working independently and at different dates, their conclusions are almost identical. Their arguments have re-inforced each other, even if Elton's interpretation is more extreme at certain points.

'Religion', Elton explained, 'is the essence of Thomas More', whose 'standard in these matters was very largely arrived at from his consciousness of original sin'. He had 'not been able to follow the call to abandon the flesh'. He was a 'sex maniac', even if this might be 'exaggerating a little'. 'Certainly', he was 'obsessed' by sex.[32] As Elton continued, his 'youthful attraction' to the Charterhouse as well as 'the manner in which echoes of that life resound through his later years' show that 'here lay his true ambition'. He was 'bound' to regard celibacy as 'the only condition really acceptable to God'. His 'inmost convictions' turned his 'inability' to remain celibate 'into a sin'. As his career unfolded once he left the Charterhouse, he adjusted himself to his 'failure'. Yet neither his career nor his domestic and family life could offset his 'conviction that he had failed to live up to what he . . . regarded as God's ultimate demand on man'. More 'knew demons'. They could be subdued, but never exorcised. Only as a prisoner in the Tower was he 'liberated' or redeemed, because he found at last 'his monk's cell'. He had 'reached his only possible cloister'. He had 'found his tonsure in the Tower'.[33]

Marius, who remains More's most persuasive modern bio-grapher in spite of the controversy he has kindled on this question, concurs with Elton's interpretation. In his view, More was perturbed for the rest of his life by the fact that he did not take holy orders. He 'considered a religious vocation and turned back'. He surrendered 'because he wanted a wife'. Few scholars, Marius argues, have 'contemplated the deep inner conflict' caused by this decision. He was burdened by 'guilt': it was 'the ruling drama of his life'. He had 'always thought that he should have been a monk or a priest'. As a result, he could 'never be single-minded' about a career in law or politics. He was 'distracted' by his search for salvation and by 'a darkness that always threatened to consume him'. In the Charterhouse, he had 'wrestled with the choice' between the religious life and matrimony. Sexual weakness had forced him to choose marriage. Only as a prisoner in the Tower could he find 'peace of mind'. In his final tribulations he was 'given the desire of his heart by a government that sought to punish him and ended by blessing him'.[34]

This interpretation is vigorously contested by the *Amici Thomae Mori* and by the contributors to *Moreana*.[35] The debate is scarcely marked by the meticulous attention to the primary sources so characteristic of the professional legacy of Elton. It is coloured, rather, by repetitions of claim and counter-claim, and by complaints against what the *Amici* consider to be a psycho-analytical approach to More's biography. Yet right is likely to be on their side. First, Roper, the most authoritative of the earliest biographers, did not claim that More was 'testing a vocation' for the priesthood. He merely said that he 'gave himself' in the Charterhouse 'to devotion and prayer . . . religiously living there without vow'. Secondly, there is a joker in the pack. It turns out that Harpsfield's 'apparent conjectures' were not, after all, based on his 'sources' in the More circle. They derived from a literalist reading of the vignette of More which Erasmus had sent to Ulrich von Hutten in July 1519. Erasmus wrote that, in the Charterhouse, More had devoted himself to the works of the Church Fathers, 'preparing himself for the priesthood'. He 'applied his whole mind to the pursuit of piety, with vigils and fasts and prayer'. He 'showed not a little more sense than those who plunge headlong into so exacting a vocation without first making trial of themselves.'[36] 'Nor did anything stand in the way of his devoting himself to this kind of life, except that he could not shake off the desire to get married.'[37] In consequence, 'he chose to be a chaste husband rather than a lewd priest.'[38]

It is striking that none of this was plundered by Roper, even though he drew extensively on Erasmus' correspondence else-where. Roper was More's son-in-law, who had no reason to misrepresent the facts or suppress evidence of an incident that occurred almost twenty years before More entered royal service. It is also obvious that Erasmus' language is playful, almost ironical, and his concluding sentiment was proverbial. To say that someone had chosen to be a 'chaste husband' rather than a 'lewd priest' was a 'merry jest' that had virtually become a colloquialism. As Margaret Paston quipped of her son whom she hoped to see married in 1473, 'I will love him better to be a good secular man, than to be a lewd priest'.[39]

Erasmus said that More in the Charterhouse was 'preparing himself for the priesthood'. Of the modern biographers, Reynolds is among those who maintain that 'this testimony . . . is important and carries more weight than Roper's much later statement'.[40] But why? And does it? Erasmus' vignette is not authoritative. It was not a private letter: it was almost immediately published and several times reprinted. It is now well understood that Erasmus' career was largely a triumph of image management.[41] In this case, his objective was to set before Europe less a factual description of Thomas More, than an idealized depiction of a Christian humanist life. He sought to create a model of decorum in which the clash between 'action' and 'contemplation' in their Christian and classical settings was resolved. It was essential to Erasmus' own 'story' that More should have carefully tested his vocation before deciding that he was 'called' to the active life. Harpsfield read Erasmus' vignette literally. He transposed the passage into a dialogue between 'Martha' and 'Mary'.[42] To achieve this, he had to embellish Roper's account. He even managed to 'explain' how and why it was that More had not chosen the priesthood. The reason was that 'God himself seemeth to have chosen and appointed' More 'to another kind of life'.[43] If this were the case, the reasons for his leaving the Charterhouse would be unassailable.

In their concern to vindicate their interpretation of More's sexual 'guilt' and 'perturbation', Elton and Marius overlook the degree to which Harpsfield's 'story' is unsupported. They proceed to what seems to be an important observation by Harpsfield, who reports that More, while imprisoned in the Tower, told his daughter Margaret 'that his short penning and shutting up did little grieve him', since 'if it had not been for respect of his wife and children, he had voluntarily long ere that time shut himself in as narrow or narrower a room than that was'.[44] Harpsfield makes this passage central to his 'story'. But, even supposing it to be a genuine comment by More, it does not by itself prove that he was a 'failed' monk tormented by his sexuality.[45] The underlying sentiment may be genuine. It resembles a passage in Margaret's 'letter' to Alice Alington, written in August 1534, which described More's incarceration in the Tower (see Chapter 9). He thanked God and the King that his fate had so far only involved loss of liberty, and not yet loss of life. The King, said More, 'hath done me so great good by the spiritual profit that I trust I take thereby'.[46] Of these benefits, 'I reckon upon my faith my [im]prisonment even the very chief'.[47] But Harpsfield is guilty of sleight of hand. His observation is taken not from Margaret's 'letter', but from Roper's *Life*, where an almost identical comment appears.[48] Yet, in Roper's narrative, it belongs to the section that portrays More's imprisonment and trial, not to that which describes the Charterhouse years. The context of the comment is entirely different.

Stapleton's is the only one of the earliest 'Lives' that supports the argument that More's ambition to become a priest or monk was frustrated by his sexuality. As he maintained, More had 'an ardent desire' for the religious life:

> But as he feared, even with the help of his practices of penance, that he would not be able to conquer the temptations of the flesh that come to a man in the vigour and ardour of his youth, he made up his mind to marry.[49]

This account has little basis in fact. It is obviously a further amplification of Erasmus and Harpsfield. It is also eccentric, since it goes on to say that More thought of becoming a Franciscan.[50] No one else has ever suggested this. It may have suited the revisionists to plunder Stapleton selectively, but he does not even mention the Charterhouse or the Carthusians. Of More's decision to marry, he adds: 'he would often speak [about it] in after life with great sorrow and regret, for he used to say that it was much easier to be chaste in the single than in the married state'.[51] Marius cites this passage with approbation. Yet it has no independent corroboration, and is almost certainly derived from an inversion of Erasmus' quip that More 'chose to be a chaste husband rather than a lewd priest'.[52]

Stapleton is the main authority for the revisionist account of More's efforts to subdue sexual arousal in his early life. He wrote that More 'even as a youth' wore a hair shirt. He slept 'on the ground or on bare boards with perhaps a log of wood as his pillow'.[53] We know that More wore a hair shirt. Roper tells us that 'for the avoiding of singularity', he did not wish this fact to be known.[54] But in Roper's *Life* the passage is disconnected from the account of the Charterhouse years. Nor is there any independent evidence that More slept with a log of wood as his pillow at any point in his life, even during his imprisonment in the Tower.

What do we actually know about More's hair shirt? In a letter of 1535 to Dame Catherine Manne, John Bouge, a Carthusian monk of Axholme, who had been More's confessor, reported that he was 'devout in his divine service and . . . wore a great hair next his skin'. According to Bouge, Alice, More's second wife, failed to discover her husband's secret for almost a year after their marriage. She begged Bouge to 'counsel' him not to wear the shirt, since it was 'hard and rough', and 'tamed his flesh till the blood was seen in his clothes'.[55] More gave his hair shirt to his daughter, Margaret, on the eve of his execution. From her it passed to her adopted sister and namesake, Margaret Gigs, through whose daughter it descended to the Community of St Monica's, Louvain, and later to the Community of St Augustine's Priory, Newton Abbot. There is no doubt about its existence: it was exhibited, preserved in a reliquary, as part of the celebrations of the quincentenary of More's birth at the National Portrait Gallery in London in 1977–8. But no one can say when More acquired it or first wore it.

In a celebrated review of Marius in the *New York Review of Books*, Elton asked, 'What purpose does a man serve who wears a hair shirt and whips himself except to "tame the flesh"?' Conveniently assuming that More already wore a hair shirt in the Charterhouse, he went on to assert that the 'evidence' was 'so strong' that 'More failed to restrain his sexual drive' that it was on this account that he was 'forced' to abandon 'his youthful ambition to enter the cloister'. Furthermore, 'this experience continued to trouble him until he found peace in the Tower'. Only 'wilful blindness' on the part of historians had 'ignored' this point for so long.[56] Elton's vaunted 'evidence', however, turned out to be Erasmus' badinage on More's marriage; the fact that Jane Colt, More's first wife, died 'after bearing four children in as many years'; the fact that More told stories of women who 'act as shrews and temptresses'; and the fact that he wore a hair shirt.

Obviously there is a link between More's hair shirt and his wish to restrain arousal. Ever since St Paul had pronounced on the matter, the Catholic Church had sought to regulate the sexual urge. What especially troubled St Augustine, whose writings More was reading in depth at this time, was the extent to which sexual desire was uncontrollable. In Paradise, according to Augustine, Adam had been able to control his sexual urge at will. Only after the Fall did he lose the ability to restrain himself. In consequence, Augustine categorized sexual arousal differently from other forms of passion, since in the case of anger the excitement did not arise independently of the mind and did not autonomously disturb the body. To wear a hair shirt, or to scourge oneself, was regarded by the Church as a discipline and an atonement for sin. All of this is far removed from the secular norms of today, but the conclusion is self-evident. More's hair shirt is a testimony to his religious faith. To this extent, Elton is correct. But it is not by itself 'evidence' that More in the Charterhouse had 'not been able to follow the call to abandon the flesh' or that he was some sort of 'sex maniac' or deviant.

The case that More was a 'failed' priest overwhelmed by sexual 'guilt' ultimately rests on the psychoanalytic theories of Sigmund Freud (1856–1939) concerning the unconscious mind.[57] In view of the defective evidence, the Charterhouse debate is likely to hit the buffers in the absence of fresh discoveries. Beyond what has already been said, we know two things. The first is that More, while resident in or about the Charterhouse, lectured on St Augustine's *City of God* at the Church of St Lawrence Jewry. Grocyn was the rector of this parish, and More's lectures were a sequel to Grocyn's own course on the *Ecclesiastical Hierarchy* attributed to Dionysius the Areopagite.[58] More's lectures were seemingly delivered extempore. No information about their contents has survived, although we do have an unconfirmed comment by Stapleton that More approached his subject not from the standpoint of theology, but from that of history and philosophy.[59]

More's biographers have considered his lectures to be suggestive. St Augustine, by his writings, and especially the *Confessions* and the *City of God*, transformed the way that the Church thought about reason and revelation, authority and tradition, grace and predestination, freedom and human nature. The thesis of the *City of God* is that the Roman Empire (and thus by implication any earthly society) was neither holy nor wicked of itself. Its moral status was determined by the piety or impiety of its members. Fallen man is subject to destructive emotions, and the State is an expression of these impulses. As the argument unfolds, an image of two 'cities' emerges: the one earthly, carnal and corruptible, inspired by pride and selfish love; the other eternal, spiritual and incorruptible, inspired by love of God in contempt of oneself. These 'cities' are mutually exclusive and radically opposed. Although on earth they would intermingle, they would be visibly divided at the end of history, when Christ will judge the living and the dead. The moral is that a Christian's duty is always to God and not to worldly vanities or powers. In the absence of true Christianity and justice, there can be no perfection of the commonwealth on earth.[60]

It is easy to see how this classic of the Middle Ages could have made a lasting impression on More. Modulations of its vision of the 'commonwealth' resonate through Book II of *Utopia*, and a number of its themes reappear in More's Tower writings. Yet a mental leap from our image of the young lawyer lecturing on St Augustine to that of the ex-Lord Chancellor, who refused to acquiesce to Henry VIII's Act of Supremacy and died for his beliefs on the scaffold, is too simplistic. A straight line cannot be drawn between More's education and his execution.

What can be said is that his education introduced him to almost all the main texts of the classical and early Christian traditions. This inference is less platitudinous than it seems. Its force is that it was exactly these texts which became central first to More's anti-Lutheran campaign begun as the King's secretary, and after 1527 to the divorce campaign and the case for the royal supremacy. Both Roper and Harpsfield understood the point, which is independently confirmed by a string of recent studies.[61] The texts with which More later grappled were those which he had first studied in his early life. And that his knowledge was unrivalled is proved by the fact that, even when deprived of his books in the Tower, he could still quote classical literature, the Bible and the Church Fathers accurately from memory.

The other thing we know about the Charterhouse is that More was 'determined ... to put before his eyes the example of some prominent layman, on which he might model his life.' At last he 'fixed upon John Pico, Earl of Mirandula.'[62] Our source is Stapleton, but his report is confirmed by Cresacre More, who noted that 'when [More] determined to marry, he propounded to himself for a pattern in life a singular layman, John Picus, Earl of Mirandula, who was a man most famous for virtue, and most eminent for learning'.[63] It was around 1504 that More completed the *Life of John Picus, Earl of Mirandula*, a translation of the 'Life' of Pico della Mirandola, the Italian humanist prodigy (1463–94), by his nephew, Giovanni Francesco, which was prefixed to the Latin edition of Pico's *Complete Works* published at Bologna in 1496. In a manuscript presented as a New Year's gift to Joyce Lee, sister of his friend Edward Lee, More translated Pico's 'Life' into fairly literal English, and rounded off the work with selected extracts from Pico's writings: an interpretation of Psalm 15, three letters, some verses on spiritual warfare and Christian love, and a prayer.[64]

The *Life of John Picus* was printed about the year 1510 by John Rastell.[65] A dedicatory epistle, unaltered from the manuscript, indicates that the work was intended for Lee's private use and that it was most likely presented in January 1505, shortly after she had taken vows at the Convent of Poor Clares in Aldgate, London. More justified his choice of texts on the grounds that nothing of comparable length would prove as profitable 'to the achieving of temperance in prosperity', 'the purchasing of patience in adversity', 'the despising of worldly vanity', and 'the desiring of heavenly felicity'.[66] These were universal Christian virtues which More advocated in his Tower writings, notably the *Dialogue of Comfort against Tribulation*. They applied to both the world and the cloister. In this sense, the *Life of John Picus* functioned as a guide to virtuous living in either vocation. And this interpretation is consistent with the fact that More, who was himself poised to leave the precincts of the Charterhouse, presented the work to someone who had just entered the cloister. It also accords with More's prefatory remark that, whatever his faults as a translator, the texts themselves would 'delight and please any person' who had a 'desire and love to God'.[67]

The *Life of John Picus* cannot contribute to a topical account of More's 'lost' vocation. This approach has been attempted by several historians, but it is not how More's mind worked.[68] There was nothing in which he took greater delight than in an open-ended debate that left competing viewpoints unresolved. The one point clarified by his translation is that Pico was called to the religious life 'by the especial commandment of God'.[69] These words were More's own interpolation into Giovanni Francesco's text of the 'Life', and established the context for the subsequent claim that Pico 'shrank' from his vocation even though it was revealed by God himself.[70] Pico, in More's eyes, had fallen victim to the sin of pride. His career was a cautionary tale, exemplifying the moral danger that Colet saw hidden in humanist scholarship, but not validating any particular standpoint as to the merits of the 'active' and the 'contemplative' lives.[71]

If, then, the riddle of More's vocation and the extent to which it was determined by his sexuality has fascinated his biographers, it has distracted attention from the humanist emphasis on philosophy. For Grocyn and Colet, the balance had tilted in favour of 'contemplation'. For More, the lure in the end was always 'action'. The significance of the Charterhouse years is likely to be that More spent his time trying to understand the proper relationship between philosophy and public life. He left the philosophical debate open-ended, but in practice opted for a legal career. We will never know how, when or why. But once that decision was taken, his career took off, and by 1518 he had entered royal service. With that step, More irrevocably abandoned 'contemplation' and accepted the 'active' life. But did he do so willingly? It is to this question that the next chapter will turn.

Notes

1 CW 3, Pt. 1, pp. 178–9; John Guy, *The Public Career of Sir Thomas More* (Brighton, 1980), pp. 210–11.
2 Three dates are possible: 6 February 1477, 6 February 1478, 7 February 1478.
3 PRO, SP 1/22, fo. 79.
4 Roper, p. 198.
5 Roper, p. 197.
6 Guy, *Public Career*, pp. 1–2.
7 J. Woolfson, *Padua and the Tudors* (Cambridge, 1998), pp. 39–72, 103–18.
8 Rogers, ed., *Selected Letters*, pp. 94–103.
9 Q. Skinner, *Reason and Rhetoric in the Philosophy of Thomas Hobbes* (Cambridge, 1996), pp. 66–99.
10 J.H. Freese, ed., *The Art of Rhetoric* (London, 1926).
11 Q. Skinner, *The Foundations of Modern Political Thought* (2 vols, Cambridge, 1978) 1, pp. 108, 115–16, 217–19, 276.
12 CW 3, Pt. 2, pp. 65–6, 294–7, 417–18.
13 CWE 1, pp. 195–7.
14 CWE 7, p. 19.
15 Rogers, ed., *Correspondence*, pp. 3–5.
16 Woolfson, *Padua and the Tudors*, p. 39.
17 E. Surtz, 'Richard Pace's Sketch of Thomas More', in R.S. Sylvester and G. Marc'hadour, eds, *Essential Articles for the Study of Thomas More* (Hamden, CT, 1977), p. 183.
18 Rogers, ed., *Selected Letters*, p. 3.
19 CWE 1, p. 230.
20 CWE 1, p. 235.
21 David Knowles, *The Religious Orders in England* (3 vols, Cambridge, 1940–59) 3, p. 224.
22 Stapleton, pp. 9–10.
23 R.W. Chambers, *Thomas More* (London, 1935), pp. 77–86; P. Ackroyd, *Thomas More* (London, 1998), pp. 93–107; A. Kenny, *Thomas More* (Oxford, 1983), pp. 11–12; E.E. Reynolds, *The Life and Death of St Thomas More* (London, 1978), pp. 27–37.
24 F. Seebohm, *The Oxford Reformers* (London, 1915), pp. 89–98; T.E. Bridgett, *Life and Writings of Blessed Thomas More* (London, 1924), pp. 19–51.
25 Roper, p. 198.
26 Harpsfield, p. 17.
27 Stapleton, pp. 9–10.

28 Cresacre More, *The Life of Sir Thomas More* (London, 1828), p. 25.
29 Harpsfield, p. 205.
30 S. Brigden, *London and the Reformation* (Oxford, 1989), p. 227; E.M. Thompson, *The Carthusian Order in England* (London, 1930); Knowles, *Religious Orders in England* 3, pp. 222–40; Ackroyd, *Thomas More*, pp. 97–8.
31 Bridgett, *Blessed Thomas More*, p. 29.
32 G.R. Elton, *Studies in Tudor and Stuart Politics and Government* (4 vols, Cambridge, 1974–92) 4, p. 150.
33 Elton, *Studies* 3, pp. 353–5.
34 Richard Marius, *Thomas More* (New York, 1984), pp. xxii–iii, 34–43, 465.
35 E.F. Alkaaoud, 'A Man for Our Season: Marius on More', *Moreana* 27 (1990), pp. 47–54.
36 *CWE* 7, p. 21.
37 *CWE* 7, p. 21.
38 *CWE* 7, p. 21 (translation adapted).
39 Reynolds, *St Thomas More*, p. 33 n. 18.
40 Reynolds, *St Thomas More*, p. 33.
41 Lisa Jardine, *Erasmus, Man of Letters: the Construction of Charisma in Print* (Princeton, NJ, 1993).
42 Harpsfield, p. 18.
43 Harpsfield, p. 18.
44 Harpsfield, pp. 17–18.
45 Marius, *Thomas More*, pp. 464–5.
46 Rogers, ed., *Correspondence*, p. 531.
47 Rogers, ed., *Correspondence*, p. 531.
48 Roper, p. 239.
49 Stapleton, pp. 9–10.
50 Stapleton, p. 9.
51 Stapleton, p. 10.
52 Marius, *Thomas More*, p. 37.
53 Stapleton, p. 9.
54 Roper, pp. 223–4.
55 *LP Add.* I.i. no. 1024; Trapp and Herbrüggen, pp. 119–20.
56 G.R. Elton, 'The Actor Saint', *New York Review of Books* (31 Jan. 1985), p. 7.
57 Elton actually cited Freud, see *Studies* 4, p. 147.
58 Harpsfield, pp. 13–14; Rogers, ed., *Correspondence*, p. 4.
59 Stapleton, p. 9.
60 St Augustine, *The City of God against the Pagans* ed. R.W. Dyson (Cambridge, 1998).
61 Roper, p. 215; Harpsfield, p. 45; B. Gogan, *The Common Corps of Christendom: Ecclesiological Themes in the Writings of Sir Thomas More* (Leiden, 1982); R. Rex, *The Theology of John Fisher* (Cambridge, 1991); R. Rex, 'The English Campaign against Luther in the 1520s', *Transactions of the Royal Historical Society*, 5th series, 39 (1989), pp. 85–106; E. Surtz and V. Murphy, eds, *The Divorce Tracts of Henry VIII* (Angers, 1988); V. Murphy, 'The Literature and Propaganda of Henry VIII's First Divorce', in

D. MacCulloch, ed., *The Reign of Henry VIII: Politics, Policy and Piety* (London, 1995), pp. 135–58; G.D. Nicholson, 'The Act of Appeals and the English Reformation', in C. Cross, D.M. Loades and J.J. Scarisbrick, eds, *Law and Government under the Tudors* (Cambridge, 1988), pp. 19–30.
62 Stapleton, p. 10.
63 Cresacre More, p. 27.
64 *EW* (1931) 1, pp. 347–96.
65 *STC*² no. 19897. 7.
66 *EW* (1931) 1, p. 347.
67 *EW* (1931) 1, p. 348.
68 S.E. Lehmberg, 'English Humanists, the Reformation and the Problem of Counsel', *Archiv für Reformationsgeschichte* 52 (1961), pp. 74–90; Lehmberg, 'Sir Thomas More's Life of Pico della Mirandola', *Studies in the Renaissance* 3 (1956), pp. 61–74; A. Fox, *Thomas More: History and Providence* (Oxford, 1982), p. 31.
69 *EW* (1931) 1, p. 359.
70 *EW* (1931) 1, p. 361.
71 Fox, *Thomas More*, p. 29.

|3|

Reluctant courtier?

Was More a 'willing' or a 'reluctant' courtier? The theme is a leitmotif of the historiography. It became an issue when Harpsfield in Mary's reign and the early Elizabethan recusants in exile in the Netherlands made More their hero and argued that his life and career had been subverted by the 'lusts' of Henry VIII. For Stapleton, whose *Life of Thomas More* formed the final part of a trilogy of saints' 'Lives', More had disdained Court life. He disliked politics and judged himself 'quite unfitted to that mode of life'. Instinctively, he 'loathed the life of the Court'. When it was plain that vice and lust ruled there in place of piety and virtue, he immediately resigned.[1]

Stapleton coloured his arguments for rhetorical effect. It was a strategy that More himself criticized in the prefatory letter to his *Translations of Lucian* (1506). He complained that writers of saints' lives often indulged in fiction: 'there is scarcely a martyr's or a virgin's life which they have passed over without inserting some falsehoods of this kind'. To such authors, it seemed as if 'truth could not stand by its own strength but had to be bolstered with lies!' And More spotted the catch: 'when the added falsehood is detected, the authority of truth is immediately diminished and weakened'.[2] This chapter will aim to show how More's legal and City career prepared him for a political career, before turning to the debate over exactly when he became Henry VIII's sworn councillor, whether he entered royal service 'willingly' or 'reluctantly', and whether he lied in order to mislead Erasmus as to the date and nature of his appointment and the extent of his ambition.

More left the Charterhouse some time during 1504. By January 1505 he had married Jane Colt, eldest daughter of Sir

John Colt, of Netherhall, near Roydon in Essex. Probably the families were already acquainted. Jane's grandfather had been a councillor of Edward IV and a leading Yorkist supporter in the Wars of the Roses, sent on diplomatic missions to treat with Charles the Bold and Louis XI. Roydon was within easy riding distance of John More's country house at Gobions, close to North Mimms in Hertfordshire. On his marriage, More leased the Old Barge, Bucklersbury, a large stone and timber house in the parish of St Stephen, Walbrook, London. His four children were born there, and Margaret Gigs was adopted as a foster-sister for his eldest daughter, Margaret.[3]

More now pursued his legal career with energy and success: there is no sign of any 'disdain' for it. According to Erasmus, 'there was no one whose advice was more freely sought by litigants', and More found himself able to command substantial fees.[4] How true this is cannot be judged. But More secured rapid advancement at Lincoln's Inn, being appointed pensioner (i.e. financial accountant) in 1507. Next, he was chosen as butler, a ceremonial office earlier held by his father. In 1510 he became marshal of the inn and was named the autumn reader for 1511. Excused service as treasurer, he was then elected as one of the inn's four governors.[5] The seniority and speed of these appointments shows that More was climbing to the peak of his profession.

On the Feast of All Saints 1514, More was designated Lent reader for 1515 at Lincoln's Inn: the highest distinction that an inn of court could confer upon a member. More's privilege was to deliver a course of lectures to the assembled society in Hall during the vacation between the Hilary and Easter legal terms. He lectured for an hour each day on an aspect of a statute or legal doctrine which interested him, and then engaged his audience in 'disputations' of hypothetical cases arising from his arguments for a further hour or so. Whether it was usual to deliver these lectures extempore or read them from a script is unknown, but neither the text nor any notes of More's reading are extant in print or manuscript.[6]

More's career advanced on other fronts. He was first returned as a member of the House of Commons in 1504. His participation in the Parliament has been disputed on the grounds that the election records for this year are missing, but there are reasons for supposing that he was indeed elected. His constituency may have been Gatton, the Surrey borough seat to which his father-in-law had been returned in 1492.[7] Roper is the authority for More's election. The value of his uncorroborated evidence was questioned by Sir Geoffrey Elton, but the accuracy of Roper's previously disputed account of the case of the Pope's ship (see below) is likely to raise his status as an independent authority. Roper recounted that in this Parliament, More opposed Henry VII's demand for an aid on the marriage of his eldest daughter, Margaret, to James IV of Scotland, and that a gentleman of the Privy Chamber, Sir William Tyler, informed the King that 'a beardless boy had disappointed all his purpose'.[8] The *History of Parliament* believes that the underlying truth of this account is supported by the known reluctance of the Commons to grant the King's request in its initial form, even if it is unlikely that More and his father were in danger after the debate, as Roper claimed. It is conceivable that More's visits to the universities of Paris and Louvain in 1508 were linked to a period of self-imposed exile that ended with Henry VII's death in April 1509, but such an interpretation is highly improbable.[9]

More's strongest connection was with the City of London. His father had been retained as legal counsel by the City as early as 1489. By the accession of Henry VIII, More was himself starting to be employed as a legal adviser or arbitrator to act in commercial disputes between Londoners or between members of the livery companies and foreign merchants.[10] In March 1509, he was admitted to the Mercers' Company 'frank and free'. According to the leading expert, livery companies were 'always ready to recruit honorary members whose services might be useful'.[11] In the following September, More was at the centre of the arrangements to receive the Pensionary (or legal councillor) of Antwerp at his visit to Mercers' Hall. By the end of the year, writs were issued for a new session of Parliament, and More was elected to the Commons on 13 December 1509 in place of James Yarford, a mercer, who, by becoming an alderman three weeks earlier, had disqualified himself.[12] The new Parliament assembled in January 1510.

In the summer of 1511, More's wife, Jane, died at the age of twenty-three, possibly in childbirth. Within a month he had married Dame Alice Middleton, a wealthy widow who was seven years older than himself. He became the subject of gossip, which embarrasses his biographers, other than those revisionists who think he was a 'sex maniac'.[13] The evidence is undisputed. John Bouge, More's confessor wrote, '[More] was my parishioner at

London. I christened him two goodly children. I buried his first wife. And within a month after, he came to me on a Sunday, at night, late, and there he brought me a dispensation to be married the next Monday, without any banns asking'.[14] Erasmus filled out the picture in his vignette to Hutten. More had married Alice against 'the advice of his friends'.[15] He himself, said Erasmus, often joked that she was 'neither a pearl nor a girl'. He had remarried 'more to have someone to look after his household than for his own pleasure'.[16] Harpsfield duly repeated this when he said that More married Alice rather 'for the ruling and governing of his children, house and family, than for any bodily pleasure' (see Chapter 4).[17]

How reliable are these reports? Bouge wrote shortly after More's execution, more than twenty years after the events he described. He was a friend of John Fisher and held More's heroism in esteem. There is no reason to treat him as a hostile witness or to doubt his account, whereas Erasmus' comments should be approached with caution. It was essential to the model of classical and Christian decorum which governed his vignette that, if More might be thought to have acted hastily, he should not appear to have done so without first seeking advice, even if he had later made his own choice. It was especially important that More did not appear to have remarried for sex. It is most unlikely that the vignette can be read as a literal description of the events of More's second marriage, which (in any case) Erasmus had not personally witnessed. A further possibility is that his remarks – as always on the subject of marriage – were playful or ironical.

More's career took a leap forward in September 1510, when he was appointed an undersheriff of London. According to Roper, his income soared to £400 a year, a substantial sum for a lawyer just thirty-three years old.[18] As an undersheriff, More was a permanent official who advised the sheriffs and sat as judge in the Sheriff's Court. Sessions were held at Guildhall, generally on Thursday mornings, and the profits of the court's jurisdiction went to the sheriffs. The undersheriffs received a fixed stipend, but they also had the right to represent the City in the central courts at Westminster as assistant legal counsel under the Recorder, London's chief law officer. It was there that More's profit lay. Legal fees in commercial or civil litigation could be considerable, and since he did not resign his undersheriff's post until July 1518, a month after he received a grant of an annuity of £100 as Henry VIII's attendant councillor, it is likely that fees from court appearances on the City's behalf made up the lion's share of his £400 salary at this time.[19]

As a prominent citizen of London, More was increasingly drawn into specially commissioned tasks on the City's and the Crown's behalf. He joined his father on a Middlesex special commission in July 1509, and again as a commissioner of sewers for the Thames district between Greenwich and Lambeth in February 1514. He assisted the staff of the Court of Chancery as a part-time examiner and arbitrator. As the City's nominees, More and his father lobbied Edward Stafford, 3rd Duke of Buckingham, and Richard Nix, Bishop of Norwich, over the Act for Corporations in December 1512. The following month, More was among those who met the King's Council 'for divers causes' on the City's behalf. He was then sent in May 1515 on the embassy to Bruges which produced *Utopia*. The aim of the mission was to renegotiate the treaty which had protected the Anglo-Flemish wool and cloth trades since 1478, but which in Henry VII's renewals of 1496 and 1506 had created loopholes for the Flemings.[20]

On his return to London, More was named to a committee to fix the price of foodstuffs in the capital. Thereafter, he was the luminary of the committee that was appointed by Wolsey and the King's Council to investigate the Evil May Day riots of 1517, a xenophobic insurgence in London during the early hours of 1 May, which was tantamount in the Crown's eyes to a political revolt. Almost a thousand rioters and looters led by a small group of disaffected apprentices had rampaged through the houses and business premises of the overseas mercantile community and released prisoners from the City's gaols.[21]

More's political career developed logically from these activities but the date and circumstances of his entry into royal service are vigorously contested. Roper blazed the trail for the earliest biographers. According to his 'story', More 'for his learning, wisdom, knowledge, and experience' came into 'such estimation' that, 'at the suit and instance of the English merchants', he was 'by the King's consent made twice ambassador in certain great causes between them and the merchants of the Steelyard'.[22] More's ability impressed the King so much that he asked Cardinal Wolsey, his leading councillor and chief minister by the end of 1514, 'to procure [More] to his service'.[23] As Roper continued, Wolsey 'earnestly travailed' to recruit More, 'alleging unto him how dear his service must needs be unto his majesty'.

But More made his excuses. It was not until his performance in the Court of Star Chamber before the Lord Chancellor and the judges as legal counsel to Pope Leo X's ambassador in the case of a confiscated cargo of alum that Henry resolved to brook no resistance, and 'for no entreaty would the King from thenceforth be induced any longer to forbear his service'.[24] More duly consented to serve the King, whereupon Henry appointed him 'Master of the Requests', and 'within a month after . . . one of his privy council'.[25]

Harpsfield followed Roper's account more or less verbatim, but added that More received 'a notable and worthy lesson and charge' from the King that 'in all his doings and affairs touching the king, he should first respect and regard God, and afterward the king his master'.[26] Harpsfield drew on More's letter of 5 March 1534 to Thomas Cromwell, in which he said that at his 'first coming' into royal service, the King had told him that he should 'first look unto God and after God unto him'.[27] Although this seems with hindsight to have been an unnervingly prophetic homily, it will shortly be shown that More's entry into royal service was indeed accompanied by an interview.

Stapleton drew on Roper and Harpsfield's descriptions, but also transcribed a letter (now lost) of More to John Fisher, written shortly after his removal to Court. According to this, More said: 'It was with the greatest unwillingness that I came to Court, as everyone knows, and as the King himself in joke often throws up in my face.' Of the Court, he said: 'I am as uncomfortable there as a bad rider is in the saddle.' And as the letter concluded, it was only to the extent that Henry VIII advanced 'in all the qualities that befit a good monarch' that the life of the Court could seem tolerable.[28] Obviously this letter is of the utmost significance. No manuscript is extant. Where did Stapleton obtain his text? William Rastell is a possible source. He had transcribed More's letters in preparation for his folio edition of More's *English Works* (1557). A copy may have been among the papers taken to the Netherlands when members of the More circle went into exile under Edward VI and later under Elizabeth. If the letter is authentic, More's own statement as well as Roper's *Life* confirms that More was a reluctant courtier. But the letter is rhetorically coloured and its provenance is suspect. At the very least, it cannot be cited uncritically.

The issue of provenance has only recently troubled historians. It did not seem to be significant, since More's reputation as a 'reluctant' politician was apparently confirmed by Erasmus. In a letter to Germain de Brie, he claimed that Henry VIII could not be satisfied until More had been 'dragged' into his most intimate counsels.[29] His vignette to Hutten reiterated the point. The King, he said, 'would not rest until he had dragged the man to his court'. As Erasmus glossed: 'I use the word "dragged" advisedly, for no man was ever more consumed with ambition to enter a court than he was to avoid it'.[30] Elsewhere, More is said by Erasmus to have 'become a courtier pure and simple, always with the King, on whose Council he is', and again, 'I should regret what has happened to More, who has been drawn into Court life, were it not that under such a King, and with so many learned colleagues, it seems rather a university than a Court'.[31]

In reality, Erasmus strongly disapproved of More's entry into politics. In the debates over the merits of 'practical philosophy' or 'action' as against those of 'idealist philosophy' or 'contemplation', he took the side of 'contemplation'. No one has ever disputed that Erasmus expressed his concern over More's entry into politics partly as a way of asserting his own intellectual independence. The issue has left an uneasy hiatus in the historiography. More's non-confessional and Catholic biographers, led respectively by R.W. Chambers and E.E. Reynolds, were equally aware of it.[32] Since leaving the Charterhouse, More had pursued his legal career in earnest and had sat twice in the House of Commons. He had also petitioned for his councillor's fee of £100. The risk was always that someone might argue that More entered Henry VIII's service 'willingly', and then refocus the debate to assert that Erasmus and More – supposedly the greatest of friends since 1509, when Erasmus had begun the *Praise of Folly* under More's roof – were different types of humanist with incompatible philosophies.

Chambers foresaw this problem but chose to smother it. His comment, 'It is not quite clear from what exact date we ought to reckon More as being in the King's service', seemed innocuous, but in a footnote he referred the reader to contradictory evidence which suggested that More had entered royal service before Erasmus knew about the matter.[33] From a different tack, Reynolds sought to reinvent the context. He conjectured that 'More had had a frank discussion with the King before entering his service'.[34] His 'source' was Harpsfield. But neither Harpsfield nor Erasmus had suggested that More had treated with the King before entering his service: the surmise that Henry VIII would have discussed terms with a subject, even in the first decade of his reign, is improbable. The inference that More expressed reservations towards Henry as early as 1518 is unwarranted, even if it is an argument that has been floated in the context of the *History of King Richard III*, which More compiled in Latin and English versions somewhere between the years 1513 and 1519, and which is at root an investigation of tyranny, inspired by More's study of the *Annals* of the Roman imperial historian Tacitus.[35]

More's political career became a shibboleth in 1970, when Sir Geoffrey Elton made it the opening salvo in his campaign to 'get at the man inside the plaster statue'.[36] The centrepiece was his 'discovery' that More was a King's councillor 'long before he allowed Erasmus to know as much' and that his 'reluctance' to enter royal service was a sham. More in his letter to Fisher was 'no doubt telling the truth, but not all the truth'. There was 'no evidence at all' that More's new position 'ran against the grain'. On the contrary, he 'followed Henry's call at so early a date that he can not have hesitated long'. He simply could not bring himself to confess this fact to Erasmus. In assessing More's place in government and politics, 'we should abandon the conventional talk about his reluctance to enter it'. More 'went with his eyes open'. He 'meant to make a career'.[37]

This was vintage Elton, and it created pandemonium. His argument was a cluster bomb, which exploded in three different places. First, it denied the truth of Roper's 'story' in his *Life of Sir Thomas More* and thereby undermined the integrity of the work as a 'primary source'. Second, it disseminated the innuendo that More was a liar who misled Erasmus as to the date and nature of his appointment at Henry VIII's Court. This attack was insidious, since no responsible historian had dared hitherto to suggest such a thing. Elton's claim almost certainly paved the way for subsequent assertions by Richard Marius that More 'distorted', 'twisted' or suppressed evidence at least twice in his career.[38] Thirdly, if More had entered royal service 'willingly' and 'meant to make a career', the significance of his 'humanism' was limited to vocational training in the narrowest of senses, and the seriousness of the debate over 'action' versus 'contemplation' and the primacy of the Greek New Testament diminished. And sure enough, Elton was soon arguing that More was not a 'proper' humanist: he was 'a humanist of sorts but always a player at the game'. He was 'no professional in the mould of Erasmus and Budé and moreover uncomfortably aware of it'. His humanism was 'superficial'. His 'real role' was always that of a lawyer, diplomat and politician.[39]

Elton's arguments greatly disconcerted the *Amici Thomae Mori*, as they were positively intended to do.[40] Germain Marc'hadour, the neo-Latin scholar and editor of the journal *Moreana*, set the trend when he announced that he would not '"wrestle" with Professor Elton'.[41] He conceded that 'perhaps too much holiness was imputed to More's motivation in earlier studies', but 'now ... we may run the risk of taking too much away from him'. His reticence served to amplify the force of Elton's iconoclasm and helped to open the way for Marius' revisionist biography, which appeared in 1984. Of course, Elton was the unrivalled authority on the public records. He was the pre-eminent archival historian in Britain. He spoke with, and commanded, authority. When Marius dealt with More's entry into royal service, he followed Elton's line, but more prudently. He circumvented the issue of whether More had lied to Erasmus, arguing that More's early position as a King's councillor was 'irregular' and so 'he did not truly think of himself as a fully-fledged councillor'.[42] This is a woolly and unconvincing theory, but it reflected the inability of historians to reconcile what seemed to be conflicting 'evidence'. Since Marius wrote, the debate has been in limbo. Despite a number of attempts to square the circle, the force of Elton's argument has largely been presumed.[43] More's most recent biographer, Peter Ackroyd, does not even attempt to revisit Elton's account of the 'evidence', despite his concern to deal with the contradictions represented by More's career.[44]

The crux of Elton's case is the alleged 'conflict' between 'ascertainable fact' and 'contemporary comment'. Whereas Roper, Erasmus, and the Venetian ambassador, Sebastian Giustinian, unanimously dated More's entry into royal service to the spring or early summer of 1518, Elton applied his expertise in the public records to argue that, when More visited Calais in the autumn of 1517 as a commercial envoy, he was already sworn as a King's councillor. Erasmus, whose correspondence with More was frequent, 'was left ignorant of this fact for the best part of a year'. The record 'leaves no doubt of this, and it calls for a reassessment of More's behaviour'.[45]

Elton's main 'evidence' was the warrant for More's attendant councillor's fee of £100.[46] On 21 June 1518, More was granted his annuity payable partly out of the Exchequer of Receipt and partly in assignments on the petty custom of London. The warrant backdated his first instalment to the previous Michaelmas (29 September), thereby 'proving' that he was already a sworn King's councillor by that date. If this were not enough, the document was not a signet warrant – the usual instrument – but a bill or petition which More himself submitted, and which when signed by the King became a warrant for the Great Seal. By this procedure, More jumped to the final stage of an otherwise more cumbersome bureaucratic process and enabled the tellers of the Receipt of the Exchequer to approve his first payment within days or weeks rather than months. The warrant suggested that More was not an 'unwilling' recipient of a grant forced upon him by a solicitous King, but a suitor. He had accepted the job, but 'had to petition for the money'. Elton concluded that 'More was promised his fee in mid-1517, when he was first appointed to the Council, but then waited patiently and in vain for the king to act'. Finally, he 'had to draw Henry's attention to the fact that nothing had been done'.[47]

Elton cited next the fact that More was not styled a 'King's councillor' in the commissions that were issued for the commercial embassy to Bruges which produced *Utopia* in 1515, whereas he was so styled in the commission for Calais in August 1517.[48] But there is nothing exceptional about styling as a King's councillor a lawyer appointed by the Crown to serve abroad as a commercial ambassador or arbitrator.[49] The councillor's style was awarded as a courtesy and as a form of diplomatic accreditation.[50] The Chancery clerks were notoriously relaxed about diplomatic status, and no political significance can be attached to discrepancies in style. Elton himself nursed doubts. He conceded that those who were styled councillors might in some cases not yet be 'formally' in the King's service, which might have applied to More. Diplomats were 'not normally in that position,' but 'exceptions certainly occurred'.[51]

The issue is therefore the warrant. Elton's case collapses when it is realized that grants or annuities might sometimes be backdated or payments made in advance. His seemingly invincible thesis is built on sand. He studied the warrant for More's fee in isolation, whereas a systematic investigation would have shown that the procedure was more nuanced than it seemed.

Bureaucrats adopt convenient fictions, and these fictions can be perpetuated in the archives. Other examples exist of backdated payments. In 1513, for example, Henry VIII ordered advance instalments of Charles Brandon's annuity as Duke of Suffolk to be paid in the month of his ennoblement as a mark of special favour.[52] Again, when Thomas Derby was appointed to the clerkship of the Council Attendant in January 1533, his annuity of £20 was backdated to midsummer 1532, probably to compensate him for his removal expenses, since he had not previously been resident at Court.[53] Elton had published a transcript of Derby's warrant in the *Tudor Revolution in Government* in 1953, but its significance had been forgotten by the time he wrote on More.

The 'ascertainable facts' of More's entry into royal service belong in the context of David Starkey's study of the relationship between the peripatetic Court and the King's Council.[54] There were two 'key events' in 1517. The first was an epidemic known as the 'sweating sickness' (a virulent form of plague or influenza), which caused Henry VIII to flee the capital and retreat to Windsor and other royal houses in Berkshire, Surrey and Oxfordshire. Wolsey fell victim to this disease in June. He was seriously ill: incapacitated to all intents and purposes for six months. The routine of official business collapsed. Henry was left 'not only without formal counsel but also without formalized methods of transacting business.'[55] Next, with a literally infectious Wolsey denied access to the King, a new set of youthful companions, spearheaded by Nicholas Carew and Francis Bryan, consolidated their hold on royal favour. Wolsey feared these men, whom he believed (probably mistakenly) to be plotting against him and abusing their influence in the Privy Chamber. The new favourites, or 'minions' as they were called, squeezed out Sir Thomas Neville, Wolsey's experienced but relatively humdrum Court 'agent', and Wolsey was in turn determined to oust them, or at the very least to place more 'sober', 'wise' and 'discreet personages' about the King, in particular to resuscitate the Council Attendant by appointing to it people he could rely on to act impartially and not to play at backstairs politics.[56]

Wolsey settled first on Richard Pace, More's friend and Linacre's protégé, who had just returned from an embassy to the Swiss. He was sent to Court early in the New Year as Henry VIII's attendant councillor. For two years Pace had officially been the King's secretary, but thus far he had largely been absent from Court on diplomatic missions and so his attendance marked a new departure. Wolsey now earmarked him as Neville's replacement, and Pace had the impossible task of watching Wolsey's back at Court and also supporting both King and minister, even when the two were at odds. By 1521, Wolsey no longer trusted Pace, whom he accused of editing the King's letters to Wolsey and misreporting Wolsey's answers, and of getting grants bestowed on his friends.[57]

By the end of March 1518, Wolsey had recruited More to assist Pace. More was expected to join John Clerk, dean of the Chapel Royal, in sifting petitions to the King and in hearing 'poor men's suits' – the traditional functions of members of the Council Attendant. By Mary's reign, the officials who performed these tasks were called 'Masters of Requests', so Roper's statement that More was appointed 'Master of the Requests' at his 'first entry' into royal service makes perfect sense.[58] More was at Court by 26 March, when the royal baggage train was about to move from Reading to Abingdon. Before leaving Reading, Henry gave 'substantial precepts to Dr Clerk and Mr More respecting their charges, especially against [i.e. concerning] forfeitures'.[59] The source is Pace's letter to Wolsey, written on the same day as the events it describes: it corroborates More's recollection in his letter to Cromwell that at his 'first coming' into royal service he received his 'charge' from Henry VIII, who told him to 'first look unto God and after God unto him'.[60] More's memory was accurate, but the context was that he and Clerk were interviewed together, and the King's 'precepts' were primarily addressed to the functions that his new attendant councillors would perform as judges of petitions and requests. Henry's main concern was 'forfeitures' due to the Crown. The reality is mundane in comparison to Reynolds' conjecture that 'More had had a frank discussion with the King before entering his service'. Henry's words later took on a significance that was possibly not intended at the time. More always remembered them: the episode offers a solid basis for reconsidering exactly what he said in his speech from the scaffold, when I believe he threw back the King's words in his face (see Chapter 11).

Otherwise, the significance of Pace's letter is that in conjunction with More's own letter to Cromwell it dates More's 'first coming' into royal service. He entered the King's Council in March 1518 and not at the time of his visit to Calais in the autumn of 1517. He did not lie about the date of his arrival at Court, nor was his appointment as a King's councillor on an 'irregular' basis, with More in a state of limbo for six months in which 'he did not truly think of himself as a fully-fledged councillor'.[61]

If Elton's chronology was mistaken, was his argument still correct? Did More enter the Council 'willingly'? Did he succumb to the lure of the 'politick life'? His career began in the City of London, where he had been appointed an undersheriff. His civic assignments, initially as a lawyer and judge, and later as a commercial agent and public orator, were considerable.[62] Again, he did not seek promotion to the grade of serjeant-at-law, the highest rank below the judiciary in the legal profession. Like Edmund Dudley, who also moved directly from the post of undersheriff to the King's Council in Henry VII's reign, he side-stepped this distinction.[63] In general, Roper's 'story' of More's entry into politics can be vindicated. There are small slips. For example, the claim that More 'by the King's consent' was 'made twice ambassador in certain great causes between them and the merchants of the Steelyard' confuses the embassy to Bruges that produced *Utopia* with More's role in the negotiations between Henry VIII and the Hanseatic League that were also held at Bruges in July and August 1520 and in the autumn of the following year.[64] The confusion is insignificant: Roper is almost certainly correct that the main way in which More came to Wolsey's and Henry's attention is through the case of the Pope's ship.

The facts of this story are newly discovered. In the spring of 1514, Charles Brandon, Duke of Suffolk, had illegally confiscated a cargo of papal alum.[65] John de Cavalcanti, a Florentine merchant in London acting as the factor for this shipment, paid Brandon a levy to release the cargo, but Brandon had already borrowed 1000 marks from Henry VIII on the security of the sale of the forfeiture in order to purchase a wardship from the Crown.[66] The alum was valued at 12 000 ducats, a considerable sum. Both Leo X and Margaret of Austria lobbied Wolsey and Henry VIII to secure the release of the cargo. In early 1515 or thereabouts, a hearing was finally arranged before Lord Chancellor Warham and the judges. According to Roper, this hearing was held in the Court of Star Chamber. Although the case has left no trace in the Court's records, this is not in itself remarkable. The registers of Star Chamber were lost in the

1640s, and only fragments of their contents are known from late-Elizabethan and early-seventeenth-century transcripts.[67] It is likely that litigation involving Florentine merchants and an illegally confiscated cargo would have been heard in Star Chamber, since exactly such litigation was sent there in the reign of Henry VII.[68] More as Lord Chancellor himself bound over two Florentine merchants in Star Chamber.[69] The case involving Cavalcanti and Brandon was decided in the plaintiff's favour and a decision must have been reached by the end of May 1515, since Leo X wrote in early June from Rome to thank Wolsey for his help in obtaining the decree.[70] His optimism was misplaced, since several years later Brandon had not paid the compensation awarded against him. The later stages of the dispute are, however, irrelevant for present purposes.

No documents from the Star Chamber proceedings are extant beyond the correspondence which confirms that the case was decided in the Pope's favour and compensation assessed. However, enough is available to support the gist of Roper's account. The litigation can be dated to the early months of 1515, and the fact that judgement may not have been handed down before the end of May, by which time More was perhaps already in Bruges, is no obstacle, since judgements were delivered in Star Chamber suits only after the publication in open court of the written depositions, and the presence of someone whose official role in the case was merely that of an interpreter was unnecessary to the final judgement.[71]

Roper's report of this Star Chamber case is likely to be sound. He claimed that once the cargo of alum had been confiscated at Southampton, the Pope's ambassador obtained leave from the King that the Pope might be legally represented and that the case against the defendant might be determined in 'some public place' in the King's 'own presence'.[72] More was appointed as counsel to the ambassador. He was to 'report to the ambassador in Latin all the reasons and arguments by the learned counsel on both sides alleged'.[73] When the case was brought before Warham and the judges in Star Chamber, More 'not only declared to the ambassador the whole effect of all their opinions', he was allowed by the Court to join in the pleadings at the bar, where he gave a 'defence of the Pope's side argued so learnedly', that the judges' opinion swung in favour of restoring the cargo, which was at length duly decreed. For this 'upright and commendable demeanour', the King would thereafter 'for no entreaty . . . be induced any longer to forbear [More's] service'. He was recruited to the King's Council and, at his 'first entry thereunto', made 'Master of the Requests'.[74]

Roper obfuscates two points. The first is the timing of More's entry into royal service, but this has been clarified by reference to Pace's letter. The second is the possibility that it was Wolsey, rather than Henry VIII, who 'dragged' More to Court – if 'dragged' he was. The King did not routinely attend the Court of Star Chamber, where the Lord Chancellor of the day presided, and so could not have heard More's speech at first hand.[75] Wolsey was not yet Lord Chancellor (his appointment did not begin until Christmas Eve 1515), but he was present in Star Chamber as the Archbishop of York in 1514 and 1515. He would have seen More in action in the case of the Pope's ship. Perhaps, as a result, he selected More for the commercial embassies to Bruges in May 1515 and Calais in August 1517? The chronology certainly fits.

Beyond this, the timing of More's arrival at Court is suggestive of Wolsey, rather than Henry, as the impresario. By the spring of 1518, Wolsey had recovered from the 'sweating sickness' and was rebuilding his Court networks. Pace and More made a natural 'pair'. Furthermore, Wolsey employed them that way in practice. Within months of his arrival at Court, More was acting as an impromptu King's secretary, and Pace and More were used without distinction to receive and dispatch letters between Wolsey and the Court.[76] Roper himself said that Wolsey had 'earnestly travailed' to recruit More to the Council, 'alleging unto him how dear his service must needs be unto his majesty'.[77]

More was not brought to Court until Wolsey was ready to reconstitute his political ascendancy and retaliate against the 'minions' in the Privy Chamber. If More had been 'dragged' to Court by Henry VIII immediately or shortly after the case of the Pope's ship, he would either have arrived on return from his first embassy to Bruges, instead of which he returned to his position as undersheriff, or else during the second half of 1517, when Wolsey was sick and absent from Court and Henry was genuinely inconvenienced by the lack of suitable attendant councillors. If Henry VIII had been as unwilling to 'forbear' More's service as Roper claimed, More would surely have been brought to Court at once instead of being sent off on another commercial mission to Calais in August 1517?

The 'sweating sickness' may itself be a clue. The branch of humanism most closely associated with Thomas Linacre, More's mentor during his years in the Charterhouse, was a form of 'medical humanism' closely linked to classical theory and models of social reform.[78] It has been argued that a flurry of humanist-related activities around 1517 and 1518 was related to this outbreak of disease. More was certainly aware of the epidemic, since it caused panic and economic disruption in London and he was among those taking precautions. If and when Wolsey sought More's presence at Court to act as a 'pair' with Pace, it is possible that More accepted, because, as Jonathan Woolfson argues, 'advanced English thinkers in this period saw themselves as putting their learning to good use' by 'healing' both the ills of their country and the illnesses of its citizens.[79]

More may have genuinely admired Wolsey at this date. He claimed that he had considered dedicating *Utopia* to the minister.[80] Later, of course, he thought otherwise. In his opening speech as Lord Chancellor to the 1529 Parliament, he compared Wolsey to 'the great wether' who had 'craftily, scabbedly, and untruly juggled' with the King.[81] Elsewhere, he said that Wolsey was '[vain]glorious ... far above all measure, and that was great pity; for it did harm and made him abuse many great gifts that God had given him.'[82] By 1529, Wolsey was disgraced. He was the man whom everyone loved to hate.

In 1517 and 1518, the prognosis was different. For all Wolsey's barely concealed ambition, he displayed a keen sense of social justice. He maintained that wrongdoing must be punished wherever it was to be found, and that justice should be 'equally' and 'indifferently' (i.e. impartially) offered to all who sought it (see Chapter 7). He sought to do right to the poor in the Courts of Chancery and Star Chamber, and to punish enclosing landlords. As well as attacking over 260 enclosing landlords from the Court of Chancery in and after 1517, he attacked food racketeers in Star Chamber. He investigated the meat trade and hauled 74 provincial graziers before the King's Council, along with dozens of butchers, for a variety of offences. Again, he issued proclamations prohibiting profiteering in cereals and enforcing traditional statutes regulating vagabonds and labourers. All of this was happening in 1517 and 1518.[83]

It is easy to imagine how More was persuaded to enter the King's and Wolsey's service. The moment was propitious and More's qualifications were ideal for the job. The gist of Roper's 'story' can be corroborated. The case of the Pope's ship is not a fiction. The revisionist critique can be exploded. Was More a 'willing' or a 'reluctant' courtier? Probably there was prevarication: Roper makes this clear. But More's 'reluctance' to enter politics was most strongly emphasized by Erasmus, who had his own agenda. Again, More's 'disdain' and 'loathing' of Court life is the 'story' of Stapleton's *Life of Thomas More* over which lies the shadow of a contested issue of provenance.

As with the Charterhouse debate, the dilemma is insurmountable. More's entry into politics can only be discussed on the basis of evidence which is inconclusive. The layers of encrusted legend are too thick. The debate has not entered a cul-de-sac, but the issue must be left open. With the collapse of Elton's argument that More was a courtier by the autumn of 1517 and had lied to Erasmus, credence must be given to the earlier traditions. On the other hand, Elton's research clarified that More's 'call to counsel' was the climax of a progression by which he steadily gained the attention of Henry and Wolsey. In a sense, this was also Roper's 'story'. More's legal and commercial work in London, Bruges and Calais between 1510 and 1517 was so extensive, and so closely linked to the interests of the Crown and State, that if it was not at least a limited form of commitment to a career in politics, what was? At a minimum, More's transition from a legal and City career to a political one was seamless.

More's lost 'letter' to Fisher, therefore, has a unique significance. Is the document genuine? Probably the bulk of it is, in which case we should have no reason to doubt More's statement: 'It was with the greatest unwillingness that I came to Court.' On the other hand, the document is highly coloured and, even if genuine, is resonant of More's ironic style:

> I am far from enjoying the special favour of the King, but he is so courteous and kindly to all that everyone who is in any way hopeful finds a ground for imagining that he is in the King's good graces; like the London wives who, as they pray before the image of the Virgin Mother of God which stands near the Tower, gaze upon it so fixedly that they imagine it smiles upon them.[84]

The sentiment is quintessential More. But where does 'fact' end and rhetorical self-fashioning begin? The greatest paradox about the political Thomas More will become his ability to dissimulate and speak the truth simultaneously.

Notes

1 Stapleton, pp. 76–80.
2 *CW* 3, Pt. 1, pp. 5–7.
3 Margaret (b. 1505), Elizabeth (b. 1506), Cecily (b. 1507) and John (b. 1509). Margaret Gigs was adopted.
4 *CWE*, 7, p. 21.
5 John Guy, *The Public Career of Sir Thomas More* (Brighton, 1980), pp. 4–5.
6 S.E. Thorne and J.H. Baker, eds, *Readings and Moots at the Inns of Court in the Fifteenth Century* (2 vols, London, 1954–90) 2, p. clxxxi, the only reference to 'More' and even this may refer to John More or the 'Thomas More' from Hampshire.
7 P. Hasler, ed., *The House of Commons, 1558–1603* (3 vols, London, 1981) 2, p. 620.
8 Roper, p. 199.
9 Hasler, ed., *House of Commons* 2, p. 620.
10 Harpsfield, pp. 312–13; G.D. Ramsay, 'A Saint in the City: Thomas More at Mercers' Hall, London', *English Historical Review* 97 (1982), pp. 269–88.
11 G.D. Ramsay, 'A Saint in the City: Thomas More at Mercers' Hall, London', *English Historical Review* 97 (1982), p. 270.
12 Hasler, ed., *House of Commons* 2, p. 620.
13 R. Norrington, *In the Shadow of a Saint: Lady Alice More* (Waddesdon, 1983), p. 4.
14 *LP Add.* I.i. no. 1024; R.W. Chambers, *Thomas More* (London, 1938), p. 109.
15 *CWE* 7, p. 21.
16 *Opus Epistolarum* 4, no. 999 (p. 19); *CWE* 7, p. 21.
17 Harpsfield, p. 93.
18 Roper, p. 200.
19 Guy, *Public Career*, pp. 5–6.
20 Harpsfield, pp. 312–13.
21 Guy, *Public Career*, p. 7; Marius, *Thomas More*, pp. 194–8; Chambers, *Thomas More*, pp. 147–51.
22 Roper, p. 200.
23 Roper, p. 200.
24 Roper, pp. 200–1.
25 Roper, p. 201.
26 Harpsfield, pp. 23–4.
27 Rogers, ed., *Correspondence*, p. 495.
28 Stapleton, pp. 76–7; Rogers, ed., *Selected Letters*, p. 94.
29 *Opus Epistolarum* 4, no. 1117 (p. 294); *CWE* 7, p. 321.
30 *Opus Epistolarum* 4, no. 999 (p. 20); *CWE* 7, p. 22.
31 Chambers, *Thomas More*, p. 169.
32 Chambers, *Thomas More*, p. 169; E.E. Reynolds, *The Life and Death of St Thomas More* (London, 1978), pp. 127–31.
33 Chambers, *Thomas More*, p. 170 and n. 2.
34 Reynolds, *St Thomas More*, p. 129.
35 *CW* 2, pp. lxxx–civ; D. Fenlon, 'Thomas More and Tyranny', *Journal*

of *Ecclesiastical History* 32 (1981), pp. 453–76; Alistair Fox, *Thomas More: History and Providence* (Oxford, 1982), pp. 75–107.

36 R.S. Sylvester, ed., *St Thomas More: Action and Contemplation. Proceedings of the Symposium held at St John's University* (New Haven, CT, 1972), p. 4.

37 G.R. Elton, *Studies in Tudor and Stuart Politics and Government* (4 vols, Cambridge, 1974–92) 1, pp. 132–3.

38 Richard Marius, *Thomas More* (New York, 1984), pp. 123, 129, 135, 141, 339.

39 G.R. Elton, 'The Actor Saint', *New York Review of Books* (31 Jan., 1985), p. 8.

40 As a student at Cambridge, I attended the first reading of Elton's paper in the Cambridge History Faculty shortly before it was presented publicly to the St John's University symposium. No doubt was left about the agenda on that occasion.

41 Sylvester, ed., *St Thomas More*, p. 4.

42 Marius, *Thomas More*, p. 198.

43 G. Marc'hadour, 'Fuit Morus in Aulam Pertractus?', in I.D. McFarlane, ed., *Acta Conventus Neo-Latini Sanctandreani* (Binghamton, NY, 1986), pp. 441–8.

44 P. Ackroyd, *Thomas More* (London, 1998), pp. 176–89.

45 Elton, *Studies* 1, p. 130.

46 PRO, C 82/463.

47 Elton, *Studies* 1, pp. 131–2.

48 Elton, *Studies*, p. 130.

49 J.F. Baldwin, *The King's Council in England during the Middle Ages* (Oxford, 1913), pp. 423–4.

50 M.M. Condon, 'An Anachronism with Intent? Henry VII's Council Ordinance of 1491–2', in R.A. Griffiths and J. Sherborne, eds, *Kings and Nobles in the Later Middle Ages* (Gloucester, 1986), p. 231.

51 Elton, *Studies* 1, p. 130.

52 *LP* II.ii, p. 1463; S.J. Gunn, *Charles Brandon: Duke of Suffolk, 1484–1545* (Oxford, 1988), p. 21.

53 PRO, C 82/664, no. 25; G.R. Elton, *The Tudor Revolution in Government* (Cambridge, 1953), pp. 334–5, 441–2. I am grateful to Dr D.R. Starkey for this reference.

54 D.R. Starkey, 'Court, Council and Nobility in Tudor England' in R.G. Asch and A.M. Birke, eds, *Princes, Patronage and the Nobility: the Court at the Beginning of the Modern Age c. 1450–1650* (Oxford, 1991), pp. 175–203.

55 Starkey, 'Court, Council and Nobility', p. 183.

56 Starkey, 'Court, Council and Nobility', pp. 182–3.

57 Starkey, 'Court, Council and Nobility', p. 183; J.J. Scarisbrick, 'Thomas More: the King's Good Servant', *Thought* 52 (1977), pp. 251–3.

58 Roper, p. 201; Starkey, 'Court, Council and Nobility', p. 183.

59 *LP* II.ii no. 4025.

60 Rogers, ed., *Correspondence*, p. 495.

61 Marius, *Thomas More*, p. 198.

62 Harpsfield, pp. 312–4; Ramsay, 'A Saint in the City', pp. 271–88.

63 E.W. Ives, *The Common Lawyers of Pre-Reformation England* (Cambridge, 1983), p. 78.
64 Roper, p. 200; Ramsay, 'A Saint in the City', pp. 286–7.
65 Alum was the term for a colourless, soluble, hydrated double sulphate of aluminium and potassium used in the manufacture of pigments, in dressing leather and sizing paper, and in medical applications.
66 *LP* I.ii. nos. 2867, 2916, 3107(11), 3205, 3241, 3490; *LP* II.i. nos. 211, 571, 849; *LP* II.ii. nos. 4561, p. 1464; Gunn, *Charles Brandon*, p. 21.
67 John Guy, 'Wolsey's Star Chamber: A Study in Archival Reconstruction, *Journal of the Society of Archivists* 5 (1975), pp. 169–80.
68 C.G. Bayne, ed., *Select Cases in the Council of Henry VII* (London, 1958), p. 13.
69 PRO, STAC 2/23/275.
70 *LP* II.i. no. 571.
71 John Guy, *The Cardinal's Court: the Impact of Thomas Wolsey in Star Chamber* (Hassocks, 1977), pp. 79–117.
72 Roper, p. 201.
73 Roper, p. 201.
74 Roper, p. 201.
75 The few occasions when the King attended were so exceptional that they were noted by the late-Elizabethan transcribers of the (lost) registers of the Court. See Guy, 'Wolsey's Star Chamber'.
76 Elton, *Studies* 1, p. 142.
77 Roper, pp. 200–1.
78 J. Woolfson, *Padua and the Tudors* (Cambridge, 1998), p. 102.
79 Woolfson, *Padua and the Tudors*, p. 102.
80 Rogers, ed., *Selected Letters*, p. 90.
81 Guy, *Public Career*, pp. 113–15.
82 A.F. Pollard, *Wolsey* (London, 1929), p. 373.
83 PRO, STAC 2/15/188–90; P.L. Hughes and J.F. Larkin, eds, *Tudor Royal Proclamations* (3 vols, New Haven, CT, 1964–9) 1, nos. 118, 121, 125, 127; Henry E. Huntington Library, San Marino, CA, Ellesmere MS. 2655, fo. 16; STAC 2/26/103; 2/32/bundle of unlisted fragments (Roger Barbor's case); Guy, *The Cardinal's Court*, pp. 30–5, 70–1; J.J. Scarisbrick, 'Cardinal Wolsey and the Common Weal', in E.W. Ives, R.J. Knecht and J.J. Scarisbrick, eds, *Wealth and Power in Tudor England* (London, 1978), pp. 45–67; Scarisbrick, 'Thomas More: the King's Good Servant', pp. 256–9.
84 Stapleton, p. 77; Rogers, ed., *Selected Letters*, p. 94.

|4|

Happy families?

Fact or spin? It is scarcely subversive to say that, apart from *Utopia* and his heroic final stand against Henry VIII on a scruple of conscience, Thomas More is best known in the public imagination less for his political and literary achievements than for what we think we know of his domestic and family life. His biographers have rarely sought to use his domestic life to make choices that underpin divergent interpretations of his career. Instead, the 'facts' of his private life have been repeated in a purely functionalist way, sometimes to fill awkward gaps in the narrative, but primarily to create an 'image' of the private foundations of his virtuous public personality. Since the methods of historical analysis have rarely been applied to these so-called 'facts', it is hardly surprising that More's biographers have almost always ended up liking him. This chapter cannot hope to resolve this difficulty, but it can at least point out some of the more obvious pitfalls. In particular, it has to be asked whether our perception of More's private life is to an excessive degree the outcome of the attention it has received from the equivalent of 'spin doctors'.

Until 1524, More and his family lived at the Old Barge, Bucklersbury, in the heart of the City of London. Between June 1523 and January 1524, he also owned the lease of Crosby Place, a large house in the parish of St Helen's, Bishopsgate, which he bought from the executors of Sir John Rest, an alderman and former mayor of London. But More himself never lived there: he sold the lease to his friend, Antonio Bonvisi, a merchant of Lucca, who had settled in London. He purchased an estate in Chelsea, then a quiet village on the north bank of the Thames some two and a half miles upstream of the palace of Westminster and four miles from the City of London. Here he built or renovated a mansion house and laid out a large garden stretching down to the river. It was complete with a private landing stage, reached from the garden through a wicket gate so that More could travel easily in his 'great barge' to Westminster Hall and the metropolis.[1]

By the time of his appointment as Lord Chancellor in 1529, More's household had grown in size. Of the immediate family who lived with him and his second wife, Alice, there were the four children of his first marriage to Jane Colt: Margaret, Elizabeth, Cicely and John. There was also Margaret Gigs, whom More had adopted, and Anne Cresacre, whose wardship he had obtained after a Star Chamber case in which Sir Robert Constable and his son, Thomas, were convicted of her abduction and rape.[2] When More's children married, their spouses settled in his household. First to wed was Margaret, who chose William Roper in 1521. Four years later, Elizabeth married William Dauncey, and Cicely married Giles Heron, another of More's wards, who attained the age of 21 and came into his inheritance shortly before the wedding.[3] Margaret Gigs, More's adopted daughter, married John Clement in 1526. Clement was already familiar to More's household as the children's former tutor. He had accompanied More to Bruges in 1515, and on his return was first appointed Wolsey's lecturer in rhetoric at Oxford and later Reader in Greek. Lastly, More's son, John, married Anne Cresacre in 1529.

By the early 1530s, eleven grandchildren had joined these family members in the mansion house. Also living there was John Harris, More's secretary and amanuensis, who married Dorothy Colly, Margaret Roper's maid; and Henry Patenson, More's fool. There was a small menagerie: a monkey, two dogs, rabbits, a fox, a ferret, a weasel, and an exotic collection of songbirds in an aviary. All contemporary writers who refer in any detail to the estate rhapsodize over its idyllic setting. But life was probably not so idyllic in the mansion house if one wanted to study, because More quickly built another house. This was called the New Building. According to Roper's description, it was constructed 'a good distance' away from the mansion house.[4] The New Building contained a chapel, a library and a long gallery. It was 'a large edifice', reserved for More's private use, when he was 'desirous for godly purposes sometime to be solitary, and sequester himself from worldly company'.[5] From the accounts of Roper and Harpsfield, it would seem that More used the New Building daily. When Alice visited him in the Tower shortly before his trial in order to appeal to him not to abandon his family for a lost cause, she couched her appeal in terms she thought he might understand: 'And seeing you have at Chelsea a right fair house, your library, your books, your gallery, your garden . . .'.[6]

More imposed an ascetic discipline on his household: he was able himself to manage without much sleep. He rose at 2 a.m. and spent the time until 7 a.m. in study and prayer. This was doubtless how he was able to write so many books even when he was Henry VIII's secretary and Lord Chancellor. A private chapel was located in the mansion house as well as in the New Building: before retiring at night, More would 'say certain psalms and collects' with his family. When the main household stirred in the morning, long after More had begun work in the New Building, he would return to the mansion house, if he had no special business elsewhere, to recite 'the Seven Psalms, Litany and Suffrages' with the children.[7] On Fridays, he always worked at home, allocating more time than usual for 'devout prayer and spiritual exercises' in the New Building.[8] He also attended Chelsea parish church, which adjoined his estate. He built a side-chapel for his household's use, and on Sundays and religious festivals no member of the family was allowed to be absent or arrive late.[9] On Good Friday, More summoned his family to the New Building, where the story of Christ's Death and Passion was read to them, usually by John Harris.[10]

A vivid impression of a centre of humanist culture, Christian piety and private decorum is created by the earliest biographers, by Erasmus in his vignette to Ulrich von Hutten, and by Holbein's portrait of More and his family group, which began as a pen and ink drawing now in the Kunstmuseum, Basel (see p. 77), made in preparation for the (now lost) canvas which hung in the long gallery of the mansion house at Chelsea.[11] By far the best of the surviving copies is the one at Nostell Priory, Yorkshire. It is largely these sources that this chapter will consider. At the forefront is Roper's claim that in all the years he lived with his father-in-law, he never saw him 'in a fume'.[12] Historians have reiterated this judgement, although Stapleton acknowledged more realistically that More lost his temper occasionally.[13] Erasmus also praised More's 'sweetness'.[14] His authority was adduced in Roper's *Life* to show that More was 'a

man of singular virtue and of a clear, unspotted conscience . . .
more pure and white than the whitest snow'.[15] Harpsfield drew
still more extensively on Erasmus: to reinforce the private
foundations of More's virtuous public personality, and to
confirm his reputation as a man who would die rather than tell
an untruth or take an oath in vain.[16]

The earliest biographers knew that More was exceptionally
devout. In Stapleton's account, he 'lived almost the life of a
monk'.[17] Every day, before all other business, he heard mass. This
self-imposed obligation was observed so strictly, 'that once when
hearing Mass he was summoned by the King, even two or three
times, but refused to leave before it was finished'.[18] At meal
times, Scripture was read aloud to the entire household. More's
daughters would take it in turns to be the readers. The passages
were 'intoned in the ecclesiastical or monastic fashion', and
readings concluded with the words 'and do thou, O Lord, have
mercy on us', as they did in religious houses.[19]

According to Roper, More urged austerity and patience in
adversity. If anyone was ill or downcast, he would remind them:
'We may not look at our pleasure to go to heaven in featherbeds.
It is not the way, for our Lord himself went thither with great
pain and by many tribulations'.[20] He believed in hell and
exhorted his family to withstand temptations. A favourite
analogy was to compare the devil to an ape:

> For, like as an ape, not well looked unto, will be busy and
> bold to do shrewd [i.e. harmful] turns and contrariwise,
> being spied, will suddenly leap backwards and adventure
> no farther, so the devil finding a man idle, slothful, and
> without resistance ready to receive his temptations, waxeth
> so hardy that he will not fail still to continue with him until
> to his purpose he have thoroughly brought him.[21]

Animals were regularly used for didactic or symbolic purposes
in the Renaissance. They were allocated attributes which had a
moral significance. The household's pet monkey, which seems to
have been Alice's favourite and in the Holbein pen and ink drawing can be seen on a chain clambering up her skirt, was symbolic
of the need to avoid worldly temptations.

The fullest account of More's domestic sphere is the vignette
by Erasmus to Hutten (1519). This was not a private letter. It was
published almost as soon as it was written and several times
reprinted. A rhetorical triumph, it constructs a model of decorum

and an image of a Christian adaptation of Plato's Academy.[22] It is often read anachronistically. It cannot refer to More's establishment at Chelsea, since Erasmus never set foot there. He paid two extended visits to More's household at Bucklersbury, one shortly after More's first marriage, and the second between the autumn of 1509 and April 1511, when the *Praise of Folly* was dedicated to More. Thereafter, he met More several times on the Continent, but the other members of More's family were unknown to him after he left Bucklersbury.

The core is the description of More himself. He was not tall, though not unduly short. His body was well-proportioned, his complexion fair, his hair blackish-brown, his beard thin, his eyes greyish-blue with a glint that suggested quick wits and a retentive memory. His manner was outgoing with a hint of banter rather than gravity or dignity. His right shoulder was slightly higher than his left. His hands were rough, since he paid little attention to his appearance. He enjoyed good, if not robust, health (later he suffered from angina). He was unfussy about his food. His diet consisted of beef, salt fish, and coarse bread rather than delicacies. (This is surely contradicted by Roper.)[23] But he enjoyed milk puddings and fresh fruit, and was especially fond of eggs. As a young man he drank water in preference to beer or wine. Later, for fear of embarrassment, he drank watered-down beer unless he could get away with filling a pewter tankard with water. He rarely touched wine, except when it was obligatory to drink a toast from a loving cup: then he would participate, but merely take a sip.

His speaking voice was gentle, but clearly audible. It was well suited to oratory, since his articulation was distinct and un-hurried. He spoke fluently, moving nimbly from one point to another, and what he said was always clear and precise. He was a brilliant extempore speaker.[24] His mind was fertile, his reactions instant. In disputations, he could take on the most learned theologian and still prove himself invincible.[25]

He liked to dress simply. He did not wear silk or scarlet, or a gold chain, except when protocol or his public duties required. He set little store by the trivial courtesies which most people thought important. He disliked blood sports and could scarcely conceal his distaste for dice, cards or the 'idle' pastimes with which other people amused themselves.[26] From greed he was entirely free. He earmarked sufficient funds for his household, but was otherwise generous and considerate. As a lawyer in private practice, he tried to persuade his clients to settle out of court or else managed their business at minimum cost.[27] As the King's councillor, he served the 'commonwealth' and his 'friends', whom he 'never forgot'.[28] Erasmus waxed lyrical on this theme. More was born for 'friendship': 'no one could take more trouble in furthering the business of his friends'.[29] Nor is the point made innocently. Erasmus' career largely consisted of a quest for patrons, and More had access to the wealthiest patrons in England by 1519. It is no coincidence that Erasmus published his vignette: he, like More, loathed flatterers, but was not above invoking flattery himself if he thought it could do some good.

What else do we know about More? Erasmus said that he collected coins and antiquities. If he saw anything rare or unusual, he bought it for the enjoyment of his visitors.[30] We know that this is true. Between 1519 and 1529, he was using a pseudo-antique gem seal on letters to his humanist friends which sported the head of the Roman Emperor Vespasian.[31] He also liked music and the arts, the *mise-en-scène* of Renaissance culture and display. His love of art is shown by his patronage of Holbein. On Erasmus' advice, the artist arrived at Chelsea from Basel in the autumn of 1526, where he lodged for at least part of his first visit to England.[32] More offered him several commissions. Preparations for the family group portrait were advanced by the end of 1527. In the same year, More sat for the superb single half-length portrait from which the detail illustrating the cover of this book is taken. As to music, Erasmus claimed that More was an aficionado, even if he lacked the talent for singing or performing himself. (Roper says that More sang in the church choir at Chelsea.)[33] Music was intrinsic to More's own image of his household. In the Nostell Priory canvas, a lute and a bass viol stand on the shelf of a buffet or cupboard at the back of the composition, which More himself asked to be placed there. Judging by the comments of Erasmus and Harpsfield, it would seem that these were the instruments played by the female members of the family.

We know that More could never resist a joke.[34] In his youth he had written comedies and acted in them. Roper said that he had 'such an angelical wit as England ... never had the like before, nor ever shall again'.[35] Not everyone liked this. The chronicler, Edward Hall, sniped at More 'the jester' and said, 'I cannot tell whether I should call him a foolish wise man or a wise foolish man'. He had 'great wit', but it was 'so mingled with taunting and mocking, that it seemed to them that best knew him, that he thought nothing to be well spoken except he had ministered some mock in the communication'.[36] Hall was an apologist of Henry VIII.[37] He was biased, but it would not be unfair to say that More was most witty when least amused. He saw the comic spirit as a correlative of the action of the Holy Spirit. What has been called his 'shrewd, sharp and ironic' wit was his way of cutting himself as well as others down to size.[38] He revelled in 'merry tales', often with sexual or scatological overtones, which, like Chaucer in the *Wife of Bath's Tale*, he recounted whenever the opportunity arose. But, whereas Chaucer told such stories for their poetic or entertainment value, More usually had a moral purpose as well. It was More who suggested to Erasmus the subject of the *Praise of Folly*. He admired the Menippean style of irony and satire exemplified by the Greek writer, Lucian of Samosata, whose work he and Erasmus translated into Latin in 1505–6. Erasmus informed Hutten that there was 'nothing in human life to which [More] cannot look for entertainment'. 'With women as a rule, and even with his wife', he relished wit and repartee.[39]

This, of course, cuts to the quick. The subject of More's quips and practical jokes at the expense of his wives is contentious. Shortly after his marriage to Jane Colt, More gave her some false jewels, pretending they were genuine. What difference, asked Erasmus in the *Praise of Folly*, did it make? She rejoiced in the fakes as if they were the rarest treasure. By his device, More won his wife's affection, saved money and enjoyed himself. The jest delighted Erasmus, whose misogynist tendencies have been remarked upon by modern critics, but greatly embarrassed the Victorian T.E. Bridgett, whose *Blessed Thomas More* contained a special appendix devoted to this prank in which he argued that since Erasmus recounted the story through the mouthpiece of 'Folly', and since More did not continue the deception for very long, it did not count. 'More', wrote Bridgett ponderously, 'after enjoying his little joke for a few days, had doubtless soon un-deceived the lady, and they both told the story to Erasmus'. The matter had to be considered carefully, he explained, 'lest the Promotor Fidei should seek to make capital out of the incident'.[40] He wrote shortly after More's beatification, and was concerned that the prospects of the cause of canonization could be put in jeopardy.

More joked elsewhere that he had only married Jane in preference to her prettier younger sister because he 'considered that it would be both great grief and some shame also to the eldest to see her younger sister in marriage preferred before her'.[41] This was typical of his way of speaking to, or about, women. Some years later, Erasmus wrote a colloquy about an unhappy wife. The story is taken even by More's hagiographers to refer to Jane Colt, since phrases in it are virtually identical to those used by Erasmus when describing Jane elsewhere.[42] Obviously the identification is plausible: Erasmus stayed with More shortly after his first marriage.[43] He knew Jane at exactly the right time. He recounted that a man, exceptionally clever and tactful, had married a seventeen-year-old girl who had lived in the country in idleness, uneducated and spending most of her time chatting to the servants. Her husband attempted to educate her: to school her in books and music, and 'repeat the substance of the sermons she heard'. The wife cried inconsolably and wished herself dead. So the 'tactful' husband suggested a visit to her parents. He secretly told her father of his difficulty. 'Use your rights and give her a good beating', said the father. 'I know what my rights are', replied the husband, 'but I would rather you used your authority.' The father feigned to be so angry with his daughter that she sought refuge 'by falling at her husband's feet in a fit of penitence'.[44] They kissed and made up. The marriage was thereafter made in heaven, a conclusion that we assume to be resonant with irony.

More joked of wives and women that 'it is not possible to live with even the best of them without any inconvenience at all'.[45] With Alice, his second wife, he developed what even his hagiographers have called 'a particular manner and tone that was quickly turned into a private family joke'.[46] Sir Geoffrey Elton, writing iconoclastically, is less charitable. To him, More's attitude to Alice is incomprehensible. 'He is supposed to have treated her with affection; yet the conviction that she was foolish and tiresome rests in great part on the sly allusions to female deficiencies scattered throughout his works.'[47] Too often, More spent his time 'sniggering about Dame Alice behind her back'.[48] According to Erasmus, Alice was a strong-willed, inflexible, ignorant woman who was not easily snubbed. He called her 'capable and watchful', using Latin words that were not intended to be complimentary.[49] Another friend, Andrew Ammonio, spoke of Alice's nose as 'the hooked beak of the harpy', a joke which became a topic of general banter.[50]

Erasmus may have exaggerated Alice's awkwardness as a foil to his characterization of More. His vignette was always a rhetorical conceit. Thus, few husbands could 'secure as much obedience from their wives by severity and giving them orders' as More did by his kindness and 'merry' humour.[51] More, by wit and persuasion, could make Alice 'do anything'. For instance, stupid as she was, he persuaded her to learn the lute, the virginals and the recorder. He assigned her 'a set piece of work every day'.[52] One can imagine how much she enjoyed this 'education', even allowing for Erasmus' hyperbole.

More introduced Alice, under the thinnest veil of anonymity, into the *Confutation of Tyndale's Answer*, which he wrote in two parts in 1532 and 1533. He tells how a husband made a futile attempt to teach his wife science, explaining the notion of the spheres from the Ptolemaic system of astronomy. More made the husband explain how, if a hole were bored through the earth, and a millstone thrown into it, the millstone would fall towards the centre of the earth and then stop. According to Ptolemaic theory, the orthodoxy at the time More was writing, the centre of the earth was the lowest point in creation, from which objects ascended in every direction. As in all More's 'merry tales', the wife would have none of this. 'As she was wont in all other things', she 'studied all the while nothing else, but what she might say to the contrary'.[53] After endlessly interrupting her husband, she summoned her maid to bring her spinning wheel with its spindle and whorl, and began a practical demonstration designed to show that if an enlarged version of the whorl were the world and the hole in its middle were the hole into which the millstone were thrown, the stone would not stop in the middle, but would emerge at the far side and would give anyone standing there 'a pat on the pate' (i.e. head) that 'would make you claw your head, and yet should ye feel none itch at all'.[54]

More constructs an image of an obstinate, opinionated, voluble female, who argues with everything her more intelligent husband says. The earliest biographies reinforce this effect. According to Harpsfield, it was necessary for More to 'frame' and 'fashion' Alice, and bring her 'to that case that she learned to play and sing at the lute and virginals' in order to make her socially presentable. Every day when he returned home, More 'took a reckoning and account of the tasks he enjoined her touching the said exercise.'[55] It is almost as if he was Orpheus taming the wild beasts in his menagerie.

There is direct criticism of Alice. Harpsfield recounted how More rebuked her for the sin of pride when she tied her hair as far back off her forehead as she could to suit the fashion of the day, and bound her waist tightly in a corset 'both twain to her great pain'. 'Forsooth, Madam,' said More, 'if God give you not hell, he shall do you great wrong, for it must needs be your own of very right, for you buy it very dear, and take very great pain thereof.'[56]

More disparaged Alice while he was Lord Chancellor. Roper reported that he 'used commonly every afternoon to sit in his open hall' at Chelsea to hear petitions and award writs of subpoena if they were justified.[57] A foolish suitor appeared one day who had entered into an elaborate deception of another man's wife. The deception backfired, and cost the suitor £92 in costs and charges. He complained to More, who dismissed the case, telling the suitor to go and tell his tale to Dame Alice. (If More delighted in folly, he never suffered fools gladly.) Unfortunately, the suitor was too stupid to realize that More spoke in jest. A year or so later, a new petition was addressed to Sir Thomas Audley, More's successor in the Court of Chancery, complaining that the case had been 'examined before the Lady More at Chelsea', but the promised redress had not materialized.[58] It was typical of More's stereotyped opinion that his instinctive reaction was that only someone as stubborn as his second wife could drum any sense into this particular suitor's head.

Harpsfield's *Life* was intended to be the 'official history' of Thomas More. It drew upon the family's collective memory as well as on Roper's earlier biography. Should we accept the truth of its anecdotes about Alice? As to the case of the stupid suitor, it comes from the records of the Court of Chancery: there is no doubt about its authenticity. In the end, Alice gave More as good as she got. When she visited her husband in the Tower, she greeted him bluntly with:

> 'What the good-year, Master More,' quoth she, 'I marvel that you that have been always hitherto taken for so wise a man will now so play the fool to lie here in this close, filthy prison and be content thus to be shut up among mice and rats when you might be abroad at your liberty and with the favour and good will both of the King and his council . . .'[59]

Roles at last seemed reversed: it was Alice calling More a 'fool', but More (or Roper) turned the tables. ' "Is not this house," quoth . . . [More], "as nigh heaven as my own?" '[60]

The ground is treacherous, because rhetorical games were being played, not just by Erasmus and More, but by More's

earliest biographers when reporting the 'sayings' of More.
'Image' and 'reflection' become confused. These writers blur
the lines between 'history' and 'story', blending truth and fiction in ways that are unimaginable today. Harpsfield allowed
the mask to slip when repeating Roper's account of the same
Tower episode. In Harpsfield's version, Alice was cast in a
specific role. She was Eve the temptress. And she was Job's
wife, who valiantly tried, but could not 'shake and overturn
any part of his good patience'.[61] Did the encounters between
More and Alice preserved in the earliest biographies really
happen, or are they rhetorical inventions? Did More love
Alice, or did they merely rub along? Did he relish what his
hagiographers delicately call his wife's 'outrageous pronounce-
ments' even while he made her the butt of his jokes?[62] We
shall never really know.

A 'story' that is less rhetorical poses an enigma. In the
Dialogue of Comfort against Tribulation, written in the Tower in
1534, More reflected on the nature of imprisonment in a parable
that Harpsfield said relates to Alice.[63] Many members of religious
orders, said More, have been content to live out their lives
imprisoned in their cells. To have a door shut on us is no real
punishment. It is merely 'a horror enhanced of our own
fantasy'.[64] To clinch his point, he told a 'story'. Once upon a
time, a woman came into a prison to visit of her charity a poor
prisoner. She found him living in a chamber that was 'meetly
fair'. He had been given mats of straw which he had carefully
positioned to keep himself warm. But 'among many other dis-
pleasures' she especially lamented that the chamber door should
be locked against him at night by the gaoler. ' "For by my troth",
quoth she, "if the door should be shut upon me, I would ween
[i.e. think] it would stop up my breath." ' On hearing her words,
the prisoner laughed inwardly, since he dared not laugh aloud.
'For somewhat indeed he stood in awe of her.' In any case, his
living costs were met by her charity and not paid for by the
Tower authorities, who were only bound to keep him locked up
and not to feed or clothe him. But he laughed, because he very
well knew that 'she used on the inside to shut every night full
surely her own chamber to her, both door and windows too'. She
locked her own bedroom door and windows on the inside, 'and
used not to open them of all the long night.' Hence 'what difference then as to the stopping of the breath, whether they were shut
up within or without?'[65]

The parable is quintessential More. The co-editors of the Yale Edition remark that it 'supplies the only glimpse we have of the interior of More's cell and the actual conditions of his confinement'.[66] They note that the prisoner in the story knows 'the intimate details of the woman's sleeping arrangements, though she was supposed to be only a casual acquaintance'. Do these statements miss the point? As the revisionist historian Richard Marius has spotted, More went out of his way to mention 'her own chamber' rather than 'their' chamber. Marius draws the inference that More and his second wife did not share a bedroom. Even if they had separate bedrooms with a connecting door or corridor as was common in the sixteenth century, Alice locked her door on the inside before retiring.[67] Marius refers to Harpsfield's statement, derived from Erasmus' vignette, that More married Alice rather 'for the ruling and governing of his children, house and family, than for any bodily pleasure'.[68] But how far can this be relied on? What he infers seems at first to be supported by the testimony of More's letter to Frans van Cranevelt, Pensionary of Bruges, in November 1528: 'I remember', began More, 'that you once wrote to me that the most pleasant sleep is in a bed without a wife'. Except that he continued: 'These are the words of husbands on the first nights after their wives have been sent away, for on the remaining nights desire comes creeping back and, unless the wife has left a proxy, it makes sleep unpleasant'.[69] Probably very little can be made of any of this. Harpsfield relied on Erasmus, whose rhetorical priority was his model of decorum. More's letters to Cranevelt were crammed with humanistic banter, especially concerning Cranevelt's wife, Elisabeth van Baussele, whom More had met and with whom he seems to have enjoyed flirting. He was effusive in his compliments to his 'mistress'. She is the 'wife who is mine by day' even as she is Cranevelt's 'by night'.[70] Such comments were highly stylized. They cannot be read literally or used to draw conclusions about More's private life.

St Augustine had said that to use a wife merely for 'bodily pleasure' and not for the procreation of children was to make her a prostitute.[71] Marius maintains that Alice is likely to have passed the menopause when More married her. He deploys this inference to argue that More may have 'used' his second marriage to a woman with whom he could not legitimately have sexual intercourse in the eyes of the Church 'to cancel a revived longing for the priesthood or the monastic life'. The 'lure of the

priesthood' may once again have become 'beguiling' on the unexpected death of Jane Colt, and Marius turns his discussion into
an apparent vindication of his interpretation (see Chapter 2) that
More's life from the Charterhouse to the Tower was a paradigm
of sin and redemption.[72] This does not seem very convincing, but
does not invalidate the force of his inference that by the time the
More household had reached Chelsea, Alice and More may have
lived together but not slept together. It is possible that More kept
a bed in the New Building, or spent the night there sometimes
without returning to the mansion house. But this is pure
conjecture.

More's attitude to women is usually excused by reference to
cultural norms and stereotypes, and by his alleged role as a
pioneer of liberal, and especially female, education. Several
humanists, notably More, Erasmus, and Juan Luis Vives, the
Spanish scholar who in 1523 succeeded John Clement and
Thomas Lupset as Wolsey's lecturer in rhetoric at Oxford,
advocated women's education. Perhaps as a result, a number of
noble or well-connected women acquired humanist and classical
learning.[73] As Bridgett put the point, 'More will ever stand fore-
most in the rank of the defenders of female culture'.[74] More
recently, historians have questioned the practical effects. It is
argued that the humanists had limited aims for the education of
women. Feminist historians even believe that the emphasis on
female passivity and chastity contributed further to the subordination of women. Some historians have suggested that the
number of genuinely learned Tudor women was limited to fifteen
or twenty prominent individuals. This may be too pessimistic,
but it is undeniable that few opportunities existed for girls to
attend schools or obtain an education beyond the confines of the
household, and the universities were closed to women until the
end of the nineteenth century.[75]

More encapsulated his philosophy of education in a letter to
William Gonell, who succeeded John Clement as tutor to his
children.[76] He stressed the role of 'moral probity', without which
learning brings nothing but 'notorious and noteworthy infamy'.
It was precisely because women's education was a novelty that
'virtue' must be visibly apparent in those who received it. A
woman who combined even modest learning with virtue would
obtain more profit than the riches of Croesus or the beauty of
Helen. What mattered was that she acquired an 'inner knowledge
of what is right'. Gonell was urged to warn More's children of

the dangers of pride. Virtue and learning were to be upheld as the way to attain piety, charity and Christian humility. Only then would a person be equipped to lead an innocent life. Conventionally, the purpose of an education was to prepare boys for public office or a career in the Church. More did not see it this way. Education was the process whereby religious and moral principles were instilled and exemplified. As long as these rules were observed, there was no difference between men's and women's education.[77]

More's letter is sententious: he intended it to be copied out by his family, translated from Latin into English, and made the subject of further correspondence. But his emphasis on 'moral probity' shows that he conceptualized education in ways that his contemporaries would have regarded as 'feminine' rather than 'masculine'. It is not a coincidence that in all the extant copies of Holbein's family group portrait, John More, like his three sisters, is shown reading a book. John, unlike his father and grandfather, was not encouraged to enter one of the professions. He did not train as a lawyer or earn a living, but lived (after More's execution) on the income from his wife's estates in Yorkshire.

Nor did More's philosophy include equipping his family to form independent judgements of religion or the world. They were to adhere to the curriculum he laid down, which followed the humanist–classical agenda and the traditions of the Catholic Church. They were to master Latin and Greek literature, logic and philosophy, and mathematics.[78] Astronomy was taught in conjunction with mathematics in 1521, when Nicholas Kratzer, whom Henry VIII had appointed royal astronomer, visited More's household.[79] Most notably, More expected his family to study the Church Fathers. His daughters were to learn St Jerome and St Augustine in particular: his own favourite authors, who had 'not only exhorted excellent matrons and honourable virgins to study', but had written them letters of instruction that were 'replete with so much erudition'.[80] When his children married, they were succeeded in what More liked to call his 'school' by his grandchildren. A continuous cycle of classical and Christian education was therefore provided for his extended family at Bucklersbury and Chelsea from around 1510 until the family's eviction from the estate after More's execution. All this seemingly conformed to Erasmus' description of More's family as a Christian adaptation of Plato's Academy, even though Erasmus had seen the 'school' in action only in its first year.[81]

For Plato and More alike, however, education was not liberal. It was designed to propagate virtue and curb moral weakness and individuality. More adored his children, especially his eldest daughter Margaret, but his educational objectives subordinated their lesser personalities to his own. It is not in the least surprising that More's and Margaret's contributions to the dialogue from the Tower contained in the 'letter' to Alice Alington can scarcely be told apart (see Chapter 9).[82] More's household may have been 'virtuous', but its norms were patriarchal. This is only to be expected, since patriarchy was the most fundamental of the concepts handed down by classical antiquity, which dictated that fathers should rule. In some ways More was an educational pioneer, but in others he was not. In particular, his 'school' was socially exclusive. No education was offered to the servants of his household or their children.

As to the domestic establishment, Erasmus stressed More's geniality. There were 'never' any troubles or disputes.[83] If anything went awry, it was remedied immediately. More had 'never' dismissed a servant. (While this may have been correct when Erasmus wrote, we know that a young servant, Dick Purser, was dismissed in *c*.1534 for attempting to communicate his heretical opinions to another servant.)[84] Once again, 'moral probity' was paramount. It was More's rule that male and female servants sleep in separate quarters, and rarely meet.[85] At least this meant that the household was safe for women servants. Sexual exploitation was widespread in Tudor domestic establishments, but More's was an exception.[86] Bridgett came close to the mark when he wrote: 'It is clear that Sir Thomas had a little Utopia of his own in his family.'[87] Again, none of the servants were permitted to waste their time. According to Stapleton, whose information came from John Harris and Dorothy Colly, responsibilities were rigorously assigned: to avoid 'idleness', the men whose duty it was to accompany More on diplomatic missions were given special gardening jobs when he was resident at home. Each was allocated a section of the garden, which would be subject to regular inspections.[88] Other servants were encouraged to sing or to play keyboard instruments in their spare time. No one was allowed to play at dice or cards, the chief of the 'idle' pastimes which Erasmus said More so despised.[89]

The exact size of More's household is a puzzle. Holbein's iconography creates the illusion of a closely-knit circle of around a dozen. The pen and ink version of the family group portrait

A drawing of the More family at Chelsea, 1527–8 (before 7 February 1528), by Hans Holbein the Younger (*Kunstmuseum Basel*).

illustrates 10 people: More and Dame Alice, More's father, Sir John (who did not live in the household at Chelsea), the three married daughters and More's son, John, Anne More (née Cresacre), Margaret Clement (née Gigs), and Henry Patenson, More's fool. In the Nostell Priory canvas, there are 12 people: the above 10 plus John Clement and John Harris. This ensemble is responsible for the notion, so attractive to the Victorians, that More and his family sat happily and cosily around the fireside. Inspired by Holbein, scholars like Frederic Seebohm could take a 'lingering look' at the 'beautiful picture of domestic happiness presented by More's home' as if it were the precursor of a late-Victorian vicarage.[90] It is this same romantic idyll that inspired Anne Manning's fanciful *Household of Sir Thomas More* (1851), which is tantamount to a novel, but was widely read and admired in an age when even the middle classes aspired to servants.

How many people were there in More's household? In 1528, following an epidemic of plague and harvest failure, Wolsey organized a national census of population and grain stocks. Most of the returns have been lost, but those for nine parishes from Acton to Chelsea are extant. More and Sir John Packington were commissioned to investigate how many people lived in every household in each of these parishes, and how much of the wheat and other cereals stored in their barns was required for domestic consumption and how much might be sold on the open market to relieve the dearth. They reported that in Chelsea, there were 2090 persons, and that More 'hath in his house daily' 100 persons.[91] This implies that in addition to the adult family members, More's grandchildren, John Harris, Dorothy Colly and the dozen or so chamber servants who waited or attended on the family, there were around 50 lesser domestic staff in the kitchens, laundry, stables and gardens, plus the eight watermen who rowed and maintained More's barge.[92] Roper later referred to the 'gentlemen and yeomen' (meaning chamber servants) who had to be found new employment after More's resignation as Lord Chancellor.[93] There was, therefore, a full domestic staff. All this is far removed from conventional descriptions, but it is corroborated by the floor plans of the mansion house at Chelsea. These have survived in the archives at Hatfield House in the form in which they were drawn in 1595, a year after Lord Burghley inherited the house from Lady Dacre, who had inherited it from the second Marquis of Winchester, the son and heir of Sir William Paulet, to whom it had been granted after More's execution. The plans are so detailed that it is even possible to work out in which room Holbein's family group portrait was painted. They show a building on two floors that was on the scale of an Oxford or Cambridge college. The Great Hall alone was 72 feet in length and the long gallery 87 feet in length. Moreover, these plans survey only the mansion house. They do not include the New Building or any domestic outbuildings.[94]

Historians have followed the earliest biographers in constructing a 'story' in which More's private and domestic life becomes the linchpin of his status as a virtuous public personality. For R.W. Chambers, to take the classic case, More's 'patience and courtesy towards heretics' can be 'revealed only to the careful student of his private life'.[95] This is a verdict that would have delighted More, who in his epitaph described himself as 'grievous' to 'thieves, murderers and heretics' but always maintained that he had acted honourably (see Chapter 6).[96] For Richard Sylvester, the most accomplished historian of More's mental world, the household at Chelsea was 'the focal point of his life'. It was through contact with his family that More kept his bearings. They enabled him to 'make sense' of his resignation and of his tribulations in the Tower. He had chosen the 'politick life' as well as a life of 'moral probity', but when the two collided, a choice was required. What made his story 'tragic' was that More was not 'the stuff of which heroes are made'. He loved his family dearly. He had a 'genius' for friendship. After his resignation, he was forced to endure the torment of a 'domestic exile' that would have broken the spirit of most people.[97]

If the revisionists have been more severe, their case is spoilt by overstatement. For Sir Geoffrey Elton, More was a misogynist: his domestic ideal a sham.[98] For Richard Marius, he was devoid of any real 'gentleness' or 'pity' until his imprisonment in the Tower turned him round. He was a superlative 'actor' or showman, who 'felt himself always on stage' to the point where we 'weary of the self-serving of his image making'. He manipulated the rhetoric of domestic affection to enhance his public reputation. 'The public spectacle he made of his real love for his family seems at times overmuch, part of the pageant he performed for an audience.' He loved his eldest daughter, Margaret, more than anything except God, but the letters he wrote from the Tower 'do not seem to be letters of comfort', but rather 'efforts to get his own view ... before the world'. Marius even excoriates More's reputed affection for animals: if a dog had entered the room in which he was sitting for the family group portrait, he 'would have booted the beast out of the house'.[99]

The revisionists realize that accounts of More's domestic and family life are built on quicksand. Traditional judgements have relied to an unacceptable degree on the attention the topic has received from the equivalent of 'spin doctors'. Can we really believe what Erasmus says in his vignette? The dilemma is that the scale of distortion is unknown. Myth-making is inherent from the start. Erasmus cited 'facts', but did not write factually. He wrote to construct an ideal.[100] The 'stories' of Roper and Harpsfield offer further snippets, but build conceptually on Erasmus' ideal. Stapleton magnifies the image reflected by Harpsfield. But how reliable is the information supplied by John Harris and Dorothy Colly? All of it lacks corroboration; much of it is resonant of Book II of *Utopia*. The upshot looks unnervingly like an inverted pyramid. No one disputes that More's domestic and family life is a key topic. In the final analysis, however, it is less a shibboleth that defines the ways in which his reputation has been imagined by historians than a source of plunder appropriated indiscriminately to bolster guesswork.

Notes

1 Roper, pp. 208–13, 226.
2 John Guy, *The Public Career of Sir Thomas More* (Brighton, 1980), pp. 25–6.
3 Guy, *Public Career*, p. 25.
4 Roper, p. 211.
5 Stapleton, p. 96; Roper, p. 211.
6 Roper, p. 243.
7 Roper, pp. 210–11.
8 Roper, p. 211.
9 Stapleton, p. 96.
10 Stapleton, p. 96.
11 By the reign of Charles I, Holbein's original version of the painting had been acquired by the Earl of Arundel. It was last heard of in the collection of the bishop of Olmütz (now in the Czech Republic) in 1671, which was destroyed in a fire at the bishop's summer palace in 1752. See L. Lewis, *The Thomas More Family Group Portraits after Holbein* (Leominster, 1998), pp. 4–5.
12 Roper, p. 217.
13 Stapleton, p. 96.
14 *CWE* 7, p. 18.
15 Roper, p. 197.

16 Harpsfield, pp. 3–218; T. Betteridge, *Tudor Histories of the English Reformations, 1530–83* (Aldershot, 1999), pp. 130–1.
17 Stapleton, p. 66.
18 Stapleton, p. 66.
19 Stapleton, p. 97.
20 Roper, p. 211.
21 Roper, pp. 211–12.
22 *CWE* 7, pp. 15–25; Harpsfield, pp. 63–99.
23 Roper, p. 226.
24 *CWE* 7, pp. 17–18, 24.
25 *CWE* 7, p. 24.
26 *CWE* 7, p. 18.
27 *CWE* 7, p. 22.
28 *CWE* 7, p. 23.
29 *CWE* 7, pp. 18, 23.
30 *CWE* 7, p. 19.
31 Trapp and Herbrüggen, pp. 32, 97.
32 The visit ended in August 1528.
33 Roper, p. 225.
34 *CWE* 7, p. 19.
35 Roper, p. 197.
36 Charles Whibley, ed., *Henry VIII* [an edition of Hall's Chronicle] (2 vols, London, 1904) 2, p. 265.
37 R.J. Fletcher, ed., *The Pension Book of Gray's Inn* (2 vols, London, 1901–10) 1, p. 496.
38 R.S. Sylvester, 'Thomas More Conference: Keynote Address', *Moreana* 16 (1979), p. 98.
39 *CWE* 7, p. 19.
40 T.E. Bridgett, *Life and Writings of Blessed Thomas More* (London, 1924), appendix B, pp. 443–4.
41 Roper, pp. 198–99.
42 R.W. Chambers, *Thomas More* (London, 1938), pp. 95–6.
43 It is, however, conjectural. See R. Warnicke, 'The Restive Wife in Erasmus' Colloquy: Mistress More or Lady Mountjoy', *Moreana* 20 (1983), pp. 5–14.
44 Chambers, *Thomas More*, p. 96.
45 C.H. Miller, ed., 'Thomas More's Letters to Frans van Cranevelt', *Moreana* 31 (1994), p. 37.
46 *CW* 12, p. cxxxvi.
47 G.R. Elton, *Studies in Tudor and Stuart Politics and Government* (4 vols, Cambridge, 1974–92) 3, pp. 345–6.
48 G.R. Elton, 'The Actor Saint', *New York Review of Books* (31 Jan. 1985), p. 8.
49 *Opus Epistolarum* 4, no. 999 (p. 19); *CWE* 7, p. 21.
50 Chambers, *Thomas More*, p. 111.
51 *CWE* 7, p. 21.
52 *CWE* 7, pp. 21–2.
53 *CW* 8, Pt. 2, p. 605.
54 *CW* 8, Pt. 2, p. 605.
55 Harpsfield, p. 94.

56 Harpsfield, p. 94.
57 Roper, p. 220.
58 PRO, C 1/706/34; M. Hastings, 'Sir Thomas More: Maker of English Law?' in R.S. Sylvester and G. Marc'hadour, eds, *Essential Articles for the Study of Thomas More* (Hamden, CT, 1977), p. 104.
59 Roper, p. 243.
60 Roper, p. 243.
61 Harpsfield, p. 98.
62 *CW* 12, p. cxxxvi.
63 Harpsfield, p. 97.
64 *CW* 12, pp. 276–77.
65 *CW* 12, p. 277.
66 *CW* 12, p. 431.
67 Richard Marius, *Thomas More* (New York, 1984), pp. 41–3, 220.
68 Harpsfield, p. 93; *CWE* 7, p. 21.
69 Miller, ed., 'Thomas More's Letters to Frans van Cranevelt', pp. 13–15.
70 Miller, ed., 'Thomas More's Letters to Frans van Cranevelt', pp. 43, 49, 55.
71 Marius, *Thomas More*, p. 42.
72 Marius, *Thomas More*, pp. 42–3.
73 Among those renowned for their classical and linguistic skills were More's eldest daughter, Margaret, Mary and Elizabeth Tudor, Lady Jane Grey and her sisters, and the five daughters of Sir Anthony Cooke, of whom the eldest, Mildred, married Sir William Cecil, and the second eldest, Anne, married Sir Nicholas Bacon.
74 Bridgett, *Blessed Thomas More*, p. 132.
75 J. Simon, *Education and Society in Tudor England* (Cambridge, 1966); S. Mendelson and P. Crawford, *Women in Early Modern England, 1550–1720* (Oxford, 1998); J. Eales, *Women in Early Modern England, 1500–1700* (London, 1998).
76 Rogers, ed., *Selected Letters*, pp. 103–7.
77 Rogers, ed., *Selected Letters*, p. 105.
78 Stapleton, p. 99.
79 Rogers, ed., *Selected Letters*, p. 146.
80 Rogers, ed., *Selected Letters*, p. 105.
81 Harpsfield, p. 92.
82 Rogers, ed., *Correspondence*, pp. 514–32.
83 *CWE* 7, p. 22.
84 Susan Brigden, 'Thomas Cromwell and the Brethren', in Claire Cross, D.M. Loades and J.J. Scarisbrick, eds, *Law and Government under the Tudors* (Cambridge, 1988), p. 35.
85 Stapleton, p. 96.
86 Mendelson and Crawford, *Women in Early Modern England*, p. 89.
87 Bridgett, *Blessed Thomas More*, p. 138.
88 Stapleton, p. 95.
89 Stapleton, p. 95.
90 F. Seebohm, *The Oxford Reformers* (London, 1915), p. 312.

91 PRO, E 36/257, fo. 55.
92 Roper, p. 226.
93 Roper, p. 226.
94 R. Norrington, *In the Shadow of a Saint* (Waddesdon, 1983), pp. 59–63.
95 Chambers, *Thomas More*, p. 86.
96 Trapp and Herbrüggen, p. 139; Harpsfield, p. 280.
97 Roper, pp. xvi–xvii, xix–xx.
98 Elton, 'The Actor Saint', pp. 7–8.
99 Marius, *Thomas More*, pp. 230, 300–1, 503, 518–19.
100 J.B. Trapp, 'Midwinter', *London Review of Books* (17–30 November 1983), p. 15.

|5|

Social reformer?

Idyll or ideal? This is the enigma of Thomas More's *Utopia* (1516). What is the book about? How was it received by More's own contemporaries? How has it been represented and interpreted since? In what ways has its significance altered in translation? What is its purpose? Does it represent More's 'ideal society'? Or is it merely intended, like Erasmus' *Praise of Folly*, to 'laugh men out of folly'? Utopian society is communist; it has abolished social degree based on private property. Such ideas were not new to *Utopia*. They derived from Plato, whose theory had been criticized by Aristotle. In turn, Aristotle's critique had been incorporated into medieval political orthodoxy by St Thomas Aquinas. But Plato's ideas (and More's – if he meant them!) denied the connection between inherited wealth and honour, reputation, nobility and social authority. Was More serious about what he said? Or is *Utopia* a humanist *jeu d'ésprit*, a literary hoax designed to show off its author's virtuosity, which is not intended as a platform for the reconstruction of society?

More imagined *Utopia* during spare moments of his embassy to Bruges in 1515. He wrote it in two halves, beginning with what is now Book II and the opening of Book I: the rest was completed on his return to London in 1516. The full title is *On the Best State of a Commonwealth and on the New Island of Utopia*.[1] Book I is fairly straightforward. It starts with a brief account of the circumstances of More's embassy to Bruges and his meeting with Peter Gillis, the friend of Erasmus and town clerk of Antwerp. After mass one day at Antwerp Cathedral, More met Gillis in the company of a Portuguese traveller, Raphael Hythlodaeus, to whom Gillis introduced him. With the entry of Hythlodaeus into the conversation, More has slipped from fact into fiction. The rest of Book I is a dialogue on a variety of political and social ills: princely ambition, court flattery, war, the perils of standing armies, unjust laws, poverty, enclosures, theft and homicide. And on a possible course of action: whether Hythlodaeus, who also turns out to be an expert in Greek philosophy, should enter a royal council to advocate the necessary reforms.

By engaging with the humanist debate on 'civic duty' in Book I, More offers a critique of the claims of 'contemplation' as against 'action': moral absolutism as against the 'politick life'. In the course of the dialogue, Hythlodaeus is the speaker who advocates moral absolutism. The now fictional 'Thomas More' puts the case for Ciceronian 'action'. As 'More' explains:

> If you cannot pluck up bad ideas by the root, or cure long-standing evils to your heart's content, you must not therefore abandon the commonwealth. Don't give up the ship in a storm because you cannot hold back the winds. You must not deliver strange and out-of-the-way speeches to people with whom they will carry no weight because they are firmly persuaded the other way. Instead, by an indirect approach, you must strive and struggle as best you can to handle everything tactfully – and thus what you cannot turn to good, you may at least make as little bad as possible.[2]

The dialogue is open-ended. It is deliberately left unresolved. It freely intermingles fact and fiction, and is indebted to parallel treatments of the same agenda in Cicero's *De officiis*, which 'More' not merely paraphrases but imitates word for word at several points.[3] Book I ends with a debate of the evils of money and private property, which leads Hythlodaeus into a description of the island of Utopia: the subject of Book II.

Book II is longer and more erudite than Book I. Couched almost entirely as a monologue by Hythlodaeus, it is a graphic but entirely fictional description of the island of Utopia, which Hythlodaeus had 'visited' with his five companions after separating from the final expeditions to the New World of Amerigo Vespucci. A clue to the riddle of Book II is etched into *Utopia*'s structure. More has created an asymmetry between reality and illusion: between the 'real' and the 'ideal'. Book I represents the 'real' world, and Book II the 'ideal' or Utopian world. Whereas

Cicero's discussion of 'civic duty' dominates the agenda of Book I, Plato's discussion of the 'ideal society' in his classic philosophical treatise, the *Republic*, dominates Book II. Plato's aim in the *Republic* is to construct an image of an 'ideal' commonwealth which exists in the mind, but which sets the standard against which actual political societies should be judged.[4] His 'ideal' is philosophical, but not remote. It belongs to the real world. But Plato is a moral absolutist, who will never accept second best. He rejects the philosopher's involvement in politics if the slightest degree of compromise is to be made. Nor will he accept second best in discussing the remodelling of society. His attitude limits the practical implementation of his project. The perfect society exists in the realm of the Platonic Form or Idea. In Plato's words, it is 'laid up as a pattern in heaven, where those who wish can see it and found it in their own hearts'.[5] Nevertheless, Plato constructs the 'ideal' society in order to perfect his own society. Is this what More also seeks to achieve? We need first to know what Book II is about.

Book II describes the island of Utopia. There are 54 cities, a federation guided by a senate of 162 members which meets annually in the capital city, Amaurot. All the cities are identical in language, customs, institutions and laws. Agriculture is the primary occupation at which everyone works. In addition, everyone learns a trade or handicraft. Everyone works for six hours a day. Some magistrates are entitled not to work, but they do not take advantage of the privilege, preferring to set a good example. Scholars are exempted from manual labour so that they may devote themselves to study, but are on a system of continuous assessment and those who fail to meet expectations are re-assigned to normal duties. In Utopia, scholars publish or perish!

Each city and its hinterland is divided into households consisting generally of blood relations and extended families. Urban households have no fewer than 10 and no more than 16 adult members; rural households have no fewer than 40 adult members. Each year 20 persons from each rural household move back into the city after completing a two-year stint in the countryside. In their place, 20 substitutes are dispatched from the town, to learn agriculture from those who are better skilled at it. The oldest member of each household is the ruler. The society is exclusively patriarchal. Wives act as servants to their husbands, children to their parents, and the younger to their elders. Women are treated 'equally', but in reality are subordinated to their husbands. They also work harder than the men – More seems quite oblivious to this point – since they are responsible for cooking and childcare in addition to manual labour. Such domestic issues as who cleans the house, who does the washing, and who does the garden are settled in Utopia by the simple expedient of not mentioning them.[6]

Utopia is a communist society. Property is held in common. Money and private wealth have been abolished. Money is needed for the conduct of trade with foreign cities, but in practice most foreign exchange transactions are handled on the basis of promissory notes. Money is required by the Utopians only when it is needed to lend to another nation, or in time of war, when it is used to hire foreign mercenaries. Otherwise, gold and silver are held to be inferior to ironwork, and are used to manufacture chamber pots or the chains and shackles of the Utopian slaves. Diamonds and pearls are given as baubles to children, who cast them aside with their toys when they grow up.

The Utopians know the difference between true and false pleasures, and between true and counterfeit nobility. They do not dress in fine clothes, they see no honour in irrelevant ceremonies, nor do they glory in empty titles of nobility. They have no need of inherited wealth or ancient ancestry. They do not waste their time, and avoid such 'idle' pastimes as gambling and hunting. They voluntarily attend public lectures before dawn in order to improve their minds. After supper they entertain themselves with music or polite conversation. Blood sports are particularly repellent to them. Hunting is seen as unworthy of free men, since it takes pleasure from killing and mutilation, and induces cruelty in humans through the condoning of brutality to animals.

The Utopians delight in education, which is provided for every child. They are keen students of moral philosophy, which they reinforce by principles drawn from their religion. When they heard from Hythlodaeus and his companions about Greek literature, they eagerly sought to learn the Greek language, which they mastered in three years. The purpose of a Utopian education is to inquire into the good of the soul and the body, to consider virtue, and to discover in what things true happiness consists. The Utopians define 'virtue' as 'living according to nature', since this is the end to which they were created. A Utopian is following nature when, in desiring one thing and avoiding another, he or she obeys the dictates of 'reason'. In the first place, 'reason' urges the Utopians to love and venerate the Divine Majesty to whom they owe their being and capacity for pleasure. In the second place, 'nature' prescribes happiness to them as the end of their being. (As we shall later see, Hythlodaeus takes care to distance himself from the opinions of the Utopians on this crucial point.)

The Utopians are pacifists. They despise war as an activity fit only for beasts and think nothing so inglorious as 'glory' achieved in combat. They go to war only for defensive reasons or to liberate an oppressed people from tyranny. As soon as war is declared, they infiltrate enemy territory and post placards promising large rewards to anyone who will assassinate the enemy prince. If assassination fails, they incite leading members of the royal family or nobility to plot for the crown. In warfare they commit their own citizens sparingly, and prefer to spend their gold and accumulated credits to hire foreign mercenaries. Since they pay the highest rates, they get the best soldiers. One prominent Utopian commands the entire army, with two others in reserve. Beyond this, no one is forced to fight abroad unless they volunteer. In the conduct of war, the Utopians are magnanimous. Truces are honoured, massacres forbidden, cities are not sacked, nor are territories laid waste. Once a war is concluded, the costs are indemnified by the conquered people who are forced to cede not only money, but also lands from which the Utopians and their allies may enjoy a perpetual income.

There is no official Utopian religion. Different forms of religion exist in the island, even within the individual cities. But the Utopians believe in a single divinity, whom they call their Father and to whom they attribute the creation and providential government of the world. Although individuals differ in various details of their religion, everyone agrees that there is one supreme power or Divine Majesty, whom they call Mithra. Religious toleration was prescribed by the original architect of Utopia, King Utopus. He laid down by law that everyone may cultivate the religion of his choice and proselytize for it, providing they do so rationally and without offending others. If persuasion fails, no one may resort to violence or abuse, and anyone who fights over religion is punished by exile or slavery.

Despite his advocacy of religious toleration, King Utopus required conformity to two basic doctrines or beliefs, because they affirm the dignity of human nature. The first is the doctrine of the immortality of the soul. The second is that the universe is ruled by divine providence and not by 'blind chance'.[7] Although these are religious principles, the Utopians see them as derived from natural reason. They constitute a 'rational' sanction for morality and a life of 'virtue'. If the soul were not immortal, and if life on earth were purely random, no one would feel inhibited from pursuing self-gratification irrespective of right or wrong. If there is no reward after death for virtue on earth, 'you have no compensation for having passed your entire existence without pleasure, that is, miserably.'[8]

Utopian religion is less 'radical' than is often represented, but because the Utopians are free of the constraints of private property (and public expenditure limits!), More could imagine a radical social environment. The cities of Utopia have public hospitals with qualified physicians in constant attendance. There are comprehensive welfare programmes, universal education, divorce, euthanasia, and women priests. Slavery is permitted, but the Utopian slaves are either prisoners of war, heinous criminals, or foreigners who have been condemned to death in their own cities. Slaves are generously treated – with the exception of those former Utopian citizens who, despite the advantage of a moral education, have resorted to crime – so much so that the labouring poor from other nations voluntarily choose slavery in Utopia, since it is so much more congenial than staying at home.

A close reading of Book II shows how restricted in practice the most radical provisions are. Divorce is conditional and extremely rare. Women priests are possible: 'but only a widow of advanced years is ever chosen, and it doesn't happen often.'[9] Euthanasia is regulated by priests and magistrates, and is never forced on anyone against their will, nor does refusal lead to a denial or restriction of medical care. In particular, euthanasia is distinguished from suicide, which is only permitted in extreme circumstances. If anyone commits suicide without prior approval, their body is thrown unceremoniously into a bog.[10] Sexual matters are also strictly ordered. Premarital sex is severely punished, as is seduction and attempted seduction. Adultery is punished by the severest form of slavery. If an innocent party chooses still to love or remained married to an unfaithful spouse, this is permitted, but he or she must share in the punishment to which the guilty party is condemned. As to the 'equality' of women, it has already been noted that any 'benefits' More had offered in educational and religious provision were extinguished in the Utopian kitchens.

The conversion of the Utopians to Christianity is integral to the structure of Book II. Utopia is a heathen society, but Hythlodaeus and his companions introduce the inhabitants to the teaching of Christ. The Utopians either 'through the secret inspiration of God' (one of More's favourite phrases in his anti-Lutheran writings), or because Christianity seemed so very like their own religion, were eager to embrace the faith. Many were converted and baptized on the spot. Unfortunately, two of Hythlodaeus' original companions had died, and among the survivors there was no priest. The Utopians could not be confirmed or given the Eucharist since these sacraments require the office of a priest. But the Utopians 'understand what these [sacraments] are, and eagerly desire them'.[11] Hythlodaeus expresses his concern that the full sacramental system of the Catholic Church should become available to the Utopians. The effect is to shift the argument in Book II from a focus on 'reason' to a focus on 'revelation'.[12] Christianity so appeals to the Utopians, once it is explained to them, because Christ 'approved of his followers' communal way of life'.[13] Hythlodaeus in his peroration in Book II invokes Christ's authority in support of Utopian communism, whereas at the conclusion of Book I, when the topic was first introduced, he had invoked only Plato's authority.

If this is what *Utopia* is about, how has the work been received and interpreted? There have been almost as many theories as there have been readers. Pluralism is endemic, not least because no consensus emerged from the relatively thin debate which followed publication of the earliest editions of the work. Which *Utopia* should we discuss? There is no holograph or other definitive text. Until recently there has never been a single *Utopia*. A standard critical edition with full scholarly apparatus was not available until the Yale Edition of *Utopia* appeared in 1965, and even then doubts must be expressed about the accuracy of the English translation which this edition provides.[14] All the earliest editions were in Latin. The first four printings were issued at Louvain (1516), Paris (1517), and Basel (March and November 1518). In preparation for the first edition, More sent a prefatory letter and his manuscript copy of the text (now lost) to Erasmus, to whom he delegated all aspects of the first printing. The marginal annotations, letters of commendation, map of the island, Utopian alphabet and other ornaments that were appended to the work, and which have been used extensively to interpret it, were added by Erasmus and Peter Gillis with the assistance of their friends. More did not know exactly what form any of the earliest editions would take until copies arrived in his hands.

When the first edition appeared, More sent corrections and fresh material, including a second letter to Gillis, for the 1517 edition, which was seen through the press by Thomas Lupset. The Basel editions of 1518 were again directed by Erasmus, to whom More sent yet another copy of *Utopia* further revised in his own hand. The last edition to appear in More's lifetime was published in Florence in July 1519, but this closely followed the Basel edition of March 1518. Subsequent Latin editions between 1548 and 1672 followed the second Basel edition of November 1518.[15] The London (Latin) edition of 1668 reprinted the text of the first edition of 1516. An edition of 1777 was a hybrid based on the texts of 1517 and 1518. After 1777, the Latin text was largely forgotten. It was not reprinted until modern critical studies of More's life and writings were inaugurated in the aftermath of his beatification. The modern publishing blitz began when the first two scholarly editions of the Latin text of *Utopia* appeared in 1895.[16]

The reactions of More's own contemporaries to *Utopia* were muted. The least ambivalent commendation was secured from Jerome de Busleyden, a prominent European statesman and councillor to Charles V. He wrote appreciatively, even if his covering letter contained the back-handed remark that he replied out of esteem for Erasmus rather than More.[17] He interpreted *Utopia* as a mimetic exercise in moral philosophy, designed to reinforce Plato's *Republic* as a counterweight to Aristotle and Cicero. He compared More's purpose to that of Plato.[18] This interpretation is the most sophisticated reading of *Utopia* from any of More's contemporaries. By contrast, Guillaume Budé, the French humanist and councillor of Francis I, hedged his bets. He was unsure whether More was writing allegorically or literally. His commendation finally interpreted *Utopia* as an exemplar of evangelical Christian humanism closer to Erasmus' *Praise of Folly* than Plato's *Republic*.[19]

The main responsibility for the critical vacuum which accompanied the first publication of *Utopia* lies at the door of Erasmus. He was uncharacteristically slow to publish his own commendation. It did not appear until 1518 and it contained implicit reservations.[20] It was also exceptionally brief. It praised

More's talent by saying (in effect) how much better it might have been if he had been trained in Italy, and if he had devoted all his attention to scholarship rather than allowing himself to marry and become distracted by a legal career. On the subject of More's purpose, especially in Book II, Erasmus was completely silent. It is this deafening silence from the doyen of northern European humanism which created space for the pluralism that later prevailed. In his vignette to Hutten, Erasmus said that *Utopia* was written 'with the purpose of showing the reasons for the shortcomings of a commonwealth'. More had 'represented the English commonwealth in particular, because he had studied it and knew it best'.[21] So Erasmus knew that *Utopia* was written to enable More to criticize his own society. But whether he thought More meant what he said about communism in Book II, and whether he fully understood the depth of More's irony, are questions that are still debated.[22]

Perhaps surprisingly, the marginal glosses inserted by Erasmus and Gillis in the earliest Latin editions are literalist. They include such comments as: 'Distribution of land', 'Food and drink', 'This smacks of Plato's community', 'Women prepare the meals', 'O sacred society, worthy of imitation, even by Christians!', 'O magnificent scorn for gold!', 'Foolish honours', 'Empty nobility', 'Marriages', 'Divorce', 'Female priests', 'O priests far more holy than our own!'.[23] And literalist readings of *Utopia* abounded. Jean Desmarez, public orator at the University of Louvain, proposed that a mission of theologians should be sent to the Utopians.[24] Erasmus omitted this letter from the 1518 editions, even though it had been printed in 1516 and 1517. When the 1518 editions appeared, one 'very foolish' reader complained that More deserved no more credit than a hack, since everything in the book that was worth reading came from the mouth of Hythlodaeus. 'All More did was write it down.'[25] Gillis and More could not contain their glee at this, and at the naïvety of those readers who were poring over maps of the New World trying to find the precise geographical location of Utopia. Their greatest mirth was reserved for the rumour that an eminent theologian had written to Cardinal Wolsey to solicit an appointment as bishop of Utopia.[26] These would provide superb examples of fundamentalist interpretations of *Utopia*, if only we could be sure that they are not themselves literary hoaxes.

Utopia was at first read only by a very small minority of humanists. More never envisaged a translation, and none appeared in his lifetime. The book was not seen as 'relevant' or commercially viable until Ralph Robinson made the first English translation, published in 1551. The context was the ferment of activity that focused on the education of the young Edward VI and the links between the Protestant Reformation and the reform of economic and social policy. The cause of 'commonwealth' reform was closely associated in 1551 with the Strasbourg reformer, Martin Bucer, whom Cranmer had appointed Regius Professor of Divinity at Cambridge. His programme sought to realize 'the Kingdom of God in this world', to which end he presented the King with a blueprint for social and political reconstruction.[27]

Robinson dedicated his translation to Sir William Cecil, later Lord Burghley. In 1551 Cecil was one of the King's principal secretaries and also principal secretary to the Duke of Northumberland, the *de facto* regent during the latter half of Edward's minority. Cecil had enjoyed a meteoric academic career at Cambridge. He stood at the hub of a Protestant network which dominated the Edwardian and early Elizabethan regimes.[28] Robinson's translation was presented to Cecil in the hope that a place might be found for him in the network. He was educated at Grantham and Stamford grammar schools, where he was Cecil's contemporary. He graduated at Oxford, and entered Cecil's service as a clerk. In 1551, he appealed to Cecil for a pay rise, enclosing some Latin verses as a New Year's Gift. As late as 1572, he was still seeking advancement.[29]

Cecil was at least a guarantee of respectability. *Utopia* was not yet an entirely safe subject, or rather More was not a 'safe' author. In his dedicatory epistle, Robinson distanced himself from More's 'blind' and 'obstinate' Catholicism, but commended his work for its 'good and wholesome lessons' which it set out 'in great abundance'. The work was 'fruitful and profitable ... pleasant and delectable'. It set forth 'the best state and form of a public weal'.[30] Unfortunately, Robinson was not a student of political thought: the philosophical depth of *Utopia* eluded him. The asymmetry between Book I and Book II is emasculated by his translation, which encouraged a literalist interpretation of Book II. Despite More's abolition of social degree in Utopia, Robinson reinstates it. His version not only has 'magistrates' and 'citizens' on the island, but also 'artificers', 'workmen', and those who practise 'husbandry'. There are 'companies of crafts' and other idiomatic signifiers of Tudor economic and social organization.

Slaves become 'bondmen' and 'slavery' bondage. *Respublica* is interchangeably 'commonwealth', 'public weal' or 'weal-public'. The latter are neutral terms, but 'commonwealth' by 1551 was coupled to Bucer's agenda and implied policies that were remote from More's own conceptualization of Book II.[31] Finally, Robinson thought that the description of Utopia and its cities was too austere. He added liberal dashes of colour to liven things up. His favourite word is 'gorgeous', so that whereas the essence of Utopian life and civic architecture is its simplicity, in his translation the streets and monuments of Utopia 'be of fair and gorgeous building', 'be very gorgeous ... of fine and curious workmanship', or have 'gorgeous and substantial arches'. The city of Amaurot is not merely an ironic analogue of London, it is indistinguishable from London itself.[32]

Despite (or perhaps because of) these deficiencies, Robinson's 1551 translation secured a virtual monopoly of the market. Four further editions appeared between 1556 and 1639.[33] Thereafter, new editions followed intermittently, culminating in those of 1869, 1887, 1893 and 1910. New translations between 1551 and the advent of modern critical scholarship were limited to those by Gilbert Burnet (1684) and Sir Arthur Cayley (1808).[34] Of these, Cayley's was the less significant. His *Memoirs of Sir Thomas More, with a New Translation of His Utopia* was distinguished neither for its depth of research nor grace of style. Burnet's work was in a different league: it was a milestone in the process whereby More's reputation was 'rehabilitated' in Protestant establishment circles. Burnet had begun his *History of the Reformation* in 1677 and the first of its three large folio volumes was published two years later. He initially wrote to defend the Anglican Church against the claims of Nicholas Sander, the leader of the Catholic recusants in exile at Louvain in Elizabeth's reign, whose *Concerning the Origin and Progress of the English Schism* had been reissued in a French translation in Paris in 1676. But within a matter of months, he was engaged in a full-scale defence of the Henrician and Edwardian Reformations, based on a comprehensive trawl of the sources.[35] The gist of his argument was that the threat to the Reformation was internal and not external. It came from the sacerdotalism of the English clergy: Burnet's view of the Reformation and its inherent logic was ultimately founded on anticlericalism.[36]

This was the context in which *Utopia Translated into English* was published in 1684. Burnet considered *Utopia* and John

Colet's famous Convocation Sermon of 1511 to be a pair. Both were reinterpreted as anticlerical tracts. Thus, Colet's sermon had attacked the clergy's role in secular affairs and had denounced their pride, covetousness and corruption. In Book I of *Utopia*, More had censured those abbots who had enclosed farm-land. He had reckoned the friars to be 'vagabonds' and the nuns 'female beggars'. He had attacked the clergy for 'corrupting' Christian doctrine. As to Book II, the Utopian priests led lives of extraordinary holiness, were commendably few in number, and exhibited a 'solid virtue much above all rigorous severities'. They were allowed to marry, and yet their piety and devotion so greatly exceeded the morals of the religious orders of More's day that 'it shows he was no admirer of [monks]'. The religion of Utopia was tolerant and permitted 'comprehension further than the most moderate of our divines have ever pretended to do'. Lastly, the role of the Utopian clergy in secular affairs was to give counsel and advice, and not to censure or punish offenders, which was left to the governor and other civil officers.[37]

Burnet's characterization of More as a Protestant reformer *avant la lettre* was achieved at a heavy price. Hereafter, *Utopia* would be interpreted in a literalist sense until the middle of the twentieth century.[38] *Utopia Translated into English* did not oust Robinson's translation from its dominant position, but it marked a watershed, since, by the mid-eighteenth century, More was becoming assimilated to the mainstream orthodoxy of Anglican conformity, his 'social' radicalism subordinated to his 'religious' radicalism. Although Burnet still regarded More's later career as intoxicated by 'popery', he was the 'best man of the popish side in that age', since 'the integrity of his whole life, and the severity of his morals' excused him from all suspicions.[39] He was a 'man of rare virtues and excellent parts', whose 'justice, contempt for money, humility, and a true generosity of mind' were a beacon to his age.[40]

With the Latin editions of *Utopia* all but forgotten and the literalism of the translations ascendant, the stage was set for the reinvention of *Utopia* in the nineteenth century. In *The German Ideology* Marx and Engels ranked More alongside the Levellers, the Owenites and the Chartists as a forerunner of socialism. William Morris announced that *Utopia* was 'a necessary part of a Socialist's library'.[41] And led by Marx, Karl Kautsky wrested More's ideas from their context in order to argue the case for his 'modernity', based on his appreciation of the 'great principle' of

Socialism: that 'man is a product of the material conditions in which he lives'.[42] According to Kautsky, *Utopia*'s intellectual roots in Plato's *Republic* and Renaissance humanism were beside the point. The 'constructive part' of *Utopia* sprang solely from the economic conditions of More's age. Utopian society had 'an essentially modern character', and the superficial resemblance to the *Republic* was 'only in externals'. More 'is one of the few who have been capable of this bold intellectual leap'. He was a 'child of his age', but was 'ahead of his time'. He was a hero of the Socialist Movement.[43]

A more nuanced, but still recognizable, version of this paradigm could be presented as late as 1949.[44] Kautsky's interpretation made its mark in the former Soviet Union, where an obelisk was sculptured on Lenin's orders immediately after the Revolution and unveiled in Moscow's Alexandrovsky Gardens. Inscribed on it are some 18 names, including those of Marx, Engels and (in Cyrillic script) 'T. More'.[45] There can be no better monument to a fundamentalist reading of *Utopia*. It is the twentieth-century equivalent of poring over atlases. More would have been unable to stop laughing. He would also have been dismayed that a State could have thought of proscribing or persecuting Christianity in conjunction with the abolition of private property and social degree. The climax of Book II of *Utopia* is precisely that the Utopians are converted to Christianity, and that Hythlodaeus invokes Christ's authority as well as Plato's for the principles of the Utopian State.

How has *Utopia* been read in the twentieth century? There are four distinctive approaches. Until the 1960s, when the Yale Edition shifted the direction of the debate, the mainstream interpretation was that *Utopia* depicts a fundamentally 'medieval' view of how rational human beings might organize society if they rely on natural reason unenlightened by divine revelation. The Utopian society depicted in Book II is an 'idyll' or 'literary conceit' designed to sharpen the reader's perception of the real world described in Book I. By this asymmetry, More aimed to 'prick the conscience' of Europe. He demonstrated that the virtues of the 'heathen' Utopians compared favourably to the conduct of the supposedly 'Christian' Europeans. Most fully amplified by R.W. Chambers, this reading was also shared by Catholic writers such as T.E. Bridgett.[46] It reached its zenith in Chambers' celebrated proposition: 'The underlying thought of *Utopia* always is, "*With nothing save Reason to guide them, the*

Utopians do this; and yet we Christian Englishmen, we Christian Europeans . . .!" '.[47] Chambers (like Bridgett) reacted against the literalism of the eighteenth and nineteenth centuries. He held that, while More 'scored a point against the wickedness of Christian Europe,' there is no sense in which he could have envisaged Book II as his 'ideal' society or as a manifesto for a reformed social order.[48] Book II was structured to create the asymmetry with Book I. It was not intended to be taken seriously. As Chambers remarked, 'When a Sixteenth-Century Catholic depicts a pagan state founded on Reason and Philosophy, he is not depicting his ultimate ideal.'[49]

Chambers' emphasis on the idyllic character of Book II was contradicted by J.H. Hexter in his brilliant introduction to the Yale Edition of *Utopia*, published in 1965.[50] Hexter stressed More's radicalism and argued that his ideal was a practical one. *Utopia* was not a literary idyll or conceit. More was one of the first 'modern radicals'. His belief was that, far from being worth preserving, 'the social order based on hierarchy is only worth eradicating'. Outside the family, 'the true principle of the good commonwealth is the very opposite of hierarchy; it is equality'.[51] The idea of 'pulling up by the roots – the starting point of radicalism – is not only implicit in *Utopia*, it is sporadically explicit.'[52] When the Utopians abolished the use of money and private property, they 'cut away a mass of troubles' and pulled up crimes root and branch. If human nature was to 'grow straight and clean', it must be transplanted in a society where there is no private wealth. Equality is justice. 'Community of property and abolition of money are *the only means* for achieving true equality'.[53] This More understood, and wished to see implemented. His vision of Utopia is an 'ideal', but it is one that ought also to exist in reality.

On a secondary level, Hexter argued that Utopia, although a heathen society, operated in More's fiction as a parallel society to Christian Europe, so that More could claim that the Utopians, by virtue of their piety and austerity, are more truly and genuinely 'Christian' than the nominally Christian societies of Europe. It is to the shame of Christians that, contrary to Christ's teaching, they have erected their so-called commonwealths on corrupt foundations in place of virtue. 'Such is the explicit judgement passed in *Utopia* on the world More lived in'.[54] *Utopia*, according to Hexter, is a Christian humanist commentary on the state of religion in the sixteenth century. It is the 'image' of a truly

Christian commonwealth. It represents the 'highest aspirations' of Christian humanists such as More and Erasmus.[55]

Whatever the merits of Hexter's case for *Utopia* as a product of More's social radicalism, the argument that the island functions as a parallel Christian society is flawed. As Quentin Skinner and Brendan Bradshaw have commented (at different times and in slightly different ways), a close reading of Book II shows that Hythlodaeus had all along distanced himself from that principle of the moral code of the Utopians which prescribed 'pleasure' and 'happiness' to them as 'the end of their being'. Hythlodaeus openly criticized this hedonism. He also made it clear that religious comprehension in Utopia was imperfect. Before his arrival on the island, the inhabitants knew nothing of the Incarnation, and even after his voyages they still lacked access to the Scriptures and to those sacraments that required the office of a priest. They lacked a knowledge of divine law, and had no understanding of the soteriological scheme outlined in the Bible.[56] If, therefore, Utopia represents More's 'ideal' of true Christianity, it follows that he did not consider Scripture, the sacraments or knowledge of Christ himself to be essential to a truly Christian existence. This is patently absurd.[57]

By the same token, it is the Utopians' reliance on 'reason' alone without the benefit of Christian revelation which enables them to approve 'radical' social measures such as divorce and euthanasia. The limitations of their moral code mislead them into supposing that actions which are mortal sins are actually pious and honourable. Skinner's scintillating critique leads him to reject the notion of Utopia as a parallel Christian society.[58] His conclusion marks, if anything, a reaffirmation of the earlier view that More sought to 'prick the conscience' of Europe. Skinner agrees with Chambers that, with revelation as well as reason at their disposal, Christians ought to be able to surpass the moral achievements of the Utopians in every respect.[59] However, he reaches this conclusion by an entirely different route. Whereas Chambers interpreted *Utopia* as both an 'idyllic' and as a fundamentally 'medieval' commentary on the political ideas of its age, Skinner has consistently maintained that the book depicts More's ideal society and represents the most avant-garde commentary on humanism that was written by a humanist north of the Alps.

If the readings of Chambers and Hexter mark two of the distinctive approaches which have emerged in the twentieth century, the third is the paradigm which sets *Utopia* in the context of the related humanist literature and argues that More planned a critique of humanism itself. Two distinct strands have converged in establishing this argument. One is Dermot Fenlon's hypothesis that More's purpose is to show that the humanist programme is misdirected. It is bound for 'Nowhere', which is why 'Utopia' is the name of the island and why the principal interlocutor is called 'Hythlodaeus'. (All the proper names in *Utopia* are puns on Greek words. 'Utopia' means 'Nowhere', and Hythlodaeus is indeed 'purveyor of Nonsense'.) According to Fenlon, *Utopia* is More's acknowledgement that the humanist enterprise is destined for failure. It rests on a fallacy, encapsulated by the asymmetry between Books I and II. More crafts *Utopia* to demonstrate that the gap between the self-interested 'egoism' of Book I, and the philosophical 'altruism' of Book II on which the humanist project must rely, is unbridgeable. Utopia, according to Fenlon, is the pattern of an 'ideal' humanist society, but it is one that More exposes as an 'illusion'.[60]

The pre-eminent modern scholar who has sought to interpret *Utopia* as a humanist critique of humanism is Quentin Skinner. His classic survey, the *Foundations of Modern Political Thought*, argues that the work 'embodies by far the most radical critique of humanism written by a humanist'.[61] More 'believes that one of the most urgent tasks of social theory is to discover the root causes of injustice and poverty.'[62] These evils are caused by the misuse of money and private property, as More's humanist contemporaries always maintained. What is 'unique' about *Utopia* is that More 'follows out the implications of this discovery with a rigour unmatched by any of his contemporaries'. His description of Utopian communism in Book II is the solution – 'the only possible solution' – to the catalogue of social evils summarized in Book I.[63] More, continues Skinner, throws down the gauntlet to his fellow humanists: he raises doubts about the coherence of their political thought. On the one hand, the humanists sought to deny that inherited wealth and ancient ancestry should be treated as qualifications for 'true nobility'. On the other, they continued to defend the traditional link between these privileges and honour, reputation, nobility and social authority. *Utopia* is the book which asks 'whether we can really have it both ways'.[64] It is true that the fictional 'More' appears in Book I in the guise of a Ciceronian humanist. At the end of Book I, he even puts the case in defence of private property. Skinner argues that the asymmetry in *Utopia* between

the views of 'More' and Hythlodaeus and between Book I and
Book II is expressly designed to enable the arguments of
Hythlodaeus to be read as an ironic inversion of the central
assumptions of scholastic and humanist political thought.[65] By
the end of Book II, the objections of 'More' have evaporated. He
'makes no attempt to restate his earlier case'. He does express
some purely practical doubts. But *Utopia* concludes on a 'wistful
and elegiac note'. 'More' says: 'I readily confess that there are
very many features of the Utopians' commonwealth which,
although I cannot have any hope of seeing, I should nevertheless
like to see, realised in our own communities'.[66] Skinner believes
that 'the thought we are left with' is that *Utopia* may indeed be
More's image of 'the best state of a commonwealth'. At this
point, his reading converges with Hexter's: *Utopia* is an 'ideal'
rather than an 'idyll'. More meant what he said. To succeed, the
humanists would have to accept the radical inferences of their
own ideology.

The interpretations of Hexter and Skinner have been critiqued
by Brendan Bradshaw, whose analysis marks the fourth
distinctive approach of recent years.[67] Bradshaw, more than any
other critic with the exception of the Jesuit Edward Surtz, has
played down the irony of Book II and rejected the notion that
More was offering an avant-garde commentary on humanism.[68]
Emphasizing the debt of Book II to Plato's *Republic*, Bradshaw
interprets More's purpose as an attack on the moral absolutism
of Plato's views of politics and philosophy. Whereas Plato in the
Republic rejected the case for pragmatism and refused to accept
second best in discussing the remodelling of society, More,
according to Bradshaw, refashions Plato's image of an ideal
society in order to argue that service to the commonwealth, and
perhaps the 'best state of a commonwealth' itself, involves state-
craft, diplomacy and compromise.

Plato's aim in the *Republic* is to create an image of a society
which exists in the mind, but which sets the standard against
which actual political societies should be judged. He constructs
an 'ideal' in order to perfect his own society. According to
Bradshaw, *Utopia* goes several stages further. The prototype is
Plato's ideal society, but More argued for urgent political
responses and pragmatic interventions which were designed to
begin the actual process of reform and nudge society as close to
Plato's 'ideal' as could be managed in the adverse conditions of
real life. If this involved compromise and expediency, and led to

reforms which were ultimately second best, then so be it. More sought not (as Skinner had argued) 'the only possible solution' for the social evils catalogued in Book I, but the 'best possible solution'.[69] More's paradigm was a 'civil philosophy' that was less remote than Plato's and far closer to Cicero's. He was a 'pragmatic' reformer who fused three 'traditions' into one: the intellectual radicalism of the Platonic *respublica*, the political radicalism of Ciceronian humanism, and the social radicalism of Scripture.

Bradshaw, unlike Skinner, does not believe that *Utopia* ends on a 'wistful and elegiac note'. He thinks it does not end at all. Whereas Plato's *Republic* reaches a final conclusion, in *Utopia* the dialogue is not concluded. It is 'merely broken off'.[70] 'More' ends by taking Hythlodaeus to supper. He remarks: 'we would find some other time for thinking of these matters more deeply, and for talking them over in more detail'.[71] Bradshaw neglects More's irony: 'Would that this would happen some day!'[72] Still, he raises the possibility that what is at issue is More's (and Plato's) belief that root-and-branch reform required the 'miraculous effort' of dialogue.[73] The debate will go on until social justice is achieved and the perfection of the commonwealth attained. The lesson of *Utopia*, according to Bradshaw, is that the possibility of progress resides neither in a tradition of 'moral absolutism' nor in the commitment of the politician to 'civic duty'. It will emerge from 'a constructive and continuing dialogue between the two'.[74]

What, then, can we say about *Utopia*? It is a profoundly complex work of classical humanism and moral philosophy, which cannot be discussed meaningfully outside of these contexts. It is also a powerful commentary on the relationship of 'reason' and 'revelation': its social principles cannot be severed from their Christian roots in order to make More a forerunner of Marx and Mao. Nor can literalist interpretations be considered helpful: Robinson's translation has sown anachronism and obliterated the extent of More's debt to the *Republic*. As to Burnet's translation, it was a milestone in the process whereby More's reputation was 'rehabilitated' in England, but the characterization of More as a Protestant reformer *avant la lettre* is a distraction that has bedevilled the debate. By subordinating More's 'social' radicalism to his 'religious' radicalism, Burnet turned *Utopia* on its head. More was 'serious' about the issues of true nobility and social justice. His book was a call to action to his fellow humanists. In many ways, *Utopia* depicts More's ideal commonwealth. It is not simply an 'idyll', a *jeu d'ésprit* or a literary hoax, even if it may sometimes have been read this way. It is a work of moral philosophy, but one that was not purely mimetic. It was a manifesto to More's contemporaries, even if we are left unsure whether he believed that communism was the 'only possible solution' to the riddle of the 'best state of a commonwealth' in practice.

Of the latest interpretations, the view that *Utopia* seeks to reconcile the rival philosophies of Plato and Cicero is highly attractive. If this reading is correct, More made the realization of Plato's ideal the mission of the Ciceronian politician. On this basis, the fictional 'More' is the key figure in *Utopia*, since by the end of Book II he seeks the best moral outcome in politics as the way of discharging the 'civic duty' of a true humanist philosopher.[75] He becomes the correlative of King Utopus. Perhaps this is why the real-life More described to Erasmus how, in his daydreams, he had been 'marked out' by the Utopians 'to be their king forever'?

> I can see myself now marching along, crowned with a diadem of wheat, very striking in my Franciscan frock, carrying a handful of wheat as my sacred sceptre, thronged by a distinguished retinue of Amaurotians, and, with this huge entourage, giving audience to foreign ambassadors and sovereigns.[76]

As Skinner infers, if a statement about More's real-life relationship to *Utopia* is required, it is that he aimed to construct 'a true understanding of the proper relationship between philosophy and public life'.[77] By following the call to 'counsel' and entering royal service in the spring of 1518, More was not succumbing to temptation: he was resisting it.[78] If entry into politics was the highest duty of a true humanist on 'moral' as well as 'civic' grounds, the temptation all along had been 'contemplation', not 'action'. Whether More sought the 'only possible solution' (Skinner) or the 'best possible solution' (Bradshaw) to the problems of social justice and the perfection of the commonwealth, *Utopia* is an 'ideal', not an idyll. And in composing it, More discovered that whether he had 'willingly' or 'reluctantly' abandoned duty in leaving the Charterhouse and embarking on a legal and political career was a question that his own philosophy had made irrelevant.

Notes

1 Logan, Adams and Miller, p. 3.
2 Logan, Adams and Miller, p. 97.
3 Q. Skinner, 'Sir Thomas More's *Utopia* and the Language of Renaissance Humanism', in A. Pagden, ed., *The Languages of Political Theory in Early Modern Europe* (Cambridge, 1987), pp. 123–57.
4 B. Bradshaw, 'More on Utopia', *Historical Journal* 24 (1981), pp. 1–27.
5 Plato, *The Republic*, ed. H.D.P. Lee (Harmondsworth, 1955), p. 369.
6 Logan, Adams and Miller, p. 129.
7 Logan, Adams and Miller, pp. 222–5.
8 Logan, Adams and Miller, pp. 160–3.
9 Logan, Adams and Miller, p. 231.
10 Logan, Adams and Miller, pp. 187–9.
11 Logan, Adams and Miller, p. 221.
12 Bradshaw, 'More on Utopia', p. 17.
13 Logan, Adams and Miller, p. 221.
14 Q. Skinner, 'More's *Utopia*', *Past and Present* 38 (1967), pp. 153–68. Subsequent reprintings of *CW* 4 contain corrections and amendments, but the most accurate translation is currently that by Logan, Adams and Miller, pp. 2–269.
15 *CW* 4, pp. cxc-cxci. There were Latin editions in 1548, 1555, 1563, 1565–66, 1601, 1613, 1629, 1663 and 1672.
16 *CW* 4, p. cxci.
17 *CW* 4, p. 287; Logan, Adams and Miller, p. 251 n. 1.
18 Logan, Adams and Miller, pp. 251–5.
19 Logan, Adams and Miller, pp. 7–19.
20 Logan, Adams and Miller, pp. 5–7.
21 *CWE* 7, pp. 23–4.
22 A. Fox, *Politics and Literature in the Reigns of Henry VII and Henry VIII* (Oxford, 1989), pp. 92–107.
23 Logan, Adams and Miller, pp. 113, 115, 119, 125, 131, 141, 143, 145, 149, 169, 173, 179, 187, 189, 191, 195, 231, 233.
24 Logan, Adams and Miller, p. 263.
25 Logan, Adams and Miller, p. 259.
26 *CW* 4, p. 292; Logan, Adams and Miller, pp. 31–9, 267–9.
27 B. Hall, 'Martin Bucer in England', in D.F. Wright, ed., *Martin Bucer: Reforming Church and Community* (Cambridge, 1994), p. 154.
28 S. Alford, 'Reassessing William Cecil in the 1560s', in J. Guy, ed., *The Tudor Monarchy* (London, 1997), pp. 238–40; Alford, *The Early Elizabethan Polity: William Cecil and the British Succession Crisis, 1558–1569* (Cambridge, 1998), pp. 14–28.
29 *Dictionary of National Biography on CD-ROM* (Oxford, 1995), *s.v.* 'Robinson, Ralph'.
30 J. Warrington, ed., *More's Utopia and a Dialogue of Comfort* (London, 1962), pp. 2–3.

31 M.L. Bush, *The Government Policy of Protector Somerset* (London, 1975).

32 J. Binder, 'More's *Utopia* in English: A Note on Translation', in R.S. Sylvester and G. Marc'hadour, eds, *Essential Articles for the Study of Thomas More* (Hamden, CT, 1977), pp. 229–33.

33 These editions were published in 1556, 1597, 1624 and 1639.

34 By 'new' in this context, I mean translations that were not derived in whole or part from Robinson's.

35 J.A.I. Champion, *The Pillars of Priestcraft Shaken: the Church of England and its Enemies, 1660–1730* (Cambridge, 1992), pp. 27–32, 77–92.

36 Champion, *Pillars of Priestcraft*, p. 81.

37 G. Burnet, ed., *Utopia Translated into English* (London, 1684), pp. 21, 37, 56, 83, 114, 130, 152, 173, 175, 177, 186, 191, 192; Burnet, *History of the Reformation of the Church of England* (6 vols, London, 1820) 5, pp. 42–7.

38 It is true, Burnet nodded in the direction of More's irony and even conceded momentarily that Utopia was 'a fable', but the literalist interpretation had prevailed.

39 Burnet, *History of the Reformation 5*, pp. xli, 46.

40 Burnet, *History of the Reformation 1*, pp. 549–50.

41 D. Baker-Smith, 'The Location of Utopia: Narrative Devices in a Renaissance Fiction', in M. Tudeau-Clayton and M. Warner, eds, *Addressing Frank Kermode: Essays in Criticism and Interpretation* (London, 1982), p. 110.

42 K. Kautsky, *Thomas More and his Utopia with a Historical Introduction* (London, 1927), p. 172.

43 Kautsky, *Thomas More and his Utopia*, pp. 1–3, 97–8, 160–2, 190, 248–50.

44 R. Ames, *Citizen Thomas More and his Utopia* (Oxford, 1949). For a literalist reading in a different genre, see M. Eliav-Feldon, *Realistic Utopias: the Ideal Imaginary Societies of the Renaissance 1516–1630* (Oxford, 1982).

45 Described in *Moreana* 21 (1984), p. 104.

46 T.E. Bridgett, *Life and Writings of Blessed Thomas More* (London, 1924), p. 104.

47 R.W. Chambers, *Thomas More* (1935), pp. 125–44 (author's italics preserved).

48 Chambers, *Thomas More*, p. 128.

49 Chambers, *Thomas More*, p. 128.

50 *CW 4*, pp. xv–cxxiv.

51 *CW 4*, pp. cxix–cxxi.

52 *CW 4*, p. cxxi.

53 *CW 4*, pp. cxxi–cxxiii.

54 *CW 4*, pp. ci–cii

55 *CW 4*, p. civ.

56 Skinner, 'Sir Thomas More's *Utopia*', pp. 140–50; Bradshaw, 'More on Utopia', pp. 6–14.

57 Bradshaw, 'More on Utopia, p. 7.

58 Skinner, 'Sir Thomas More's *Utopia*', p. 151.

59 Skinner, 'Sir Thomas More's *Utopia*', pp. 151–2.
60 D.B. Fenlon, 'England and Europe: Utopia and its Aftermath', *Transactions of the Royal Historical Society,* 5th ser., 25 (1975), pp. 115–36.
61 Q. Skinner, *The Foundations of Modern Political Thought,* (2 vols, Cambridge, 1978) 1, pp. 255–62.
62 Skinner, *Foundations* 1, pp. 261–2.
63 Skinner, *Foundations* 1, p. 262.
64 Skinner, 'Sir Thomas More's *Utopia*', pp. 154–5.
65 Skinner, 'Sir Thomas More's *Utopia*', p. 155.
66 Skinner, 'Sir Thomas More's *Utopia*', pp. 156–7.
67 Bradshaw, 'More on Utopia', pp. 1–27.
68 *CW* 4, pp.cxxv-clxxxi.
69 Bradshaw, 'More on Utopia', p. 20.
70 Bradshaw, 'More on Utopia', p. 26.
71 Logan, Adams and Miller, p. 249.
72 Logan, Adams and Miller, p. 249.
73 A.J. Slavin, 'Platonism and the Problem of Counsel in More's *Utopia*', in G.J. Schochet, P.E. Tatspaugh and C. Brobeck, eds, *Reformation, Humanism, and 'Revolution': Proceedings of the Folger Institute Center for the History of British Political Thought* (Washington DC, 1990), pp. 207–34.
74 Bradshaw, 'More on Utopia', p. 27.
75 Skinner, 'Sir Thomas More's *Utopia*', p. 135.
76 Rogers, ed., *Selected Letters,* p. 85.
77 Skinner, 'Sir Thomas More's *Utopia*', p. 135.
78 Bradshaw, 'More on Utopia', p. 24; Skinner, 'Sir Thomas More's *Utopia*', p. 135.

|6|

Heresy hunter?

No topic has done more to crystallize opinions of More's reputation than his role as an alleged inquisitor. He said himself that he took no pleasure in the prosecution of heresy, but regarded the work as necessary and 'well done'. A relapsed heretic was 'the devil's stinking martyr', who had 'taken his wretched soul with him straight from the short fire to the fire everlasting'.[1] Heresy was 'poison'. It was an 'incurable canker' to be excised. It was 'an incurable and contagious pestilence' to be treated 'according to justice by sore painful death, both for example and for [to avoid] infection of other'.[2] For his view of heresy, More would be condemned by Hume and Voltaire. Charles Lamb described the Preface to More's *Confutation of Tyndale's Answer* (1532–3) as 'penned with a wit and malice hyper-satanic'.[3] Such excoriations are based on moral rather than historical criteria. In his epitaph, More declared that he had been 'grievous' to 'thieves, murderers and heretics'.[4] The claim is highly sensitive. The original text, which he wrote himself, was etched in stone on his tomb in Chelsea Old Church, but when the monument was restored and the inscription slab remade, the phrase was truncated and a gap left in the marble. Since 1833 at the latest, a visitor to his tomb would have discovered that More had only been 'grievous' to 'thieves and murderers'.[5]

Opinion was changing in the sixteenth century. Erasmus welcomed the burning of heretical books, but disapproved of burning people at the stake. He made the inaccurate claim that no heretic was put to death while More was Lord Chancellor.[6] Within months of his resignation, More was under attack for his actions. His opponents complained to the Privy Council and their allegations were carefully examined. The charges were found to be 'very shameless false', but the fact that they were investigated at all is indicative of a mental shift.[7] More dealt with every one of these accusations in his *Apology*, the book he published in the spring of 1533, almost exactly a year after his resignation as Lord Chancellor, to defend his reputation. He summarized his position in the penultimate chapter:

> As touching heretics, I hate that vice of theirs and not their persons, and very fain would I that the one were destroyed, and the other saved. And that I have toward no man any other mind than this (how loudly so ever these blessed new brethren [the Protestants] the professors and preachers of verity belie me) if all the favour and pity that I have used among them to their amendment were known, it would I warrant you well and plain appear, whereof if it were requisite I could bring forth witnesses more than men would ween.[8]

More was an experienced controversialist, but in the *Apology* he made a fatal mistake. In order to refute the grievances of his opponents, he had repeated them, and it was these shibboleths that the Protestant martyrologist, John Foxe, incorporated into the first English edition of his *Acts and Monuments*, published in 1563. It will be helpful to summarize the accusations levelled by Foxe.[9] The gist is that More personally interrogated at least three of the heretics burned at the stake while he was Lord Chancellor. Two of these victims were imprisoned at his house at Chelsea so that More could examine them at will, and a fourth suspect was set in the stocks which More kept at home, and forced to incriminate his associates. (This suspect eventually escaped and fled to Antwerp.) A fifth suspect was imprisoned for distributing Tyndale's English New Testament. A sixth initially evaded capture on a warrant issued by More, but was later arrested and imprisoned in the Tower when he was spied attempting to embark ship for the Continent.

According to Foxe, More used the full panoply of his powers to pursue and investigate suspected heretics, but had also acted illegally. He had imprisoned heretics at his house, instead of committing them to the Tower or the bishop's prison. He had conducted a retrospective Star Chamber examination of witnesses present at the death of Thomas Bilney in the Lollards' Pit at Norwich, in order to prove that Bilney had recanted his heresies before his death and had not made a last minute appeal for justice to the King. To extract confessions, More had resorted to violence. He had flogged at least three suspects in his garden at Chelsea. One was John Tewkesbury, later burned at the stake, whom More had also tortured with ropes until 'the blood started out of his eyes'.[10] (This accusation was among several withdrawn by Foxe in the second edition of the *Acts and Monuments* in 1570.) He had flogged the young servant, Dick Purser, whom he had dismissed from his household in *c.*1534 for attempting to communicate his heretical opinions to another servant. A final victim was a mentally-deranged man who had fallen into 'frantic heresies' and lifted up women's skirts in church, whom More in his *Apology* admitted was severely whipped.[11]

It was Foxe's 'story' which was vindicated by the accession of Elizabeth I in 1558. The Church of England became officially Protestant and history was rewritten. This is not to say that Foxe was disingenuous. His efforts to obtain full documentary transcripts from 'credible witnesses' are legendary. His text was amended and revised in the manner of a computer database. He did not deliberately propagate fictions, although 'he wove his material into forms that were as fictive as they were factual'.[12] Some of the worst accusations against More were omitted even from the 1563 edition of the *Acts and Monuments*. But history is written by the winners: the Protestants were ascendant in politics (and publishing!) when the *Acts and Monuments* appeared. More's *Apology* was printed only in a single edition in 1533. It was included by William Rastell in his folio edition of More's *English Works*, but thereafter went out of print. The next edition was the one prepared for the Early English Text Society in 1930.[13]

More's earliest biographers circumvented his role as an inquisitor. Roper and Harpsfield wrote late in Mary's reign, when the heresy laws had been revived and some 287 Protestants burned.[14] Opinion was inflamed by the proceedings against Cranmer and his companions. Roper scarcely alluded to the topic of heresy. Harpsfield praised More's loathing of it, but made no reference to the trials and investigations in which he was involved.[15] A discussion of his anti-Lutheran writings was incorporated into the literary survey which followed Harpsfield's description of his family and domestic life.[16] But the purpose was not to justify More's confessional standpoint, which required no defence in Mary's reign, but to demonstrate 'the integrity, the sincerity and uprightness' that he had displayed in controversy.

The Protestants (and some humanists) had attacked the pungency of More's polemical style, and Harpsfield needed to refute this criticism in order to perfect his characterization of More as a virtuous personality.[17] His defence was that More sought only the truth in controversy and had never misrepresented his opponents or taken their words out of context, which had been More's own reply to his critics.[18]

Little was attempted by Stapleton and the recusant tradition to dislodge Foxe's verdict on More. Change had to wait for the publication of the third volume of Gilbert Burnet's *History of the Reformation* (1714), which assimilated More to the anti-sacerdotalist view of the Reformation by claiming that he had been an anticlerical 'radical' in 1516.[19] When he wrote *Utopia*, according to Burnet, he had expressed his 'first and coolest thoughts'.[20] If he had died at that time, he would have been reckoned among those who, although they had accepted the authority of Rome, saw clearly 'the errors and corruptions of that body'.[21] It followed that More was a Protestant reformer *avant la lettre*, one of those Catholics who lacked the 'opportunities of declaring themselves more openly for a Reformation'.[22]

More's radicalism in *Utopia* made his heresy proceedings almost inexplicable. As Burnet continued:

> It is not easy to account for the great change that we find afterwards [More] was wrought up to: he not only set himself to oppose the Reformation in many treatises, that, put together, make a great volume: but when he was raised up to the chief post in the ministry, he became a persecutor even to blood; and defiled those hands, which were never polluted by bribes, by acting in his own person some of those cruelties, to which he was, no doubt, pushed on by the bloody clergy of that age and church.[23]

Horace Walpole encapsulated the dilemma when he said that More was 'that cruel judge whom one knows not how to hate, who persecuted others in defence of superstitions he had himself exposed'.[24]

If, however, More was a reformer *avant la lettre*, his later career had even more relevance than it had before. After the Revolution of 1688, he was depicted as an historical figure who would rather die than tell an untruth or take an oath in vain. If he had been 'cruel' or 'zealous' in the persecution of heresy, the blame lay squarely on the shoulders of Rome. In the *Memoirs of*

the Life of Sir Thomas More (1758), the Reverend Ferdinando
Warner wrote:

> But amidst all the Encomiums which I think are due to the
> Memory of Sir Thomas More ... I must not conceal from
> the Readers, what was a great Allay to all his Virtues, his
> furious and cruel Zeal in the Persecution of Hereticks.
> Much of this, however, if not the Whole, must be attributed
> to the Ignorance and Superstition of the Age and Religion
> He had been bred in.[25]

To attack More's 'cruel zeal' only to exonerate him on the
grounds of the influence of 'superstition' was to strike a
trenchant blow against the 'subversive' influence of Catholicism.

The Victorian historian, James Anthony Froude, carried on
where Foxe and his successors had left off. He began writing his
*History of England from the Fall of Cardinal Wolsey to the
Defeat of the Spanish Armada* in 1854. The first two volumes,
covering the 1530s, appeared in 1856. Froude has been called the
earliest of the 'professional' historians of England for two
reasons. He was the first to exploit fully the resources of the State
Paper Office, and later the Public Record Office, as well as the
dispatches by foreign ambassadors to London in the archives at
Paris, Simancas, Vienna and Brussels. He was also the first
historian of the English Reformation who was not a wholly
committed Christian. Froude was not an unqualified secularist.
He rejected the view that people were governed by self-interest
alone. And he believed that history, and in particular the study of
history, had profound moral implications. 'We learn in it', he
said, 'to sympathise with what is great and good; we learn to hate
what is base.'[26]

Froude defended the reputation of Henry VIII and the Church
of England on social and political grounds. His argument led him
to interpret John Fisher and Thomas More as the unavoidable
casualties of change, especially Fisher, whose conversations with
Eustace Chapuys, Charles V's ambassador, on the subject of
Henry VIII's excommunication and deposition by the Pope, were
uncovered by Froude's researches in Simancas. His exposé of
Fisher caused a sensation, but at least it was based on quanti-
fiable evidence. In More's case, Froude drew extensively, if not
uniformly, on the charges in the *Acts and Monuments*, so that he
found it impossible to sustain his claim that he was not motivated
by partisan or doctrinal considerations.

Froude's treatment of More was arguably the least professional and historical portion of his *History*, since it was based
almost exclusively on moral outrage. He wrote movingly of
More's trial and execution, but jibed disparagingly of his
chancellorship. Tactically, this was unwise. His irony was unsubtle and has not worn well. When More became Lord
Chancellor, declared Froude, a 'bloody page' was inscribed in
English history. More was guilty of 'fanaticism'. The stake
'recommenced its hateful activity', and was 'more often lighted'
in three years than during the whole of Wolsey's chancellorship.[27]
The Protestants had 'not loved Wolsey', but 'it was better to bear
a faggot of dry sticks in a procession' than to be incinerated.
Within a year of their exposure to the 'philosophic mercies of Sir
Thomas More', the reformers 'would gladly have accepted again
the hated cardinal'.[28] There was in More, 'a want of confidence
in human nature, a scorn of the follies of his fellow creatures',
which, as he became more religious, 'narrowed and hardened his
convictions'. In this way, the 'genial philosopher' who wrote
Utopia was turned into a 'merciless bigot'.[29]

Froude's final flourish smacked of sarcasm:

> Wolsey had chastised them [the Protestants] with whips; Sir
> Thomas More would chastise them with scorpions; and the
> philosopher of the *Utopia*, the friend of Erasmus, whose
> life was of blameless beauty, was to prove to the world that
> the spirit of persecution is no particular attribute of the
> pedant, the bigot, or the fanatic, but may co-exist with the
> fairest graces of the human character.[30]

In reply, the Catholic historian, Father Bridgett, set out the case
for an historical rather than a moral or psychoanalytical critique,
and coolly put three questions. Whom does More designate as
heretics? In what way did he trouble or 'molest' them? Did he
remain within, or did he go beyond the law as it existed in
his time?[31]

Bridgett saw the way to exit from the cul-de-sac, but proved
unable to take it. The problem was that modern critical editions
of More's *Answer to Luther*, the *Dialogue Concerning Heresies*
and the *Confutation of Tyndale's Answer* were the precondition
of a systematic analysis. Lacking these, Bridgett could scarcely
begin. In consequence, he attempted a defence mainly from the
perspective of the degree of consistency between More's opinions
in Book II of *Utopia* and his later career as described in the

Apology. While this conformed to the agenda laid down by Froude, it did not advance understanding of More's definition of heresy or his role as an inquisitor. Discussions of these topics were still less than the sum of their parts.

The debate was reopened in 1935, when R.W. Chambers launched a spirited defence of More in his classic biography designed to exculpate him from all charges. Chambers' rebuttal was patronizing in tone and selective in its citation of evidence, but was not without merit, since it referred the reader to More's own words and challenged the degree to which Foxe and Froude had taken their allegations out of context.[32] But Chambers relied on three idiosyncratic distinctions. The first was that it was only 'seditious' and not doctrinal heresy that More abhorred. His actions were rooted in a 'fear of sedition, tumult and civil war' and not in 'religious bigotry'.[33] The second distinction concerned the extent of More's reach. Chambers knew that, with only one exception, the six Protestants burned while More was Lord Chancellor had gone to their deaths after February 1531.[34] He argued that, although in office, More was not 'in power and favour' after that date. It was no longer More who directed the attack on heresy, but Bishop Stokesley of London.[35] Finally, Chambers distinguished between heresy cases in London and elsewhere. He called the diocese of London 'More's diocese', even though, as Lord Chancellor, More had intervened elsewhere and was responsible for issuing writs of signification (the writs which authorized the sheriffs and lay officials to burn heretics at the stake after their conviction in the Church courts) throughout the whole of England.[36]

By virtue of his last two distinctions, Chambers was able to assert that 'during the dozen years when More was increasingly in power or favour', there was *'not one death sentence pronounced on a heretic in the diocese of London'*.[37] By virtue of his first, he could maintain that even the investigations that did occur, and which involved More, were concerned with civil unrest and not confessional orthodoxy.

Chambers' special pleading held the field for almost fifty years, but did not pass unchallenged. In *The Statesman and the Fanatic: Thomas Wolsey and Thomas More* (1982), Jasper Ridley made Froude's attack on More seem measured by comparison. In fifteen years, More had changed from a 'brilliant intellectual' into 'a sycophantic courtier and then into a persecuting bigot'. He was 'the worst kind of intolerant fanatic', who had lambasted

Protestantism with a sexual and scatological explicitness shocking even to a modern audience.[38] He was a liar, and 'a far more zealous persecutor than Wolsey'.[39] He was an intolerable ideologue. Had he lived in the twentieth century, he would have been a Stalinist or a Nazi.[40]

Ridley's was an extraordinary diatribe, which looked even more incongruous when it was discovered that the North American edition had been retitled *Statesman and Saint* in order to protect sales. Writing in *Moreana*, Anne Lake Prescott revelled in 'a libel on More [which] can be almost enjoyed as a sort of tonic, like an exercycle for the spirit'.[41] Ridley's argument was bold, but breathtakingly unsubtle. More's treatment of heresy was the crux of his double biography, and yet his analysis was crude and unconvincing. In its conceptual framework, it was stale. As a *tour de force* it was purely rhetorical. As an evocation of More, it was less historical than Bridgett's *Blessed Thomas More*, which had an underlying confessional bias, but at least asked better questions.

A quantum leap followed the entry of the revisionist historian Richard Marius into the arena.[42] The pre-eminent authority on the anti-Lutheran campaign, his verdict on More's role as an inquisitor was uncompromising. More was deeply committed to a policy of censorship and to the extirpation of heresy, and *pace* Chambers the basis of his attitude was confessional. His legal powers were used 'to wage unrelenting war against the enemies of the faith'.[43] Although he lost power and favour with Henry VIII, this did not stop him. 'His methods were not gentle.'[44] 'He fought hard against heretical books and those who peddled them.'[45] He repeatedly intervened, to assist the bishops in bringing suspects to trial, to obtain the confessions necessary to secure convictions in the Church courts, or else to prove in Bilney's case 'that the traditional way of dealing with heretics was the right way'.[46] His activities were 'utterly single-minded'. There was never 'any flash of mercy or tolerance'. 'Heretics were enemies of God, servants of Satan, minions of hell.' More believed passionately 'that they should be exterminated, and while he was in office he did everything in his power to bring that extermination to pass'[47]

The *Amici Thomae Mori* find this description 'distressing'.[48] But Marius' achievement is less his characterization of More, which is provocative and will continue to be disputed, than his willingness to refocus the debate: not simply to chronicle what

More allegedly did as an inquisitor, but to explain why he did it. As a distinguished co-editor of the Yale Edition, Marius draws on the full repertoire of More's writings. In the process, Chambers' false distinctions are dissolved. Previously, the evidence on both sides of the argument was quarried from Foxe's *Acts and Monuments* and More's *Apology*. The circularity of this process takes its toll. In every case, the truth of the examples, and the exemplariness of the truth, depend upon the rhetoric. The historiography is less a discussion of the problems of these sources than a series of stereotyped confrontations or appeals to the confessional or moral prejudices of readers.

Marius points the way to a new paradigm.[49] Whereas Foxe's *Acts and Monuments* and More's *Apology* give the impression that More's preoccupation with heresy began with his appointment as Lord Chancellor, Marius argues that the ideological pattern was defined earlier. It began to be shaped in 1521, when More became Henry VIII's 'theological councillor' and a linchpin of the King's own anti-Lutheran campaign. His role as an inquisitor developed from there. He made the transition from 'theological councillor' to 'public defender of the faith' in 1525, when appointed Chancellor of the Duchy of Lancaster. He played a leading part in Henry's and Wolsey's drive to regulate the book trade and prohibit the import of translations of Scripture and other Lutheran books from the Continent.[50] In this phase, the foundations of his understanding of Catholic 'consensus' and 'conscience' were laid down. His exposure in depth to these concepts was the direct consequence of his role as the King's surrogate against Luther.[51]

This interpretation is a landmark, and needs to be explored in more depth.[52] The King's anti-Lutheran campaign was inaugurated by Wolsey's promulgation of the papal condemnation of Luther at St Paul's in May 1521, an event which began with a sermon by Fisher and culminated in a bonfire of heretical books.[53] More was a linchpin from the outset. According to Roper, his recruitment was 'by [the] appointment' of Henry VIII.[54] He was asked to edit the King's *Defence of the Seven Sacraments* (1521). Next, he was asked to write the *Answer to Luther* (1523). Between December 1525 and February 1526 he wrote the *Letter to Bugenhagen*. He then assisted Henry VIII in composing the *Letter in Reply to Martin Luther*, published in December 1526. By the time that he completed the *Dialogue*

Concerning Heresies (1529), the platform for his defence of Catholic tradition was established.

The chronological sequence is clear. The *Defence of the Seven Sacraments* was written by Henry VIII with the assistance of a committee of theologians possibly steered by Archbishop Warham or Bishop Tunstal. The *Defence* was Henry's reply to Luther's *Babylonian Captivity of the Church* (1520). More was appointed to edit the book in the spring of 1521, and did so with the 'consent' of Henry's panel of advisers.[55] We know that he read the work closely and debated its contents with the King. He later recalled to Cromwell that the initial draft had taken a maximalist view of the papal primacy.[56] More spotted these arguments 'at the first reading', and had 'moved the King's Highness either to leave out that point, or else to touch it more slenderly'.[57] The final version of the *Defence* was presented to Pope Leo X in a private consistory (2 October 1521), securing Henry VIII the title of 'Defender of the Faith'.

In 1522, Luther attacked the *Defence* with a vituperative tirade *Against Henry VIII of England*. Henry did not condescend to answer personally, and conscripted More and Fisher to rebut Luther on his behalf. Fisher's contribution was a theological blockbuster: his *Refutation of Martin Luther* (1523) ran to 200 000 words and was tantamount to a complete critique. More replied pseudonymously with his *Answer to Luther* (1523), which appeared in two separate versions and concentrated on the issue of authority in the Church.[58]

The *Answer to Luther* evolved intellectually from More's work on the *Defence* and logically from his duties as a King's secretary, since the secretary was the King's public orator and official mouthpiece as well as his amanuensis. As Sir Geoffrey Elton always maintained, the key to More's role as an attendant councillor is provided by the duties he was asked to perform.[59] These were not primarily political in the King's Council, or even legal in the Courts of Star Chamber or Requests. Almost from the moment More arrived at Court, Wolsey and Henry exploited his humanist skills by using him as a supernumerary King's secretary.

Starting in 1518, and with increasing regularity, the flow of royal correspondence was channelled through More. He became the King's public orator, and accompanied Henry and Wolsey to the Field of Cloth of Gold in 1520. He was next with Wolsey at Calais and Bruges. When he returned to Court, he was again the King's secretary; probably he was keeping a close eye on Richard

Pace, the official secretary, whom Wolsey had come to distrust. In
December 1521, Pace was sent away on an embassy to Rome.
Richard Sampson obtained his post, but the following year he,
too, was shipped off by Wolsey as ambassador to Spain.
Thereafter, More alone served as the King's secretary.[60] And he
gained advancement in the post. He was knighted and appointed
to the sinecure of Under-Treasurer of the Exchequer (May 1521),
given lands and perquisites which enabled him to purchase his
estate at Chelsea,[61] and made Speaker of the House of Commons
in 1523, a blatant attempt by Wolsey to manipulate Parliament,
but one from which More carefully distanced himself.[62]

The years in which More was the King's sole secretary were
dominated by the anti-Lutheran campaign. They began with the
Answer to Luther and ended with the *Letter to Bugenhagen*, an
open letter ostensibly written in reply to one of Luther's closest
associates that was intended for the German Princes.[63] Its
purpose was to refute the false rumour of England's imminent
conversion to Lutheranism. In the event, the *Letter* was
consigned to a drawer. It was pre-empted by the arrival of a letter
from Luther addressed directly to the King, which Henry
rebutted personally with More's assistance, an open letter
published as the *Letter in Reply to Martin Luther*.[64]

While More was the King's sole secretary, he had almost
unlimited access to Henry. Roper says that they discussed
astronomy and geometry as well as theology.[65] Marius does not
say so, but it is likely that More's ideas and Henry's were
synergetic until 1526 or thereabouts. More began the *Answer to
Luther* tentatively, but was soon building confidently on the
arguments as expressed in the *Defence of the Seven Sacraments*.[66]
The co-editors of the Yale Edition have illustrated the process
whereby the ideas on authority and tradition in the Church in the
Answer, the *Letter to Bugenhagen*, and later the *Dialogue
Concerning Heresies*, evolved into a comprehensive, and in some
respects original, synthesis of Catholic ecclesiology.[67] It will be
helpful to interpolate a brief summary of these ideas, since they
provide the earliest rationale not only for More's defence of
tradition but for his later rejection of the royal supremacy.

Luther had argued in the *Babylonian Captivity* that the Word
of God was the authority for salvation, and that the Bible set the
standards by which the Church and clergy should be judged. This
was not a literalist claim: the Holy Spirit had to speak through
the writing and inspire faith in people's hearts. But Scripture was

the decisive authority in the eyes of the reformers. And some of them, including the English Lutherans, William Tyndale and Robert Barnes, began to treat 'Scripture' and the 'Word' as synonymous terms. Soon they were suggesting that Scripture was 'plain as a pikestaff' and 'its own interpreter'. The reformers also suggested that the 'true' Church was not the 'visible' Catholic Church, but an 'invisible' community of believers comprising only the 'elect'.

More denounced these claims as heresies. No 'invisible' or 'church unknown' comprising only the 'elect' could be believed.[68] The true 'Catholic Church' was that which had prevailed since the time of the Apostles and only this Church had the authority to distinguish the divine from the human elements of Scripture.[69]

When More attacked the reformers, he knew that the vital terrain was not papal authority, but Catholic tradition. The reformers rejected tradition, but More argued that Catholic tradition had prevailed since the time of the Apostles. There were two types of Christian revelation: one written (Scripture), the other unwritten (oral), and More pointed to an oral tradition which had been handed down from the Apostles and safeguarded by the Church.[70]

More ridiculed the notion that the 'gospel' taught by the Church could be proved wrong by Luther.[71] The 'gospel' had been revealed by Christ. But Christ had not written a book. For fifteen centuries the true 'gospel' had been protected by the Church, which had collated the texts of canonical Scripture. The Holy Spirit, which inspired consent, had permitted this process. Christ spoke to the whole Church when he promised that the Holy Spirit would lead men into truth and the Holy Spirit was omnipresent, constrained neither by time nor space. 'On the heart, therefore, in the church of Christ, there remains inscribed the true gospel of Christ *which was written there before the books of all the evangelists*'.[72]

More revered tradition, which might even override Scripture. God had 'inscribed' faith so indelibly on the Catholic Church 'that no deceptions of heretics can erase it'.[73] The Church's authority was independent of Scripture: it did not matter how many texts, apparently disproving this or that, were cited by heretics. The 'true gospel of Christ' had been revealed to the Church before the Bible was compiled. The Church was not to be judged by individual opinions. 'Conscience' was to be anchored to the consensus or 'common faith' of Christendom, even if the heretics believed that their opinions were rooted in what they individually believed to be Scripture.

The most subversive heresy that More could imagine was the notion that Scripture stood in opposition to the teaching and practice of the Catholic Church. From his perspective, the division between the 'known church' and the 'Word of God' which the reformers had constructed was the crux of the Reformation divide. This explains why the notion of 'consensus' or the 'common faith' of Christendom became More's most important ideological concept, culminating in his refusal to accept the Act of Supremacy on the grounds that the explicit and implicit 'consensus' of General Councils of the Catholic Church and of the faithful was the infallible sign of the authenticity of a dogmatic position (see Chapter 10). More's standpoint on 'consensus' was embryonic in the *Defence of the Seven Sacraments* and the *Answer to Luther*.[74] It would become axiomatic by 1534, when he was imprisoned in the Tower. The irony is that it was first stimulated, if not originally derived, from his agenda as Henry VIII's surrogate against Luther.[75]

More's role as an inquisitor developed from this. The stage was set for his transition from 'theological councillor' to 'public defender of the faith'. The pattern was established before he was appointed Lord Chancellor. In 1524, Wolsey, Archbishop Warham, Fisher and Bishop Tunstal were nominated to censor the book trade.[76] Tunstal immediately summoned the London booksellers and warned them against printing, importing or handling heretical books.[77] The campaign was intensified in the latter part of 1525, when Wolsey heard that the first sheets of Tyndale's New Testament were coming off the press at Cologne. On the King's instructions, another ceremonial bonfire was held at St Paul's (February 1526). Robert Barnes, the most prominent English reformer to be put on trial by Wolsey, was forced to abjure and perform public penance before the fire was lit. Also compelled to abjure at the book-burning were four merchants of the German Steelyard in London, converts to Luther's teaching and importers and propagators of his writings.[78]

The German merchants had been captured following a series of raids by More on the Steelyard. The first raid was on 22 December 1525 under the pretext of checking on coinage.[79] The second followed on 26 January, when More burst into the Steelyard precincts and posted guards at all the exits. He justified the raid on the grounds that one of the Germans had recently been imprisoned for clipping English coin, but the real aim was to search for translations of the Bible and other Lutheran books. When nothing was found, More left. The next day he returned with two clerks. The merchants were asked to swear that they would destroy any heretical books in their possession. Their living accommodation was then searched. The four Germans forced to abjure at St Paul's were suspects detected by More, whom Wolsey immediately referred to his legatine commissaries for trial. Each confessed to having seen or possessed books or Bible translations by Luther. At least two confessed to doctrinal beliefs that the commissaries judged heretical.[80]

More's raids followed his appointment to the position of Chancellor of the Duchy of Lancaster (September 1525). This relatively onerous post was based in the Duchy Chamber at Westminster, and not at the royal Court.[81] By the middle of 1526, More had left Henry's Court and the duties of King's secretary were performed by William Knight, although More was briefly back in 1527 and 1528, when Wolsey suspected intrigue and needed someone he could trust.[82] As Chancellor of the Duchy, More was attached to Wolsey's censorship commissioners: it was in this capacity that he raided the Steelyard. Next, he was present when the King's Council devised a censorship order against heretical books and preaching. It marked a watershed in Wolsey's attack on Lutheranism (8 July 1527).[83] Tyndale's New Testament was now on the streets of London: the anti-Lutheran campaign shifted from polemic to heresy prosecutions. In November 1527, Wolsey established a legatine court at Westminster Abbey to try Thomas Bilney and Thomas Arthur, two leading East Anglian reformers, together with Richard Foster, a yeoman usher of the Crown. The three abjured, and More took a keen interest in Bilney's case, which he attended daily and discussed in his *Dialogue Concerning Heresies*.

The following March, More was commissioned by Tunstal to take command of a crash programme of anti-Lutheran propaganda. To equip him for the task, Tunstal sent under sealed cover a bundle of prohibited books, which More was licensed to read.[84] The commission paved the way for the *Dialogue Concerning Heresies*, the first refutation of Luther and the reformers that More wrote independently of Henry VIII. By the time the book appeared in June 1529, the transition from 'theological councillor' to 'public defender of the faith' was complete.

When reassessing More's inquisitorial role as Lord Chancellor, Marius revisits the cases discussed in More's *Apology* and Foxe's *Acts and Monuments*.[85] The evaluation is fair, if censorious in tone. Whether More was a heresy hunter is ultimately in the eye of the beholder. If his reputation is judged against moral and humanitarian considerations, he was a persecutor. If narrowly defined criteria are applied, he was not. There is no dispute over his crusade against heresy. Writing to Erasmus, he glossed the claim in his epitaph that he had been 'grievous' to 'heretics' by saying: 'I wrote that with deep feeling. I find that breed of men absolutely loathsome, so much so that, unless they regain their senses, I want to be as hateful to them as anyone can possibly be.'[86]

In More's eyes, to defend the Catholic Church was a religious obligation. Before the break with Rome it was also a secular one.[87] The latter point is almost invariably forgotten. The Act *De Heretico Comburendo* had been passed by Parliament in 1401. It prohibited unlicensed preaching or books contrary to Catholic doctrine. Books or writings owned by heretics or their supporters were to be surrendered to the bishops within forty days; those disobeying were to be arrested on suspicion until they had purged themselves, or had abjured and performed penance. First-time offenders convicted in the Church courts were to be punished at the discretion of the bishops by imprisonment or fine, while relapsed heretics, or those refusing to abjure their heretical opinions, were to be surrendered to the secular arm to be burned. In 1414, a supplementary Act commanded secular judges and officials from the Lord Chancellor downwards to assist the Church in the task of detecting, investigating and extirpating heresy. Their oaths of office were amended to incorporate these obligations. The Act also empowered secular judges to inquire into heresy by presentment and indictment at common law. Persons attached in this way were to be securely held, and delivered to the bishops or their commissaries for trial in the Church courts within ten days after their arrest.

Although Foxe and Froude maintained that More had acted illegally in his treatment of heretics, no irrefutable proof has been produced. He stretched his legal powers to the limit: it is unlikely that any of the suspects held at Chelsea were first presented at common law before he questioned them, since his intention was to deliver them to Bishop Stokesley. But More was on the commission of the peace for Middlesex, and thus had summary powers of arrest in that county. Irregular in comparison was the retrospective investigation of Bilney's alleged recantation at the stake at Norwich by special proceedings in Star Chamber. More used the findings of this inquiry in the *Confutation of Tyndale's Answer* to claim that the eyewitnesses at Bilney's burning had heard him recant his heretical beliefs. Although not involved in Bilney's second trial for heresy, even as an observer, More decided to summon the eyewitnesses by writs of subpoena, because a rumour had started that Bilney had appealed at his trial to Henry VIII as 'Supreme Head of the English Church' and then had declined to read the bill of recantation that was presented to him at the stake.[88] More invoked his powers as Lord Chancellor to demand testimony on oath from the eyewitnesses, proceeding inquisitorially, without bill or information filed in proper form, and thus contrary to Star Chamber's due process.[89]

The main target of More's campaign against heresy was the traffic in prohibited books. In his first year as Lord Chancellor, he secured a Star Chamber decree and a royal proclamation to reinforce Wolsey's censorship measures.[90] Over a hundred titles were formally proscribed on an index of heretical books. When the distributors of Tyndale's New Testament and other colporteurs were caught and brought before More in Star Chamber, he applied the full severity of the law in the punishments which he handed down.[91] The booksellers were fined and imprisoned. Their stocks of heretical literature were publicly burned. Lastly, they themselves were forced to perform public penance: being paraded on market days through the streets of London on horseback, sitting back-to-front, their coats 'pinned thick' with the proscribed books, while they were pelted with rotten fruit.[92]

None of this was illegal. Yet 'legality' has little to do with justice, as More himself told the common-law judges during the debate over equitable decrees in Chancery (see Chapter 7). In the last resort, More's excuse was that heresy was so dangerous, it demanded the 'rigour' of the law in every case. His rationale was set out in the Preface to the *Confutation of Tyndale's Answer* and in his *Apology* and *Debellation of Salem and Bizance*. Heresy was a heinous crime. It was treason against God and the Church. It was a crime against the King. Henry VIII desired nothing more on earth than the 'maintenance of the true Catholic faith'. This was why he was so deservedly styled 'Defender of the Faith'. Had not he written his *Defence of the Seven Sacraments* against

Luther? Had he not personally come to the Star Chamber (on 25 May 1530) to instruct the secular magistrates to impound heretical books? As the King's 'unworthy' Chancellor, More was bound to 'follow the example of his noble grace'. It was his 'part and duty'.[93]

More's plea is transparently honest. His exculpation by Chambers is based on misrepresentation and special pleading. But it is far from the case, as Foxe implied in the *Acts and Monuments* and Froude emblazoned in the *History of England*, that More set out to launch a self-appointed inquisition. Or that he succumbed to a 'furious and cruel zeal', as Warner maintained. Or that he 'set himself' to oppose the Reformation, as Burnet argued in the *History of the Reformation*. On the contrary, More was 'set' to the anti-Lutheran campaign by Henry VIII in the context elucidated by Marius. In attacking heresy as Lord Chancellor, he was continuing the King's agenda. His actions were increasingly disowned as opinion changed in Parliament and Henry flirted with reformers such as Simon Grinaeus and Robert Barnes in the hope of securing progress on the divorce, thereby making More's position untenable.[94] All this makes more sense of what otherwise has seemed 'irrational' behaviour on the part of the author of *Utopia*, even to those who deny that he was a radical in 1516. In Burnet's resonant phrase, it helps to explain 'the great change' in More between 1516 and 1529.[95] But it does not make complete sense. More's confession to Erasmus that 'I find that breed of men absolutely loathsome ... I want to be as hateful to them as anyone can possibly be', is too severe. For this reason, the schizophrenia created by More's dual roles as author of *Utopia* and inquisitor in heresy cases will never be dispelled. It is too deeply ingrained and no final reconciliation is possible on the available historical evidence.

Notes

1 CW 8, Pt.1, pp. 16–17.
2 CW 8, Pt. 1, pp. 3–40; Pt. 2, p. 979.
3 CW 8, Pt. 3, p. 1208 n. 4.
4 Trapp and Herbrüggen, p. 139; Harpsfield, p. 280.
5 Harpsfield, pp. 278–80.
6 CW 9, p. xxx n. 4.
7 CW 9, p. 127.
8 CW 9, p. 167.
9 G. Townsend, ed., *The Acts and Monuments of John Foxe* (8 vols,

London, 1843–9) 4, pp. 643–52, 664, 670–1, 688–94, 697–707; 5, pp. 3–11, 29, 99–100, 181.

10 Townsend, ed., *Acts and Monuments* 4, p. 689.

11 *CW* 9, p. 118.

12 P. Collinson, 'Truth, Lies, and Fiction in Sixteenth-Century Protestant Historiography', in D.R. Kelley and D.H. Sacks, eds, *The Historical Imagination in Early Modern Britain* (Cambridge, 1997), p. 37.

13 *CW* 9, p. xc.

14 John Guy, *Tudor England* (Oxford, 1988), p. 238.

15 Harpsfield, pp. 207–8.

16 Harpsfield, pp. 105–31.

17 Harpsfield, p. 108.

18 Harpsfield, pp. 108–9.

19 J. Champion, *The Pillars of Priestcraft Shaken: the Church of England and its Enemies, 1660–1730* (Cambridge, 1992), pp. 77–82.

20 G. Burnet, *History of the Reformation of the Church of England* (6 vols, London, 1820) 5, p. 45.

21 Burnet, *History of the Reformation* 5, pp. 45–6.

22 Burnet, *History of the Reformation* 5, pp. 45–6.

23 Burnet, *History of the Reformation* 5, p. 46.

24 T.E. Bridgett, *Life and Writings of Blessed Thomas More* (London, 1924), p. 253.

25 F. Warner, *Memoirs of the Life of Sir Thomas More* (London, 1758), pp. 67–8.

26 J.P. Kenyon, *The History Men* (2nd edn., London, 1993), pp. 118–20.

27 J.A. Froude, *The History of England in the Reign of Henry VIII* (3 vols, London, 1909) 1, p. 177; J.A. Froude, *The Divorce of Catherine of Aragon* (London, 1891), p. 186.

28 Froude, *History of England* 1, p. 105.

29 Froude, *History of England* 1, p. 222.

30 Froude, *History of England* 1, p. 339.

31 Bridgett, *Blessed Thomas More*, p. 253.

32 R.W. Chambers, *Thomas More* (London, 1935), pp. 274–82.

33 Chambers, *Thomas More*, p. 282.

34 Chambers, *Thomas More*, pp. 278–9; John Guy, *The Public Career of Sir Thomas More* (Brighton, 1980), p. 164.

35 Chambers, *Thomas More*, pp. 280–2.

36 Chambers, *Thomas More*, pp. 279–81.

37 Chambers, *Thomas More*, pp. 279, 281 (author's italics preserved).

38 J. Ridley, *The Statesman and the Fanatic: Thomas Wolsey and Thomas More* (London, 1982), p.i.

39 Ridley, *The Statesman and the Fanatic*, pp. 238–62.

40 Ridley, *The Statesman and the Fanatic*, pp. 292–3.

41 A.L. Prescott, 'A Sharper Look at Ridley's Book', *Moreana* 21 (1984), p. 98.

42 Richard Marius, *Thomas More* (New York, 1984), pp. 276–91, 386–406.

43 Marius, *Thomas More*, p. 386.
44 Marius, *Thomas More*, p. 395.
45 Marius, *Thomas More*, p. 402.
46 Marius, *Thomas More*, p. 401.
47 Marius, *Thomas More*, p. 406.
48 E.F. Alkaaoud, 'A Man for Our Season: Marius on More', *Moreana* 27 (1990), p. 47.
49 The paradigm is also latent in R. Marius, *Thomas More and the Heretics* (Yale PhD, 1962; University Microfilms, Ann Arbor, 1971).
50 Marius, *Thomas More*, pp. 325–50.
51 Marius, *Thomas More*, pp. 276–91. Minor criticisms may be levelled at the way Marius develops his case. More's role in the anti-Lutheran campaign was as a polemicist, not as a theologian. The leading theologian in the group was Fisher. Again, Marius upbraids More for the 'witless vulgarity' and 'monotonous scatology' of his *Answer to Luther*, but it was precisely a polemicist able to beat Luther at his own game that Henry VIII required. Cf. Marius, p. 282. There is no vulgarity or scatology in More's *Letter to Bugenhagen*.
52 Further support comes from Sir Geoffrey Elton, who has independently argued that More showed 'no special interest' in the anti-Lutheran campaign until Henry VIII recruited him. Thereafter, his involvement is 'plainly documented'. G.R. Elton, *Studies in Tudor and Stuart Politics and Government* (4 vols, Cambridge, 1974–92) 1, pp. 147–8.
53 R. Rex, *The Theology of John Fisher* (Cambridge, 1991), pp. 78–92; R. Rex, 'The English Campaign against Luther in the 1520s', *Transactions of the Royal Historical Society*, 5th series, 39 (1989), pp. 85–106.
54 Roper, pp. 234–5.
55 Roper, p. 235.
56 Rogers, ed., *Selected Letters*, p. 212.
57 Rogers, ed., *Selected Letters*, p. 212.
58 *CW* 5, Pt. 2, pp. 715–803.
59 Elton, *Studies* 1, pp. 129–54.
60 Guy, *Public Career*, pp. 15–16.
61 Guy, *Public Career*, pp. 24–5.
62 Roper, pp. 202–7; Guy, *Public Career*, pp. 15–24; John Guy, 'Wolsey and the Parliament of 1523', in C. Cross, D.M. Loades and J.J. Scarisbrick, eds, *Law and Government under the Tudors* (Cambridge, 1988), pp. 1–18.
63 *CW* 7, pp. xvii–xxxvi; Guy, *Public Career*, pp. 15–19.
64 *CW* 7, pp. xxix, xxxv–xxxvi.
65 Roper, p. 202.
66 *CW* 5, Pt. 2, pp. 732–74; *CW* 6, Pt. 2, pp. 494–535; *CW* 7, pp. xlii–lxiv.
67 *CW* 5, Pt. 2, pp. 732–74; *CW* 6, Pt. 2, pp. 494–535; *CW* 7, pp. xlii–lxiv.
68 *CW* 5, Pt. 1, pp. 180–5.
69 *CW* 5, Pt. 1, pp. 242–4; *CW* 6, Pt. 1, pp. 116–21, 180–2, 253–5.
70 *CW* 5, Pt. 2, pp. 735–7.

71 *CW* 7, pp. 15–17, 29–31.
72 *CW* 5, Pt. 1, p. 101 (my italics); *CW* 6, Pt. 1, pp. 143–4.
73 *CW* 5, Pt. 1, p. 101.
74 *CW* 5, Pt. 1, pp. 301–5, 413–17, 627–9; Pt. 2, pp. 740–5; B. Gogan, *The Common Corps of Christendom: Ecclesiological Themes in the Writings of Sir Thomas More* (Leiden, 1982), p. 363.
75 Guy, *Public Career*, pp. 160–1.
76 Rex, *The Theology of John Fisher*, p. 83.
77 *CW* 8, Pt. 3, p. 1138.
78 *CW* 7, pp. xxxi–xxxii; S. Brigden, *London and the Reformation* (Oxford, 1989), pp. 158–9.
79 *CW* 6, Pt. 2, p. 456, n. 2.
80 *CW* 7, pp. xxxi–xxxii; *LP* IV.i. no. 1962; Elton, *Studies* 1, p. 148.
81 M. Hastings, 'Sir Thomas More: Maker of English Law?' in R.S. Sylvester and G. Marc'hadour, eds, *Essential Articles for the Study of Thomas More* (Hampden, CT, 1977), pp. 104–18; Guy, *Public Career*, pp. 26–30.
82 Guy, *Public Career*, pp. 16, 21.
83 BL, Lansdowne MS. 160, fo. 312; Guy, *Public Career*, p. 13.
84 *CW* 8, Pt. 3, pp. 1137–9.
85 Marius, *Thomas More*, pp. 394–406.
86 Rogers, ed., *Selected Letters*, p. 180.
87 *CW* 10, pp. xlvii–lxvii.
88 Marius, *Thomas More*, pp. 396–401; Guy, *Public Career*, pp. 167–71.
89 Guy, *Public Career*, pp. 170–1.
90 BL, Lansdowne MS 160, fo. 312ᵛ; P.L. Hughes and J.F. Larkin, eds, *Tudor Royal Proclamations* (3 vols, New Haven, CT, 1964–9), 1, pp. 193–7; Guy, *Public Career*, p. 171; *CW* 6, Pt. 2, p. 883.
91 Guy, *Public Career*, pp. 171–4; Brigden, *London and the Reformation*, pp. 179–87.
92 Guy, *Public Career*, pp. 173–4.
93 *CW* 8, Pt. 1, pp. 3–40; *CW* 9, p. 136; *CW* 10, pp. lxxix–lxxxi, 76–83.
94 Marius, *Thomas More*, pp. 391–4.
95 Burnet, *History of the Reformation* 5, p. 46.

|7|

Law reformer?

Thomas More's legal career has generally been taken for granted. As in the case of his private and domestic life, the so-called 'facts' laid down by the earliest biographers have been recycled down the centuries in an uncritical and purely functionalist manner. Roper and Harpsfield sought to create an image of More that would underpin his heroic status and in Harpsfield's case support the view that More's career was subverted by the 'lusts' of Henry VIII. Their 'stories' were nurtured by Erasmus' vignette to Hutten, which had already set the agenda by claiming that More was a judge of 'absolute integrity' and that 'no one ever determined more cases'.[1] By his description of More's domestic life, Harpsfield crystallized his image of More as a virtuous personality. His strategy was so successful that it hardly seemed necessary to elaborate on More's judicial career other than to follow Roper's lead in citing examples of his virtue in refusing privileges to his own family circle and his meticulous care in awarding injunctions.[2] Roper and Harpsfield also emphasized More's scrupulousness in refusing bribes, but for strategic reasons their discussions of this topic were deferred until later in their narratives.[3] To reinforce the impression of a systematic campaign of royal vindictiveness, they linked More's successful defence of his integrity against charges of judicial corruption to his defence against the charge that he had conspired with Elizabeth Barton, the Nun (or Holy Maid) of Kent, to prophesy Henry VIII's deposition or death if he divorced Catherine of Aragon and married Anne Boleyn (see Chapter 9).

More's legal career was not considered irrelevant. Roper and Harpsfield treated the Courts of Chancery and Star Chamber as the arena in which More's private and public virtue converged. Both inserted their accounts of More's judicial career into the space in their narratives between the fall of Wolsey and the initial hesitant steps towards the break with Rome that were signalled by the summoning of the Reformation Parliament and the enactment of anticlerical legislation in the final months of 1529. In Harpsfield's more comprehensive version, this was the section that immediately preceded his discussions of More's private and family life and his role as a defender of the Catholic faith.

Harpsfield's 'story' also had a deeper intent. He aimed to point up the contrast between More's and Wolsey's careers as Lord Chancellor. His desire was polemical, since Harpsfield (more so than Roper) was the source of the recusant tradition that it was Wolsey, and not Bishop Longland of Lincoln, the King's confessor, who had been 'the first author and incenser' of the divorce.[4] Harpsfield believed that Henry VIII's first divorce campaign was the beginning of the Reformation in England. He sought to confute the thesis circulating among the Marian exiles that a genuine Protestant grass-roots movement was stimulated by Lollardy and Lutheranism, the thesis that became the bedrock of John Foxe's *Acts and Monuments*. At the core of Harpsfield's anti-Protestant polemic was the *Treatise on the Pretended Divorce of King Henry VIII from Catherine of Aragon*, which was originally planned as an appendix to the 'Life' of More, but which quickly became the tail that wagged the dog.[5]

In consequence, two distinct elements have come to dominate representations of More's legal career. The first centres on the blackening of Wolsey's reputation, which is a shibboleth of the recusant tradition and inspired the claim that More was appointed Lord Chancellor to clear up the mess left by his predecessor. The second relates to More's independent achievements as Lord Chancellor, both in the courts of law and in the House of Lords, which raises the question of whether he was still a Utopian reformer in 1529.

More received the Great Seal from the hands of Henry VIII and was appointed Lord Chancellor in a private ceremony at Greenwich palace on 25 October 1529.[6] A fortnight earlier, Wolsey had pleaded guilty to a charge of *praemunire* in the Court of King's Bench. He confessed that he had illegally promoted the Pope's jurisdiction in England as a papal legate *a latere* in derogation of the royal prerogative and the laws and customs of the realm. These charges were fabricated, but they served their purpose. A sentence of life imprisonment was imposed on Wolsey, whose true offence was his failure to obtain an annulment of Henry VIII's marriage to Catherine. In addition, his offices and property were forfeited to the Crown. Henry VIII genuinely liked Wolsey and spared him the humiliation of lengthy imprisonment. He restored him to his archbishopric of York and allowed him to travel to his diocese to engage in pastoral work. However, Wolsey was an instinctive politician who could not keep his head below the parapet. His overtures to the French Court were betrayed to the Duke of Norfolk by his physician, and he was summoned to return to London. He succumbed to dysentery on the journey south from York, and died at Leicester Abbey (29 November 1530).

More was sworn in as Lord Chancellor in Westminster Hall by the Dukes of Norfolk and Suffolk and others of the Privy Council the morning after his appointment by the King.[7] By way of introduction, the Duke of Norfolk delivered a speech, to explain to all those assembled in the law courts 'how much all England was beholding [*sic*] to Sir Thomas More for his good service', how 'worthy he was to have the highest room in the realm', and how 'dearly' Henry VIII 'loved and trusted him'.[8] What this really meant was that the Duke, who was at this point the dominant political force in the Privy Council, had persuaded the King to appoint a layman as Wolsey's successor, but was not qualified to act as Lord Chancellor himself, since he lacked the necessary legal expertise. A lawyer, who was also an experienced King's councillor, was required to preside in the Courts of Chancery and Star Chamber. More as a former Chancellor of the Duchy of Lancaster was perfect for the job. In fact, he was doubly qualified, since the Master of the Rolls, who deputized for the Lord Chancellor in Chancery, and the Six Clerks, who administered the court's procedure, were still civil or canon lawyers. They were trained in Roman or ecclesiastical law rather than common law, which is why the Lord Chancellor had usually been a bishop and not a layman. We know that More had more than a superficial knowledge of Roman law, since he had been admitted as an honorary member of Doctors' Commons in December 1514.[9] (Doctors' Commons was the equivalent of an 'inn of court' for civil and ecclesiastical lawyers.) At this stage, More's legal expertise and ability to succeed Wolsey in the Courts of Chancery and Star Chamber offset the fact that he could not support Henry VIII's divorce (see Chapter 8).

Led by Harpsfield and informed by Roper's account of More's scrupulousness as a judge, the recusant tradition focused on Wolsey's failings, and turned to the articles of impeachment that were levelled against him in the House of Lords in the first session of the Reformation Parliament. More had signed these articles, which catalogued Wolsey's alleged 'misdeeds' under a string of itemized headings.[10] According to the charges, Wolsey had stifled discussion in the King's Council, banging his fist on the table in fits of impatience; taken the Great Seal abroad illegally; exaggerated his influence on the King when boasting to ambassadors; taken the King's name in vain; failed to prevent the spread of Lutheranism at Cambridge; and so on.

A leitmotif of the articles was the claim that Wolsey had obstructed justice. He had 'delayed' litigants, whom he had compelled to appear before himself at Hampton Court or at his many other residences, or whose suits he had reserved solely to his own discretion, even though he was so busy (and the cases so numerous) that 'ten of the wisest men in England' could not have been sufficient to clear the backlog. He had examined cases in the Court of Chancery 'after judgement had been given on them by the common law', and had illegally reversed common-law judgements to the derogation of the King and his judges. He had granted injunctions from the Chancery staying lawsuits in the other courts of justice 'when the parties were never called, nor bills put in against them'.[11] According to this litany, Wolsey failed as Lord Chancellor. His arrogance, incompetence and whim had been vexatious to litigants and the legal profession. He appropriated lawsuits to himself and clogged the courts with frivolous suits by encouraging everyone with a grievance to bring their cases before him. In particular, he was a plaintiff's judge. He had awarded injunctions and writs of subpoena on impulse, without first insisting on the taking of sureties or the formalities of written complaints. In effect, he had acted arbitrarily. He had made decisions based purely on hearsay or on *ex parte* arguments to the loss and prejudice of honest defendants.[12]

It is true that Wolsey had urged suitors who were unable to obtain justice at common law, especially before local magistrates, to file petitions in Star Chamber, where (in his own words) 'the complainants shall not dread to show the truth of their grief'.[13] There were occasions when he had overstepped the mark. He did from time to time live up to his reputation for impulsive treatment of litigants. There was, for example, his reception of

George Bayen's suit against William Underhill in 1527. After futile litigation in King's Bench, Common Pleas and the Court of Requests, Bayen came before Wolsey in Star Chamber to try out his luck. Wolsey was sympathetic and the plaintiff (like Shylock in the *Merchant of Venice*) praised him as a 'noble judge'.[14] The defendant, who was summoned by a writ of subpoena but who initially had refused to appear, was successfully brought before the court in 1529, and a day was set for a final hearing in the next Michaelmas term. Wolsey's fall intervened. The plaintiff therefore made suit to More in Hilary term 1530, but received in reply what the new Lord Chancellor considered to be a fully-justified rebuff. More regarded the suit as frivolous, and would not accept it for hearing, which eventually led to a further petition to his successor, Sir Thomas Audley.

Legal historians fascinated by More's role as Lord Chancellor always appreciated that it would be necessary to verify the claims of Roper and Harpsfield. Preliminary investigations by Sir James Mackintosh and Lord Campbell in the nineteenth century proved inconclusive, probably because the full archival resources of the Public Record Office were not exploited until the 1970s.[15] In fact, the recusant tradition remained the basis of the standard view as late as 1976. Richard J. Schoeck summarized this interpretation, when he argued that Wolsey 'had progressively alienated common lawyers and judges'. 'We can only infer that Henry was persuaded that the situation was at least potentially grave.' More brought 'immense prestige' to the post of Lord Chancellor. He played an 'extraordinary role' in mitigating the ideological breach caused by Wolsey's 'arrogance, ignorance of legal customs, and at times deliberate insulting of the judiciary'. More brought reconciliation into the Chancery and Star Chamber, where he restored 'harmony' between the Lord Chancellor and the common lawyers and judges.[16]

The latest research has shown that these perspectives are misleading. Wolsey's achievements as Lord Chancellor were considerable and his serious indiscretions few.[17] His most significant initiative was his law-enforcement policy, unveiled in the King's presence in Star Chamber on 2 May 1516 and reiterated in May 1517 and October 1519.[18] It emphasized, first, that wrongdoing must be punished wherever it was to be found, irrespective of the social or political influence of those committing offences; and, secondly, that justice should be 'equally' and 'indifferently' (i.e. impartially) offered to all who sought it. In effect, Wolsey launched an attack on judicial corruption and sleaze. He insisted that the King's councillors, the nobility, and those local magistrates who served as sheriffs or justices of the peace in their localities, should apply to others the standards that they expected for themselves and their friends.

Next, Wolsey introduced an element of philosophy into the legal system. In an age when access to justice was determined by social status or the ability to pay expensive legal fees, he advocated the principle that the people should have justice as a right. As Lord Chancellor, he insisted that litigants should be allowed to present their complaints, if necessary, to him personally. His system was largely of his own creation. He expected suitors to follow the procedures he laid down, to submit to independent arbitration wherever possible, and to be governed by the golden rule of equity: 'Do as you would be done by' – as Christ himself commanded in the Sermon on the Mount. In the eyes of some professional lawyers, this was an unwarranted interference in due process of law! Some litigants were even allowed to sue *in forma pauperis* (i.e. without payment of fees), although most of these cases were not heard in Chancery or Star Chamber, but were sent to the Court of Requests.[19] Rarely do judges canvas the ideal of better justice so blatantly. Lord Ellesmere, Lord Chancellor to James I between 1603 and 1617, criticized Wolsey as a judge who had 'stirred up suits' and 'so brought water to the mill'.[20] Certainly Wolsey underestimated the attractions of his initiatives. A flood of litigation swamped his courts by 1525, and he was obliged to refer a large proportion of these additional cases for adjudication before local commissioners or the assize judges.[21]

But this was far from the whole story. A more insidious migration of business from the courts of common law to Chancery and Star Chamber had begun in the mid-fifteenth century. The workload of King's Bench and Common Pleas had fallen by almost half between 1440 and 1515, and had dropped further by 1525. A recovery by 1529 to roughly the level in 1515 partially reversed the trend, but was hardly reassuring. Over the same period, the Courts of Chancery and Star Chamber gained in business, confidence and prestige. It seemed as if the older courts were 'losing out' to the newer courts of equitable jurisdiction, which were generally more flexible and able to deal with trusts, debts and ownership disputes in ways that were more relevant to society's needs. In particular, Chancery was able to assist landowners to protect their estates from the full extent of feudal and inheritance taxes, which made its jurisdiction especially attractive.[22]

As a result, Chancery and Star Chamber built up stakes in specific areas of jurisdiction. While Wolsey was Lord Chancellor, 7476 suits were filed in Chancery. Of these, 46 per cent were disputes over land or personal property, 30 per cent were commercial or mercantile suits, and 24 per cent were essentially miscellaneous. In the same period, 1685 suits were filed in Star Chamber. Only a quarter of the Star Chamber cases are sufficiently complete for their subjects to be properly identified, but of this sample 41 per cent concerned land or personal property, while the remainder sprang from riot or trespass, corruption of justice, or other misdemeanours. In other words, the largest proportion of cases in Chancery and a substantial proportion in Star Chamber lay in the sphere of land and personal property with a sizeable proportion concerning commercial and mercantile matters. No wonder that the common lawyers felt threatened, since these were the most lucrative areas of legal work. The rise of Chancery and Star Chamber must have meant a significant loss of income for practitioners in King's Bench and Common Pleas.[23]

All this might seem to vindicate the recusant tradition: to explain why More was chosen as Lord Chancellor. Is it possible, after all, to argue that his role was to heal 'a dangerously widening breach between Chancery and the common law'?[24] The answer is a resounding no. There could not have been an ideological breach between the common lawyers and the Chancery, because far from the common lawyers boycotting the courts of equitable jurisdiction, they provided the expert services without which neither Chancery nor Star Chamber could function. Although civil and canon lawyers were predominantly the clerks and officials in these courts, the legal counsel who advised litigants and pleaded their causes were exclusively common lawyers by 1500. The same learned counsel acted as arbitrators, mediators, umpires, referees and valuers in these courts.[25] There were thirty or so common lawyers who practised almost exclusively in Chancery and Star Chamber, and who made their fortunes there. The debate in the legal profession by the mid-1520s was between those common lawyers with Chancery and Star Chamber practices, and those with King's Bench and Common Pleas practices. It was at the climax of the controversy between these rival interests that More was appointed Lord Chancellor.

What colours the accounts of Roper and Harpsfield upon which almost all subsequent biographers have relied is their selective emphases. Far from reversing Wolsey's policies as Lord Chancellor, More vigorously continued them. He left his predecessor's law-enforcement policy intact, and continued to meet the needs of suitors in Chancery and Star Chamber.[26] In Chancery, the level of litigation rose steeply. More was presented with 2356 suits in the 31 months of his office. His chancellorship saw the most substantial growth in litigation since the reign of Edward IV, and the subjects of these cases were identical to those received by Wolsey. Of More's suits, 48 per cent were disputes over land or personal property, 15 per cent were commercial or mercantile suits, and 37 per cent were miscellaneous. In Star Chamber, the pattern also followed that established under Wolsey. Around 400 suits were filed under More, of which 167 are well enough documented to discuss. Of these 167 suits, 44 per cent concerned land or personal property, and 56 per cent dealt with riot or trespass, corruption of justice, or other misdemeanours.[27]

The nature and scope of the work discharged by More was directly comparable to that undertaken by his predecessor. More's policy involved no jurisdictional innovations, no obvious changes of direction within existing jurisdictions. The number of commercial suits in Chancery declined somewhat, but the proportion of cases concerning land and personal property in both Chancery and Star Chamber remained as high as under Wolsey. In this respect, it is remarkable that More, himself a common lawyer, made no attempt in Star Chamber to foreclose on the court's jurisdiction over property matters, since medieval legislation prohibited it from determining cases touching title to freehold land. Star Chamber circumvented these rules by settling 'possession' rather than 'title' to land. It used its coercive power to exclude sitting tenants or claimants from occupying land to which they had no title and to restore the interests of legitimate claimants in their lawful possession, but it enforced these decisions without formally determining the strict issue of 'title', which it left to the courts of common law. In this legal subterfuge, More followed in Wolsey's footsteps, although it must be said that he was more careful than his predecessor to secure the explicit assent of the common-law judges to each of these decisions.[28]

Despite his care, More himself ran into trouble with the common lawyers. The intermittent controversy between the Lord Chancellor and the judges over injunctions did not end with Wolsey's fall: not surprisingly, since More's injunctions were identical in scope to those awarded by his predecessor.[29] Injunctions were an essential procedural weapon of the Courts of Chancery and Star Chamber, especially in property and commercial cases. More resolved to reconcile legal opinion to his (and therefore Wolsey's) use of them. According to Roper, he instructed John Croke, one of the Six Clerks of Chancery, to prepare a docket of injunctions issued since Wolsey had left office. He then invited the judges to dine with him in Star Chamber. After dinner was concluded, he 'broke' with the judges 'what complaints he had heard of his injunctions'. He then went on to demonstrate 'both the number and causes of every one of them in order'. This he did 'so plainly' that, following a full debate, the judges 'were all enforced to confess that they in like case could have done no otherwise themselves'.[30]

Roper's narrative, although uncorroborated, is convincing. We know that More had secured the approval of the judges for those of his Star Chamber decisions which were potentially contentious, and he took the trouble to cancel those outdated injunctions of Wolsey's still on the file after his arrival as Lord Chancellor.[31] The preparation of a docket summarizing More's injunctions would have been something easily achieved by reference to the *contrabrevia* (i.e. office copies) held in Chancery. The postprandial debate of queries in the Star Chamber or Exchequer Chamber was likewise a traditional judges' procedure. There is no reason to doubt the bare facts of Roper's account.

But his perspective is skewed. Roper, and later Harpsfield, sought to describe More's care in awarding injunctions sparingly in order to point up the contrast with Wolsey.[32] They moulded their accounts to maximize the force of this rhetoric. They aimed to show that, despite a challenge from the judges even in relation to those few injunctions which More himself had issued, he had vindicated his actions in the name of justice. He had countered that:

> if the judges of every court – unto whom the reformation of
> the rigour of the law, by reason of their office, most
> especially appertained – would upon reasonable considera-
> tions by their own discretions, as they were as he thought in

conscience bound, mitigate and reform the rigour of the law themselves, there should from henceforth by him no more injunctions be granted.[33]

When the judges refused to accept this reasoning, More delivered the *coup de grâce*: ' "Forasmuch as yourselves, my lords, drive me to that necessity for awarding out injunctions to relieve the people's injury, you cannot hereafter any more justly blame me." '[34]

The earliest biographers played down the fact that, in constructing this defence, More simultaneously raised the issue of law reform and defended Wolsey's policy of equitable relief. Wolsey's philosophy had been that litigants should have justice as a right. If the common-law judges were unwilling to recalibrate their system to match these values, then a new generation of common-law chancellors would offset this by refining Wolsey's scheme whereby law enforcement and attacks on judicial corruption became the distinctive function of the Court of Star Chamber, while property and commercial litigation flooded increasingly into Chancery. These reforms could not be postponed indefinitely. In the 1540s and 1550s, the common lawyers did reform (mainly) the Court of King's Bench. They introduced new substantive remedies and replicated the most popular and successful features of Chancery and Star Chamber procedure to simplify and expedite litigation. In this transformation, William Roper, as Chief Clerk or Prothonotary of King's Bench, played a decisive role.[35]

But these reforms post-dated More's resignation. His agenda as Lord Chancellor was therefore one of streamlining the system he had inherited: the problems he tackled were practical in nature. One of Wolsey's failings had been his almost naïve belief that if private parties, especially those at issue over property ownership, were given unrestricted access to idealized forms of 'justice' and 'equity', good order could be preserved. In common with many of his contemporaries, Wolsey underestimated the persistence and chicanery of what legal historians have called 'the new-style litigant' who was 'bent less upon asserting a right than not forgoing an advantage, less on winning than not losing in court, and always questing for another court in which to continue battle with his adversaries.'[36]

Wolsey's facility of free access to Chancery and Star Chamber had left him open to the charge that he was a plaintiff's judge who had awarded injunctions and writs of subpoena on impulse. More resolved not to restrict access to the courts. According to Roper, he sat 'in his open hall' at Chelsea in the afternoons: 'to the intent that, if any persons had any suit unto him, they might the more boldly come to his presence'.[37] As a safeguard, More pursued a policy of strict scrutiny. He supposedly read 'every' bill of complaint himself before a writ was awarded. If the plaintiff averred 'matter sufficient worthy a subpoena', More would approve the writ by his signature on the bill, or else 'cancel it'.[38] Roper's account of these proceedings can be checked. Only one-tenth of the bills extant in the Chancery Proceedings for More's period of office carry his endorsement. Again, numerous writs were issued which relate to bills which he had not signed.[39] The comprehensive scrutiny envisaged by Roper may have been desirable (and it no doubt appealed to Roper, whose income as Chief Clerk of King's Bench was directly affected by the popularity of the Chancery and Star Chamber), but it was impracticable. The pressure of work in the courts, Parliament and the Privy Council was too great for the Lord Chancellor to vet all bills himself. Obviously More sampled these bills, itself a step in the right direction. However, he did not insist that plaintiffs should offer pledges to prosecute, as in the fifteenth century. Nor did he require bills of complaint in Star Chamber to be signed by legal counsel, as later became standard practice.[40]

One reform introduced by More was his decision that defendants in Chancery might be allowed to appear by attorney rather than in person. This could apply only to Chancery; in Star Chamber the defendant was required not only to be sworn to the truth of his answer to the bill of complaint, but was also examined in court upon interrogatories. In Star Chamber, criminal allegations were usually at stake, despite the essentially civil issues at base. In Chancery, the court's jurisdiction was entirely civil. As More was well aware, appearances by attorney were allowed in civil actions in the common-law courts, and he decided to allow this in Chancery in suitable instances. He wrote *'per se vel per atturnatum'* ('either in person or by attorney') in his own hand on the dorse of several bills of complaint authorizing the issue of process against defendants.[41] The concession was useful, and was retained by More's successors. It saved many honest defendants the time, trouble and expense of travelling to London.

More's main contribution to the refinement of Wolsey's system came in the field of the better enforcement of equitable decrees.[42] In Star Chamber, Wolsey had used fines or imprisonment as a final sanction. Those who otherwise refused to obey were attached for contempt of court. In addition, defeated parties might be bound over under penalties to comply with the court's decrees or else pay fines or compensation to the successful party by instalments. More used all of these methods, and was not reluctant to enforce decrees for the recovery of land or personal property by injunction. His imposition of double damages for non-compliance was an innovation. In the face of direct disobedience, More streamlined the method by which a writ of assistance was addressed to the local sheriff, commanding him to enforce a decree, using force if necessary, and to bind those who resisted to 'good abearing' and to their immediate appearance before Star Chamber for contempt of court.[43]

Those who resisted More's decrees were automatically gaoled. He was the first Lord Chancellor to rule that contempts committed in Chancery were punishable in Star Chamber. This is what lay behind Roper's garbled report of More's 'flat' decree in Chancery against his son-in-law, Giles Heron, when the latter presumed too much of his favour and 'would by him in no wise be persuaded to agree to any indifferent order'.[44] Heron expected More to show favour to members of his own family circle, but More refused. Roper said that he made 'a flat decree' against Heron. He refused to proceed further with Heron's suit in Chancery, and bound him in 1000 marks (£666) to his appearance in Star Chamber, when he was to 'abide' such 'order and determination' as should be thought expedient. The alternative was imprisonment in the Tower.[45] These terms were unusually stiff. A notorious contempt must have been committed by Heron.

Roper and Harpsfield cited Heron's case as an example of More's virtue in refusing privileges to members of his own family. While the case can certainly be read that way, its legal significance is that it was one of the first cases in Chancery to test the reach of the court in the enforcement of compliance. Wolsey had often been tentative, even irresolute, perhaps hoping that parties would agree to settle their differences in a spirit of mutual compromise. Such altruism was rarely found, and litigants tended to walk away from the court if they failed to secure the decision that they believed was justified. More would not accept that suitors could pick and choose in this way. Once they had subjected themselves to the jurisdiction of the court, he brought the relative severity of the common lawyer's approach to the notion of the 'final end'.

More's virtue as a judge is no longer in question, but this issue was fundamental to his earliest biographers. Roper opened his narrative of More's chancellorship in this vein. He described how another son-in-law, William Dauncey, had complained that, whereas Wolsey had allowed his servants to profit from arranging audiences for suitors, More was so accessible that nothing was to be gained in that way. The slur on Wolsey was mean but predictable. In reply, More listed the other ways by which a judge could help his intimates: by showing favour by word or letter, by appointing biased commissioners to hear and end a suit, or by referring parties to arbitration to the detriment of the one who would have won in a judgement. The Victorian Lord Chancellor John, Lord Campbell was scandalized by this passage, but More's point is simple. Why get involved in anything so crude as bribery? The passage is also ironic. More (and Roper) knew that the practices More described were rampant among magistrates in the sixteenth century and were not unknown in the central courts at Westminster. In any event, More's conclusion was uncompromising: ' "I assure thee on my faith, that if the parties will at my hands call for justice, then all were it my father stood on the one side and the devil on the other, his cause being good, the devil should have right" '.[46]

The earliest 'Lives' highlighted More's refusal of bribes. He had received a gilt cup from the wife of a grateful Chancery suitor, brought as a New Year's gift, but had immediately returned it after pledging her health in wine.[47] And when 'Mistress Crocker' brought a pair of gloves and £40 in gold, More kept the gloves but refused the money.[48] Finally, 'one Master Gresham', probably John Gresham, a prominent citizen and mercer of London, whose suit was pending in Chancery, sent More 'a fair gilted cup'. More knew that acceptance was unthinkable, but thought the opportunity for a 'merry jest' too great to pass up. Gresham's cup was beautifully wrought, but its legal worth was its bullion value alone. More therefore exchanged it for a cup of inferior workmanship but greater bullion value from his own collection. By the exchange, he obtained the superior cup, rebuked the donor, and preserved his integrity.[49] (This 'jest' is comparable in its multiple ironies to More's gift of false jewels to Jane Colt, described in Chapter 4.) Such subtleties were not universally appreciated, and More found these cases were brought in evidence against him by the Boleyn faction after his resignation.[50] The allegations were investigated by the King and Privy Council: he was cleared on all counts, but as late as the 1920s Lord Justice Russell wrote: 'Sir Thomas More's integrity emerged unscathed from these charges; but I confess his conduct over the Gresham cup strikes me as injudicious, and I should have liked to see Mistress Crocker committed for contempt of court'.[51]

More's reputation stands high among the modern legal profession. A haze of mythology envelopes his outlook as a judge. An endemic myth is that he was an uncompromising advocate of the common-law jury system in criminal trials. In reality, his *Debellation of Salem and Bizance* (1533) shows that he was not. In this book, written in his 'retirement' after his resignation, More defended his opinion, expressed earlier the same year in his *Apology*, that trial juries could not be relied on to convict: he himself would 'trust the truth of one judge, as well as the truth of two juries'.[52] More wrote in reply to Christopher St German, the author of the legal classic *Doctor and Student* and a barrage of other works which attacked both the legislative independence of the English Church in Convocation and *ex officio* proceedings in the Church courts in cases of suspected heresy (see Chapter 9).[53] This was a highly visible controversy. By publishing such an iconoclastic opinion when and where he knew that his critics would immediately seize on it, More shows that it must have been a considered view, and one that was strongly held.

Legal legend also maintains that More's diligence was such that he dispatched more cases in Chancery than any other judge before or since. Although suits had been pending there for 20 years, he cleared away the backlog and kept pace with current litigation. In a fable omitted by Father Bridgett but avidly retailed by the undiscriminating R.W. Chambers, More's 'day of triumph' came when, one morning, he called for the next case and was told that 'there was no man or matter to be heard'.[54] 'This he caused to be enrolled in the public acts of that court.'[55] The incident, says Chambers, 'gave More his traditional reputation', reflected in the popular ditty:

> When More some time had Chancellor been,
> No more suits did remain.
> The like will never more be seen
> Till More be there again.[56]

It is possible that More worked harder and faster than his predecessors or successors in determining suits: this statement cannot be tested in the absence of quantitative data. But the notion that More kept abreast of current litigation and left no backlog is romantic fiction. It is certain that much of the business begun under More, and a good deal of that which had accumulated under Wolsey, was not concluded when Sir Thomas Audley succeeded More in Chancery.[57] While More indeed heard suits which were twenty years old, there is no evidence to suggest that he was any more successful than his predecessors in ending them. As to the inference that one day he had no current work in Chancery, this (if it happened at all) could only have been a freak of timetabling. Nor could he have caused anything to be 'enrolled' in the 'public acts' of the Court of Chancery. The story is anachronistic, since the introduction of decree and order rolls was a reform implemented at the time of Sir Thomas Wriotheseley's appointment to the chancellorship.[58]

Was More a Utopian reformer as Lord Chancellor? Were his actions governed by a philosophical impetus towards social justice and the perfection of the commonwealth despite the limitations of his campaign against heresy? The evidence is inconclusive, but unpersuasive. More was adamant that Wolsey's system of access to 'equal' and 'impartial' justice irrespective of social status should be maintained. If the common-law judges would not 'mitigate' the 'rigour' of the law on grounds of equity, then he would continue to award injunctions 'to relieve the people's injury'; and to this end, he streamlined the procedure of Chancery and Star Chamber, notably in respect of the 'finality' of decrees.

But this was no more than the Lord Chancellor was bound to do by virtue of his oath of office. If equitable jurisdiction is itself to be equated with Utopian reform, then Wolsey was as much a Utopian reformer as More. The Lord Chancellor swore to 'do right to all manner of people, poor and rich, after the laws and usages of this realm'.[59] This was the essence of the job. The case in favour of equity was that interventions by the Lord Chancellor were necessary to mitigate the rigour of the common law. General rules of law should in difficult cases be interpreted flexibly and fairly, and not in ways that were technically 'legal' but detrimental to 'justice'. The case against was that equity allegedly 'violated' the oaths of the King at his coronation and of the judges on their appointment that they would 'uphold' the 'laws and customs of England'. According to this reactionary view, the 'law' of the Chancery and Star Chamber was fickle, uncertain and injurious to the commonwealth, since it encouraged chicanery and fraud. It fostered the assumption that people could default on their debts and abandon their contractual obligations. It also encouraged individual chancellors to develop personality cults.[60]

The lines of this debate were settled under Wolsey. More's intervention on injunctions kept the issue of law reform firmly on the agenda, but did not alter or transform the argument. Nor was there anything socially 'radical' about his orders and decrees in Chancery and Star Chamber, the bulk of which concerned rights over private property, and which upheld the claims of legitimate proprietors and occupiers. The notion that Utopian communism was the solution – 'the only possible solution' – to the catalogue of social evils in the reign of Henry VIII was entirely alien to More's practical outlook in the courts, whatever relevance it still bore to his abstract philosophy of justice.

There are tantalizing signs that More would have liked to have done more as a legal reformer in the House of Lords. At the opening of the first session of the Reformation Parliament on 3 November 1529, he delivered the speech from the throne in the absence of the King. The bulk of the speech was concerned with a justification of Wolsey's fall. This had to be carefully pitched, since Wolsey's disgrace had been sudden. It had also been precipi- tated by his failure to obtain Henry VIII's divorce rather than for the reasons for which he had been officially condemned. Wolsey's 'failure' to reform the evils of the commonwealth was made the centrepiece of More's address, and the speech ended (according to a cryptic note on the Parliament Roll) with a 'long and elegant' exposition of these 'errors and abuses' and what was required to reform them.[61] The Roll does not record what More said beyond the fact that he said it. The chronicler, Edward Hall, who sat in the House of Commons as MP for Wenlock, reported that he called for the reform of laws which 'by long continuance of time and mutation of things' were 'very insufficient and imperfect'. He also attacked 'new enormities' which had 'sprung amongst the people' and which required legislation 'to reform the same'.[62]

In this session Parliament enacted anticlerical statutes reform- ing mortuary and probate fees, clerical pluralism, and clerical non-residence and absenteeism, legislation which More could not personally have condoned and which led to an appeal to Rome by three bishops led by John Fisher, who sought an annulment of these statutes by the Pope on the grounds of their infringement of ecclesiastical immunity from secular jurisdiction.[63] But six other statutes streamlined aspects of the legal system, and perhaps marked the beginning of a 'lost' programme of reform that More envisaged, but which in later sessions was frustrated by the rise of the divorce issue and by the demands of his rearguard defence of Catholicism in the House of Lords (see Chapter 8).

The first Act made fraudulent embezzlement by servants a felony, as long as the stolen items were worth 40 shillings or more. This remedied a long-standing legal loophole. Servants routinely handled money, jewels, plate and other goods and chattels on behalf of their masters or employers. Before the new Act, they could not be held to have stolen or embezzled such items at common law, even if they had misappropriated them, as long as they had been put in possession of them lawfully in the first place. After the new Act, prosecutions for embezzlement were permitted at common law. This reform would have appealed to a common-law chancellor, since it meant that it was no longer necessary for the owner to sue for redress in Chancery or Star Chamber. Temporary at first, the Act was made permanent in 1563.[64]

A second Act empowered the common-law judges to order thieves to restore stolen goods to their true owners at the discretion of the court. This reform resembles an aspect of the customs of the Polylerites as described by Hythlodaeus in Book I of *Utopia*.[65] Whereas by common law, the property of convicted thieves (including stolen goods) was forfeited to the Crown, the new statute distinguished between stolen goods in the thief's possession and the other goods which he should forfeit on his conviction. While this did not address the principal irony to which Hythlodaeus drew attention – the fact that by common law convicted murderers and thieves were punished equally with death, so there was little incentive not to commit murder during a burglary – the Act dealt with another issue that in default of legislation had previously been the preserve of the Court of Chancery rather than the common law.[66]

The other four Acts reformed aspects of civil procedure. All dealt with specialized issues of land law and inheritance. The most important statute protected leasehold tenants from fictitious or collusive recoveries of the freehold estate that led to their eviction or harassment by new owners. The Act protected tenants from predatory freeholders. It also provided guaranteed enjoyment of the long lease, and enabled leases to be developed as a legal basis for contriving family settlements and arranging mortgages. Once again, this Act dealt with abuses which, until the new legislation, could only be remedied in Chancery, Star Chamber or the Court of Requests. The other significant Act empowered landlords to collect their rents and customary dues even when (because of recoveries, secret enfeoffments and sub-leases) they were no longer able to identify their tenants by name. The Act worked entirely to the benefit of landowners, but dealt with a genuine problem of rent avoidance by unscrupulous tenants and squatters.[67]

The extent to which More promoted all or any of these Acts cannot now be determined: the sources are defective. The Lords' Journals do not cover the proceedings of 1529 and the original parchment Acts for this session were lost as early as the sixteenth century. All these statutes were printed and enrolled. But without the Acts in the form in which they received the royal assent, we do not even know if these measures were introduced in the House of Lords rather than in the Commons. The measures share a common theme: the redress at common law of grievances which previously could be remedied only in the courts of equitable jurisdiction. This connection is suggestive, but it cannot be made the linchpin of an argument. On the evidence we have, More's agenda included law reform, but he was not a Utopian reformer. What he might have achieved had he become Lord Chancellor earlier, and if the King's divorce and the royal supremacy had not destroyed him, is an elusive question. But it is one to which there can never be an answer. There is no more certainty to be gained from an examination of the legal records than there is from a reading of *Utopia*.

Notes

1 *CWE* 7, p. 22.
2 Roper, pp. 219–22; Harpsfield, pp. 51–6.
3 Roper, pp. 231–3; Harpsfield, pp. 152–5.
4 Harpsfield, pp. 40–2; Roper, pp. 213–14.
5 Harpsfield, p. cciv.
6 PRO, C 54/398 (no. 18).
7 PRO, C 54/398 (no. 18).
8 PRO, C 54/398 (no. 18); Roper, pp. 218–19.
9 K.R. Massingham, 'Thomas More, "Laicus", gent.', *Moreana* 22 (1985), pp. 25–35.

10 *LP* IV.iii. no. 6075.

11 *LP* IV.iii. no. 6075 (pp. 2712–13).

12 For recent investigations of these allegations, which show that they were largely untrue, see John Guy, *The Cardinal's Court: the Impact of Thomas Wolsey in Star Chamber* (Hassocks, 1977); Guy, *Christopher St German on Chancery and Statute* (London, 1985), pp. 64–81; Franz Metzger, *Das Englische Kanzleigericht Unter Kardinal Wolsey 1515–1529* (Erlangen-Nürnberg PhD, 1976).

13 Guy, *The Cardinal's Court*, p. 121.

14 PRO, STAC 2/3/244–6, 2/19/375, 2/20/340; STAC 10/1/41.

15 John Guy, 'The Development of Equitable Jurisdictions, 1450–1550', in E.W. Ives and A.H. Manchester, eds, *Law, Litigants and the Legal Profession* (London, 1983), pp. 80–6; Guy, 'Wolsey's Star Chamber: A Study in Archival Reconstruction', *Journal of the Society of Archivists* 5 (1975), pp. 169–80; Guy, *The Public Career of Sir Thomas More* (Brighton, 1980), pp. 37–93, 204–5; E.W. Ives, *The Common Lawyers of Pre-Reformation England* (Cambridge, 1983); J.H. Baker, ed., *The Reports of Sir John Spelman* (2 vols, London, 1976–7).

16 R.J. Schoeck, 'The Place of Sir Thomas More in Legal History and Tradition', *Moreana* 51 (1976), pp. 85–90.

17 Peter Gwyn, *The King's Cardinal: the Rise and Fall of Thomas Wolsey* (London, 1990); John Guy, *Cardinal Wolsey* (Oxford, 1998); Guy, *The Cardinal's Court*; J.J. Scarisbrick, 'Cardinal Wolsey and the Common Weal', in E.W. Ives, R.J. Knecht and J.J. Scarisbrick, eds, *Wealth and Power in Tudor England* (London, 1978), pp. 45–67.

18 Guy, *The Cardinal's Court*, pp. 23–78, 119–31; John Guy, 'Thomas More as Successor to Wolsey', *Thought* 52 (1977), pp. 275–92.

19 John Guy, 'Wolsey, the Council and the Council Courts', *English Historical Review* 91 (1976), pp. 481–505; Guy, *The Cardinal's Court*, pp. 40–5, 109.

20 Ellesmere's view of Wolsey was derived from Hall's Chronicle, Henry E. Huntington Library, Ellesmere MS. 2810.

21 Guy, *The Cardinal's Court*, pp. 45–50.

22 Guy, *Public Career*, pp. 37–49.

23 Guy, *Public Career*, pp. 38–40; Guy, *The Cardinal's Court*, pp. 51–3.

24 Schoeck, 'Sir Thomas More in Legal History and Tradition', pp. 85, 90.

25 Guy, *Christopher St German*, pp. 65–6; Guy, *Public Career*, pp. 40–2; Guy, 'Thomas More as Successor to Wolsey', pp. 278–9; J.H. Baker, 'Lawyers Practising in Chancery, 1474–1486', *Journal of Legal History* 4 (1983), pp. 54–76; Metzger, *Das Englische Kanzleigericht*, pp. 204–14.

26 Guy, *Public Career*, pp. 50–79.

27 Guy, *Public Career*, pp. 50–79, 204–5.

28 Guy, *Public Career*, pp. 56–64.

29 Guy, *Public Career*, pp. 52, 56, 57–9, 60, 83–4, 86–9, 91, 92.

30 Roper, p. 221.

31 PRO, C 263/3/9A, 11, 13A; Guy, *Public Career*, p. 84 n. 27.

32 Roper, p. 221; Harpsfield, pp. 54–6.
33 Roper, pp. 221–2.
34 Roper, p. 222.
35 Baker, *Reports of Sir John Spelman* 2, intro., pp. 53–7.
36 T.G. Barnes, 'Star Chamber and the Sophistication of the Criminal Law', *Criminal Law Review* 64 (1977), pp. 316–26.
37 Roper, p. 220.
38 Roper, p. 220.
39 Guy, *Public Career*, p. 90 and n. 46.
40 Guy, *Public Career*, p. 90; Guy, *The Cardinal's Court*, pp. 80–1.
41 Guy, *Public Career*, p. 90 n. 49.
42 Guy, *The Cardinal's Court*, pp. 134–5.
43 Guy, *Public Career*, p. 91.
44 Roper, p. 220.
45 PRO, C 54/400 (entry for 18 Dec. 1531).
46 Roper, p. 220.
47 Roper, pp. 231–2.
48 Roper, p. 232.
49 Roper, p. 232.
50 Roper, pp. 231–2.
51 R.W. Chambers, *Thomas More* (London, 1935), pp. 270–1.
52 CW 10, pp. lxxxiv–lxxxv, 134–5.
53 John Guy, 'Thomas More and Christopher St German: the Battle of the Books', in Alistair Fox and John Guy, eds, *Reassessing the Henrician Age: Humanism, Politics, and Reform* (Oxford, 1986), pp. 95–120.
54 Chambers. *Thomas More*, pp. 273–4.
55 E.V. Hitchcock and P.E. Hallett, eds, *The lyfe of Syr Thomas More, sometymes Lord Chancellor of England* (London, 1950), p. 69; Chambers, *Thomas More*, p. 274.
56 Chambers, *Thomas More*, p. 274.
57 Guy, *Public Career*, p. 92 n. 59.
58 PRO, C 78/1–3.
59 PRO, C 54/398 (no. 18).
60 Guy, *Christopher St German*, pp. 19–21, 67, 71–3, 77, 81–94, 106–26.
61 PRO, C 65/138, m. 1; Guy, *Public Career*, pp. 113–15.
62 Charles Whibley, ed., *Henry VIII* [an edition of Hall's Chronicle] (2 vols, London, 1904) 2, p. 164.
63 S.E. Lehmberg, *The Reformation Parliament, 1529–1536* (Cambridge, 1970), pp. 76–104; Guy, *Public Career*, pp. 117–39.
64 Guy, *Public Career*, pp. 122–3.
65 Logan, Adams and Miller, pp. 71–3.
66 21 Henry VIII, c. 11.
67 Guy, *Public Career*, p. 123.

|8|

Politician?

Politician or saint? For Thomas Stapleton, whose *Life of Thomas More* was completed as the Spanish Armada sailed up the English Channel, the roles were diametrically opposed. The politician's mantle was repugnant to a man of virtue. More 'loathed the life of the Court'. He 'judged himself to be quite unfitted to that mode of life'.[1] He had tolerated his position as a councillor and King's secretary in the 1520s only because the Court of Henry VIII enjoyed a 'high reputation for virtue'.[2] On Wolsey's fall, More was promoted Lord Chancellor: the highest office in the State, and the post which Cardinal Morton, to whom he was indebted for his humanist education, had occupied. But More was increasingly uncomfortable. When 'lust began to rule in place of virtue', he did not condone the King's policy. He was prepared to speak the truth, rather than merely say what was expedient. He discharged his duty to the King, but did so by counselling him privately. Finally, he petitioned to resign.[3] His request was not greeted with approbation. It was a matter of 'the greatest difficulty'. But when at last Henry acceded, More was 'freed from the servitude of the Court'.[4]

Roper and Harpsfield are less otherworldly in their perspective, but their 'story' is the same.[5] More was caught up, but not implicated, in politics. He was not associated with those who, like Fisher, John Clerk (Bishop of Bath and Wells) or Thomas Abel, opposed the divorce outright. If More would not support the King, neither would he 'oppose' him. He kept out of trouble. He was not 'political' in his actions. There was no dissimulation or pretence. He expressed his opinion privately to the King three times according to Roper, four according to Harpsfield. Otherwise, he resisted

Henry's blandishments. He reminded the King that 'at his first coming into his noble service', Henry had willed him 'first to look unto God, and after God to him'.[6] The King had conceded that if More 'could not therein with his conscience serve him, he was content to accept his service otherwise'.[7] He would employ other councillors on the divorce. Despite this, More was required to present to Parliament the favourable opinions which the King had secured from a number of European universities. Although he managed not to express his own opinion of the divorce in Parliament, More realized that the King would not yield in his desire to have his marriage to Catherine of Aragon annulled. He therefore asked to resign: he perceived the 'disturbance' which the King's intentions would precipitate in Christendom.[8]

The agenda of the earliest biographers is overt. When More had given his opinion on the divorce privately to the King, he had been promised that Henry would 'continue his gracious favour towards him and never with that matter molest his conscience after'.[9] By attacking in 'retirement' a man who had not opposed him, Henry had been vindictive. He had pursued More to the death, acted tyrannically and also committed perjury, since he had reneged on a promise. Eager to exculpate More on every count, Harpsfield even argued that, since there had been no opposition, it followed that More could not have displeased the King.[10] He had negotiated his resignation with the King through the intercession of the Duke of Norfolk purely on the grounds of ill health.[11] Harpsfield chose to suppress Roper's unequivocal statement that More 'pretended himself unable any longer to serve'.[12] Ill health was the pretext, not the cause, of More's resignation. Roper was More's son-in-law, who had reason to know and no motive to lie. Harpsfield omitted Roper's evidence in favour of More's own account of his resignation, which he put out for public consumption, and which maintained that he had 'retired' entirely on his doctors' advice (see Chapter 9).[13] More's account stretched poetic licence to its limit. What he said was true (he suffered from angina): it was simply not the whole truth. Harpsfield does not have this excuse. He wrote in Mary's reign, when there was no fear of reprisals against the More circle should a neglect of tact be exposed. He chose to follow More's account and suppress Roper's, because the former had been published and the latter remained in manuscript. He was writing what he supposed to be the 'official history' of Thomas More: he sought to avoid the discrepancy becoming obvious.

More wrote his own account of his role in politics. On 5 March 1534, a month before his imprisonment in the Tower, he sent it in the form of a letter to Thomas Cromwell.[14] It is a comprehensive defence of his conduct since late September 1527, when he returned to England from Amiens after assisting Wolsey with the ratification of the Anglo-French alliance. In his lawyer's way, More was putting his own version of the facts on record. His letter achieves for his political career what the *Apology* attempts less successfully for his campaign against heresy. It is the keystone of all subsequent interpretations. More said that as soon as he returned from France, he 'repaired' to Hampton Court to report to the King. Independent evidence confirms that Henry was at Hampton Court between 12 and 17 October but at no other time that autumn, hence the week in which the interview took place is established.[15] According to More, the King, 'walking in the gallery, break with me of his great matter'. Henry explained that 'it was now perceived' that his marriage to Catherine of Aragon 'was not only against the positive laws of the Church and the written law of God', but also 'against the law of nature'. The defects of the marriage were so serious 'that it could in no wise by the Church be dispensable'.[16]

Henry had married Catherine by virtue of a papal dispensation of the impediment of affinity which her former marriage to the King's deceased elder brother, Arthur, had created between them. More knew that Henry's matrimonial scruple had first arisen in the spring of 1527 before he left for France. The 'greater hope of the matter' then lay in the fact that a legal defect discovered in the original dispensation, and in the 'brief' which had amended it, might be enough to persuade Clement VII to grant Henry's annulment speedily, so that the politically explosive issue of the Pope's dispensing power would not arise.[17]

The prospect of a quick annulment on technical grounds had evaporated. In Henry VIII's opinion, whether his marriage to Catherine was against divine law was the crux.[18] It is likely that More suspected this from the beginning. Judging by the rumours at Court before he left for Amiens, he would have known that Henry had set his heart on divorcing Catherine on the grounds that the Levitical prohibition on marriage to a brother's wife (Leviticus 20:21 in the Old Testament) was God's law and thus of equivalent status to the Ten Commandments. The King rejected a conflicting text (Deuteronomy 25:5) which seemed to authorize his marriage. He denied its relevance on the grounds that it merely reflected a custom of the Jewish nation (the 'levirate') which was not binding on Christians. And he later went further. He asserted that sexual intercourse with a brother's wife was tantamount to incest, which was against the law of nature. In his letter to Cromwell, More said that the first he knew that the King's marriage might be 'in such high degree against the law of nature' was at Hampton Court. Henry had laid open the Bible before him and read aloud passages which, in the King's view and that of his team of advisers, proved his case.[19]

More was unconvinced, but told the King he was not in a position to confirm his opinion without studying the authorities. Henry 'benignly accepted' this reply, and referred him to Edward Foxe, one of the King's research team, who was writing the first of a series of King's 'books' on the divorce.[20] (These 'books' were compiled iteratively by teams of lawyers, theologians and rhetoricians in a similar manner to the *Defence of the Seven Sacraments* which More had edited in 1521.) More read Foxe's manuscript, but his opinion remained unchanged. The King then left More alone until shortly after he was appointed Lord Chancellor, when he entreated him to 'look and consider his great matter' again.[21]

> And if it so were that thereupon it should hap me to see such things as should persuade me to that part, he would gladly use me among other of his councillors in that matter, and nevertheless he graciously declared unto me that he would in no wise that I should other thing do or say therein, than upon that, that I should perceive mine own conscience should serve me, and that I should first look unto God and after God unto him, which most gracious words were the first lesson also that ever his Grace gave me at my first coming into his noble service. This motion was to me very comfortable . . . .[22]

More agreed to revisit the King's case, and Henry assigned Thomas Cranmer, Edward Lee, Edward Foxe and Nicholas de Burgo, an Italian friar, to assist him. This was a new research team which had superseded the earlier one. By the autumn of 1530, it had produced the first version of the *Collectanea satis copiosa*, a composite source collection for the later King's 'books', which provided the intellectual justification for the Act in Restraint of Appeals and Act of Supremacy.[23] When More consulted the team in the last weeks of 1529, its work on the *Collectanea* had barely begun. The group was still working on the final revisions to the first sequence of King's 'books', designed to uphold the thesis that the prohibition on marriage to a brother's wife was divine law which the Pope cannot dispense, and that sexual relations between a man and his brother's widow were against the law of nature – the same arguments that Henry had explained to More at their first discussion of the divorce at Hampton Court.[24]

More read 'as far forth as my poor wit and learning served me', but it was no good. He returned to Henry, to whom he professed that 'to do him service', he would 'have been more glad than of all such worldly commodities as I either then had or ever should come to', if only he could have agreed with the King's opinion. And Henry accepted defeat with considerable grace. The King, said More, would never 'put any man in ruffle or trouble of his conscience'. He would only use those in the pursuit of his suit 'whose conscience his Grace perceived well and fully persuaded upon that part'.[25] After this, concluded More, he had done nothing in the matter of the divorce. He neither wrote a word to the prejudice of the King's case, nor did anyone else by his 'procurement'. He settled his mind 'in quiet to serve his Grace in other things'. He would not read the numerous treatises in favour of Catherine's cause by Fisher and Abel which circulated in print and manuscript. When belatedly he had discovered in his study a treatise in favour of Catherine which John Clerk had lent him in 1529, he had burned it.[26]

The iconic power of More's letter to Cromwell caused R.W. Chambers to attempt to exculpate him from Lord Acton's criticism that he had evaded his moral and political responsibilities as Lord Chancellor. According to Acton, who had written on Henry VIII's divorce in 1877, More 'put off the hour of trial that was to prove the heroic temper of his soul'. Despite believing steadfastly in the validity of Henry VIII's first marriage, he dissembled and declined to state his opinion, even though he occupied the highest office of State.[27] A close friend of Gladstone and the most eminent Catholic historian in Victorian England, Acton had resisted the promulgation in 1870 of the dogma of papal infallibility by the First Vatican Council, which put him at the centre of a political storm. He held that More ought to have stood up earlier for his principles.

Chambers poured scorn on this verdict. He ridiculed Acton, 'who demands that More should have been simultaneously Chief Minister and Leader of the Opposition'.[28] But Acton's point stood. It was only a matter of time before the shibboleth that More had 'loathed' politics and not 'dirtied his hands' provoked the counter-argument that he should either have stood up for his beliefs as Lord Chancellor or not accepted the office in the first place. Chambers could remain aloof from this only because he was bewitched by the magic of More. He exonerated him first on the grounds that Henry must have forced him into office, an interpretation justified only by a dubious remark in the notes of William Rastell.[29] He then defended his inaction on the grounds that if Henry, having heard his opinion on the divorce at Hampton Court, had 'promised to give him freedom of conscience' as Lord Chancellor 'and to employ him in other matters', then More 'had no option but to serve the King'.[30]

Not only did this argument fail to answer Acton's criticism that More should have spoken out sooner, it was also based on the false assumption that More had been promised freedom of conscience before, rather than after, he accepted his appointment as Lord Chancellor. To achieve this sleight of hand, Chambers superimposed onto the appointment itself the last interview with the King that More had described in his report to Cromwell. This was a blatant distortion, but it enabled Chambers to make his case. If More knew in advance that he had been excused from any association with the King's 'great matter' and was to concentrate on other tasks, his acceptance of the highest office in the State was less open to criticism on moral grounds.

The a priori methods of Chambers are misplaced. As early as 1879, fresh evidence had come to light which added considerably to the standard narrative and More's letter to Cromwell. It provided a basis for the hypothesis that More was deeply involved in politics. Yet it was largely ignored, even by J.A. Froude who had used similar evidence in his exposé of Fisher in the *History of England from the Fall of Wolsey to the Defeat of the Spanish Armada*. The new material took the form of abstracts of the dispatches of Eustace Chapuys, Charles V's ambassador in London.[31] In one, dated 20 September 1530, Chapuys had reported:

> The King has discovered of late that what passed in his Privy Council got wind, and now he has taken such rigid measures and precautions that it is impossible for the Queen or anyone else to learn the least thing of any importance except by means of bribery and pensions.[32]

He continued:

> The Chancellor, I hear, has spoken so much in the Queen's
> favour that he has had a narrow escape of being
> dismissed.[33]

While the dispatches of Chapuys are not unimpeachable (the
ambassador had a vivid imagination and the abstracts in the
printed calendars are not always correctly translated), they
remain suggestive. It was this, and other evidence in the Public
Record Office which Chambers either ignored or misinterpreted,
that led Sir Geoffrey Elton to argue that More, far from 'keeping
silence' or 'concealing his principles' as Lord Chancellor, had
done exactly what Lord Acton had demanded on moral grounds.
He had fought for his beliefs as Lord Chancellor, thereby
'opposing' Henry VIII. He had 'maintained some contact with
the centre of intrigue, the emperor's ambassador', and had
'contributed frank opinions in policy debates with king and
Council'.[34] More's letter to Cromwell had not mentioned this
political activity in order to create a smokescreen. The earliest
biographies had followed More's own account, because their
purpose was 'obviously' hagiographical.

Elton first presented his findings in a paper on 'Thomas More
and the Opposition to Henry VIII', which was published in
1968.[35] A schematic summary appeared a decade later in *Reform
and Reformation*, Elton's classic text book reflecting his mature
views.[36] My own book, *The Public Career of Sir Thomas More*,
later offered a fuller analysis of the Public Record Office
material.[37] My interpretation differs in several respects from
Elton's, but since the main divergences relate to the political
theory of the Acts of Appeals and Supremacy and the status of
Thomas Cromwell as Henry VIII's second minister, they are not
important here. Our accounts of More's role in politics converge,
except that our understanding of what Elton called More's 'frank
opinions in policy debates with king and Council' is different.
The significance of this will be explained in its proper place.

Elton argued that a 'battle for control' of the King's policy was
waged in the Privy Council and Parliament while More was Lord
Chancellor. These were not 'years without a policy', as he had
previously held in *England under the Tudors* (1955). They were
years in which rival groups defined ideological positions that
competed to win Henry's attention.[38] The battle centred on the
King's divorce and on the campaign in the House of Commons to

curtail the legislative independence of the English Church as guaranteed by chapter 1 of Magna Carta: the chapter that said 'that the English Church shall be free' ('*quod Anglicana ecclesia libera sit*') – free, that is, to legislate in its own Convocation (or ecclesiastical parliament) and to control its own courts independently of the State.[39] The Commons' agitation was directed spontaneously towards the alleged abuses of *ex officio* procedure in the Church courts in cases of suspected heresy, but it was implicitly linked to the divorce, since the King's most radical supporters believed that the subordination of the Church to the Crown was the Trojan horse which would enable the King to obtain his divorce by unilateral action in England. More as Lord Chancellor lay at the heart of both these struggles, and to a large extent provided the bridge between them.

As defined by Elton, the rival cabals comprised the Queen's supporters in the divorce suit; those radicals like Cranmer and Foxe (whom Cromwell later joined) who were compiling the *Collectanea satis copiosa* in order to justify the King's divorce by unilateral action in England; and lastly the nobles who, if not an ideologically based faction, were a major political force, even if they were 'barren of ideas and merely echoed what the King was saying'.[40] The Queen's group included the Earl of Shrewsbury, Fisher, William Peto (head of the Franciscan Observants of Greenwich), Bishop Cuthbert Tunstal, Nicholas Wilson (archdeacon of Oxford), and Bishops West, Clerk, and Standish. They had a close ally in More, whom they assisted in his efforts to eradicate heresy and pre-empt the attack on Catholicism that he could see was coming.[41] A cohesive party determined to defend the Church, they carefully monitored moves by the King such as the letter signed by the Great Council in favour of the divorce which was sent to Rome in July 1530,[42] or the *praemunire* charge filed in the Court of King's Bench against the English clergy which forced Convocation to concede that Henry VIII was 'Supreme Head of the English Church as far as the law of Christ allows'.[43] And they countered such moves in public sermons and propagandist treatises.[44] Fisher wrote seven or eight books against the divorce and in defence of the Church's legislative independence; and Peto preached that if the divorce went ahead, the dogs would lick Henry's blood as they had Ahab's.[45]

The Queen's party had allies in Parliament and Convocation. They were represented in the House of Commons by members of the Queen's Head group, an inchoate band of Catholic members who dined and talked politics together at the Queen's Head Tavern. Among them was Sir George Throckmorton, a Warwickshire MP, whose brother later served Cardinal Pole as his private secretary. Throckmorton confessed in October 1537 to engaging in parliamentary opposition at the behest of More and Fisher. More had summoned him to a little room off the Parliament Chamber; interrupting a conversation with John Clerk, he called Throckmorton a good Catholic, and added: 'if ye do continue in the same way that ye began and be not afraid to say your conscience, ye shall deserve great reward of God and thanks of the king's grace at length'.[46] By this, More evidently meant that when Henry VIII lost his infatuation with Anne Boleyn and came to his senses, he would appreciate the true worth of subjects who had shown that their first loyalty was to God and to the whole 'corps' of Christendom. (It was exactly this appeal to Henry's Catholic orthodoxy that More deployed in the Preface to his *Confutation of Tyndale's Answer* when discussing the basis of the anti-Lutheran campaign.)

In Convocation, the Queen's party was represented in the Upper House by those bishops who acted as Queen Catherine's legal counsel, and in the Lower House by a diehard group: Peter Ligham (a friend of Fisher), Thomas Pelles, Robert Clyff, John Baker, Adam Travers, and Rowland Phillips. All these men were excluded from the pardon granted by Henry VIII to the clergy in the parliamentary session of 1531, and were indicted afresh for *praemunire* for opposing the King in Convocation and defending papal authority and the legislative independence of the Church in a letter sent to Clement VII at Rome.[47]

Aligned against Queen Catherine's party were Anne Boleyn's supporters: Cranmer, Foxe, Cromwell, Thomas Audley (Speaker of the House of Commons), and Sir George Boleyn. Their opportunity to grasp the reins of power and promote radical reform in Church and State lay in resolving the divorce crisis. At his trial for heresy in Mary's reign, Cranmer justified his actions under Henry VIII as necessary 'to improve the corrupt ways of the Church as Primate of the realm'.[48] Cromwell shared these aims. He had recovered from Wolsey's fall by becoming Henry VIII's councillor and parliamentary manager. And if the radicals were ambitious, they were not afraid to extend royal power at the clergy's expense. More said to Cromwell (as Roper recounted):

> If you will follow my poor advice, you shall, in your
> counsel-giving unto his grace, ever tell him what he ought
> to do but never what he is able to do. . . . For if a lion knew
> his own strength, hard were it for any man to rule him.[49]

Yet Cromwell was not ascendant before More's resignation.
The most powerful cabal after Wolsey's fall included the Dukes
of Norfolk and Suffolk, the Earls of Wiltshire and Sussex,
Stephen Gardiner (promoted Bishop of Winchester), Lord Darcy,
and Lord Sandes. They had helped to destroy Wolsey and wished
to please the King; but they rejected radical ideas until Henry
himself endorsed the strategy of the *Collectanea satis copiosa*. In
particular, Norfolk, Darcy, and Gardiner recoiled from schism.
Darcy later opposed the break with Rome, becoming a prime
mover of the Pilgrimage of Grace. Norfolk was a traditional
Catholic, whose beliefs were close to those of More. He and
Gardiner were the mainstays of the conservative Act of Six
Articles (1539) and led the faction on the Privy Council in 1540
that helped to destroy Cromwell by persuading Henry VIII that
his chief minister had protected radical Protestants at Calais.

On 30 March 1531, More accepted an unwelcome duty. He
was required to present to Parliament the favourable opinions on
the divorce which the King had gathered from various European
universities. It was a task he viewed with evident discomfort. He
began in the House of Lords, explaining that he was there to
deny that Henry sought a divorce out of love for a woman rather
than for genuine scruples of conscience. He then asked the clerk
to read the opinions. When Catherine's supporters protested, the
Duke of Norfolk quickly intervened to say that the King had sent
the opinions to Parliament for information and not debate.[50]
More left the Lords, but not before someone managed to ask him
his own opinion of the divorce. He replied 'that he had many
times already declared it to the King; and he said no more'.[51] The
report comes from Chapuys, but its authenticity can scarcely be
doubted.

When More went down to the Commons, his speech was
recorded by the chronicler, Edward Hall, MP for Wenlock:

> You of this worshipful house I am sure be not so ignorant
> but you know well that the king our sovereign lord hath
> married his brother's wife, for she was both wedded and
> bedded with his brother Prince Arthur, and therefore you
> may surely say that he hath married his brother's wife. If

this marriage be good or no, many clerks do doubt. Wherefore the king like a virtuous prince willing to be satisfied in his conscience, and also for the surety of his realm hath with great deliberation consulted with great clerks, and hath sent my lord of London here present to the chief Universities of all Christendom to know their opinion and judgement in that behalf.[52]

The Bishops of London and Lincoln then addressed the Commons. They 'took it on their consciences that the marriage of the King and Queen was more than illegal'.[53] This was in striking contrast to More, who had chosen his words with care, 'not showing of what mind himself was therein'.[54] The Commons received everything in silence, and More and the others departed. The next day Parliament was prorogued.[55]

Roper was right to infer that More could only have done this 'at the King's request'.[56] Was he also right that the job was compromising enough to make More ask the Duke of Norfolk for help in resigning his office? We will never know for certain. But if so, why did More not resign immediately? Why did he remain in office for another year? Both Roper and Harpsfield omit the period from April 1531 to May 1532 from their narratives: they create the illusion that More's resignation followed immediately from the events in Parliament. My own belief is that More did not resign because he believed that the battle in the Privy Council could still be won.[57] Or as Elton argued, More only resigned after 'a last battle' in which he 'finally jeopardized what remained of the king's favour'.[58] Nothing was settled in 1531. There was a vigorous policy debate, but no agreement. The King still considered the *Collectanea satis copiosa* too radical. He was doctrinally conservative, in spite of his quarrel with the Pope. Cromwell was outnumbered in the Privy Council, where the nobles and Queen's party were in the majority, and shortly after More laid the opinions of the universities before Parliament, Henry and Anne Boleyn had a tiff. The King complained to the Duke of Norfolk that her insolence was insufferable. She abused him daily in ways that Catherine had never contemplated.[59] Anne next crossed swords with Sir Henry Guildford, Comptroller of the King's Household, and the King had to intercede between them.[60]

More was fighting for what he believed. He was described by Chapuys as 'having conducted himself most virtuously in this matter of the Queen'.[61] In recognition of his services, Charles V wrote a letter of thanks. Written in Brussels on 11 March 1531, this reached London on the 22nd.[62] More received word of its arrival shortly after he spoke in Parliament. But he would not accept the letter. He evaded Chapuys, and refused him access to his house at Chelsea. Always scrupulous, More became obsessed by the need for discretion. Chapuys told Charles:

> He begged me for the honour of God to forbear, for although he had given already sufficient proof of his loyalty that he ought to incur no suspicion, whoever came to visit him, yet, considering the time, he ought to abstain from everything which might provoke suspicion; and if there were no other reason, such a visit might deprive him of the liberty which he had always used in speaking boldly in those matters which concerned your Majesty and the Queen. He said he would not hold them in less regard than his life, not only out of the respect which is due to your Majesty and the Queen, but also for the welfare, honour, and conscience of his master, and the repose of his kingdom.[63]

This is one of More's most important statements. It confirms that he had offered what Elton called 'frank opinions' on Queen Catherine's behalf, whether privately to the King or in debates in the Privy Council. It also confirms that his activities were sufficiently 'political' for More to know that he would be ruined should his contact with Charles V's ambassador become known. Lastly, it confirms that More was anxious not to lose such influence as he had over policy – itself an admission that he did have influence still. His remark that he would avoid contact in order to 'incur no suspicion' is compelling. From Henry VIII's standpoint, More had shown a degree of compliance by speaking on the divorce in Parliament. Despite the casuistry of his words, his mere presence in Parliament would have bolstered royal hopes that he might one day be won round to supporting the divorce, which was always Henry's aspiration, whereas More himself must have seen the value of compliance in terms of continued influence over policy. As he told Chapuys, his objective was Henry's and England's welfare and domestic peace in the long term: the same argument he used to encourage Throckmorton to speak his mind in Parliament.[64]

A year later, More lost both the battle and the war. In March 1532, the Catholic cause suffered a setback when, as part of the King's campaign to extract papal concessions on the divorce, Parliament yielded to the Act in Conditional Restraint of Annates. The payments clerics made to Rome on their appointment to benefices were to cease and, if the Pope ordered an interdict, it was to be ignored. When the first version of the bill provoked an outcry, Henry conceded a clause that made the Act's validity conditional upon later confirmation. He then had to appear in the House of Lords on three occasions to quell opposition. When the Commons proved equally uncooperative, the King returned again to Parliament, ordering those who would support his bill to one side of the Chamber, and those who would oppose it to the other. Several of the bill's opponents immediately capitulated. Only in this way was a majority obtained and the Act passed.[65]

Next, Cromwell brilliantly exploited the grievances of the common lawyers in the Commons, especially those concerning heresy trials. The rationale of the common lawyers' attack on *ex officio* proceedings in the Church courts was their belief in the common-law rights of presumed innocents whom the bishops suspected of heresy, but whom no one would accuse. Sometimes these suspects were examined on interrogatories by the bishops or their commissaries, and made to abjure and perform public penance even though they had not yet been convicted by a Church court. Sometimes suspects were put on trial, but no accusers or witnesses were produced in open court, and the suspects were convicted on the strength of their answers to the bishops' interrogatories or on the basis of evidence collected in secret. All of this was technical: the extent to which ordinary MPs understood the debate is disputed. None the less it was widely appreciated that canon law treated suspects differently to common law. The Church courts assumed that there was no smoke without fire (More himself took this line in the *Debellation of Salem and Bizance*); the common-law courts worked on the assumption that suspects were innocent until proved guilty by the verdict of a jury.[66] Hall wrote of the debate in Parliament:

> After Christmas the xv. day of January the Parliament began to sit and amongst divers griefs which the Commons were grieved with, they sore complained of the cruelty of

the Ordinaries, for calling men before them *ex officio*: that is, by reason of their office: For the Ordinaries would send for men and lay Accusations to them of Heresy, and say they were accused, and lay Articles to them, but no Accuser should be brought forth, which to the Commons was very dreadful and grievous: for the party so cited must either Abjure or be burned, for Purgation he might make none.[67]

The Commons' grievances were collated in a string of petitions that culminated in the 'Supplication against the Ordinaries'. Elton argued that Cromwell had even drafted the 'Supplication' in advance of the session, assimilating copies of petitions on *ex officio* procedure prepared by Commons' committees in 1529 and 1531 into a composite document which was introduced in almost final form when Parliament reassembled in 1532.[68] Whatever the truth of this, the 'Supplication' was presented to the King on 18 March. At first, he seems not to have realized its significance. He passed it to Archbishop Warham for answer by Convocation, and no more was heard about it for weeks. It was the 'Answer of the Ordinaries' which fired Henry's anger. The clergy's reply was intransigent, and included a vigorous defence of the Church's independent legislative authority grounded upon Scripture and tradition 'which must also be a rule and square to try the justice and righteousness of all laws, as well spiritual as temporal'.[69] A supplementary 'Answer' even maintained that the Church's immunity from secular interference was ordained by God. In consequence, canon law could not be referred to the King for scrutiny and the royal assent, as the Commons had demanded. The King might offer advice, but only canons which did not concern the Catholic faith might be submitted for confirmation.[70]

Henry was incandescent. On 10 May, Edward Foxe was sent to Convocation, where he exhibited three articles on the King's behalf.[71] A stand-off ensued, during which Henry summoned Audley and a delegation of the Commons and informed them that the clergy were 'but half our subjects, yea, and scarce our subjects'. He complained: 'For all the Prelates at their consecration make an oath to the Pope, clean contrary to the oath that they make to us, so that they seem to be his subjects, and not ours'.[72] The remark that the clergy were but half the King's subjects was one of Cromwell's favourite phrases: transcripts of the conflicting oaths had been prepared by him in advance. Cromwell next exploited the King's mood to engineer the Submission of the Clergy to the Crown (15 May 1532). The exact sequence of events will never be known.[73] Henry, or more probably Cromwell, lost control of the House of Lords on 12 or 13 May, either over a bill to require Convocation's subordination to Parliament, or over a bill to prevent the bishops making arrests for heresy. Parliament was prorogued on 14 May, but the bishops were defending the Church's immunity from royal interference so volubly, they were almost doing Cromwell's work for him. Chapuys described the debates in the House of Lords on 13 May: he linked More to the resistance. The Lord Chancellor and the bishops, he said, 'oppose' the King. Henry was 'very angry, especially with the Chancellor and the bishop of Winchester, and is determined to carry the matter'.[74]

On 13 May, Convocation offered to compromise. Henry's response was to raise the stakes: once on 13 May and twice on the 15th. The *coup de grâce* came when Convocation was told that it 'always hath been and must be' assembled only by royal writ. A writ was issued for the prorogation of Convocation, where on the 15th a delegation of nobles appeared to demand instant compliance with the King's articles without any reservation. Archbishop Warham duly polled Convocation for its approval of the Submission. A majority in the Upper House grudgingly agreed. It is unlikely that a majority consented in the Lower House, but the vote was rushed and the motion deemed to be carried. Warham immediately announced the prorogation.[75]

On 16 May, the Submission was inscribed on parchment in a ceremony at Whitehall before commissioners who included Cromwell.[76] Convocation was not in future to assemble without the King's permission; no new canons were to be enacted without royal assent; existing ones were to be vetted by a royal commission; and any deemed prejudicial to the royal prerogative were to be annulled. More immediately resigned. We know the exact time: 3 o'clock in the afternoon. He went to Whitehall, where in the King's privy garden, watched by the Duke of Norfolk, he handed back the white leather bag containing the Great Seal to Henry VIII in a symbolic ceremony.[77] He asked to be allowed to withdraw from public life: in his own words, 'to bestow the residue of my life in mine age now to come, about the provision for my soul in the service of God'.[78]

The King (as More later claimed) was gracious. He discharged him affably, promising that for the service which he had previously given, 'in any suit that I should after have unto your Highness, which either should concern mine honour ... or that should pertain unto my profit, I should find your Highness good and gracious lord unto me'.[79] But More was skating on extremely thin ice. Appearances were all. His resignation and the Submission of the Clergy were lineally connected. This is the force of Elton's case. It was vital that the King did not appear to have been snubbed. The events had to be depicted as unconnected – hence the account of his resignation which More put out for public consumption.

How does this evidence tally with More's own account of his role in politics? *Pace* Elton, he had not opposed the King's divorce in public. There is no reason to question his letter to Cromwell on that point. Chapuys believed that he had 'spoken so much in the Queen's favour' in 1530 'that he has had a narrow escape of being dismissed'.[80] A year later, More admitted speaking 'boldly in those matters which concerned ... the Queen'.[81] The venue of what Elton called More's 'frank opinions in policy debates with king and Council' is never stated, and even if it was the Privy Council, a case can be made that these debates remained within the private and not the public sphere. The Privy Council's mandate was to advise the King and seek his approval for its confidential recommendations. Privy councillors were still the King's servants: it was not until Elizabeth's reign that the Privy Council began to assert itself as an independent political force. Elton would not agree. His view of the Privy Council equates it to the Cabinet under Gladstone or Disraeli, rather than to the *Conseil Privé* of Francis I or Henri II.[82] Parliament would be a different case, but the care with which More chose his words in both Houses in March 1531 is documented by Roper and Harpsfield, and independently corroborated by Hall.

Yet More was not obliged to keep silent concerning the attacks on the Church by the common lawyers, especially those relating to *ex officio* procedure in cases of suspected heresy. He 'opposed' the attack on the Church in the House of Lords on 13 May 1532. He defended the campaign against heresy in the *Confutation of Tyndale's Answer*, the first part of which had been published in January 1532 (see Chapter 6). On this agenda, he stood up for his principles, as Lord Acton had demanded. He was politically active, and he was in trouble with the King. As Chapuys reported, the King was 'very angry, especially with the Chancellor and the bishop of Winchester'.[83] Furthermore, More had almost crossed the line, since the issue of the Church's immunity was implicitly linked to the divorce: it was only when Convocation was subordinated to the Crown that the divorce plan in the *Collectanea satis copiosa* could become feasible.

In Elton's verdict More 'had been right at the centre of affairs' as Lord Chancellor 'and had not kept silent'. He had backed 'a losing policy, and when that policy was lost he had taken himself off out of sight'.[84] Later, to insulate himself as far as possible from reprisals, he had reported in his letter to Cromwell only that part of his role in politics that concerned the 'great matter'. On the narrowest interpretation he was 'safe'. The King, he reminded Cromwell, had promised that he would never 'put any man in ruffle or trouble of his conscience'.[85] By March 1534, when the letter was written and it increasingly began to look as if Henry might insist on More's conformity to the Act of Succession, whether the King would continue to keep his promise was the rub.

Elton's argument lacks the iconoclastic hubris of his later revisionism. Unlike his views of More's sexuality and entry into royal service, his interpretation of the politics of More's chancellorship has generally commanded assent. By this token, More was a politician, even if he failed. He was not merely 'caught up' in politics: he was deeply implicated. He was prepared to 'dirty his hands', to fight for his beliefs. It is a far cry from the notion that the politician's mantle was repugnant to a man of virtue. Politician or saint? For Stapleton, it is a straight choice. For the historian, it is a false choice. The recusant argument was invented because More lost the battle. He failed in his objectives. The immunity of the English Church from royal jurisdiction was abolished: the Submission of the Clergy wiped chapter 1 of Magna Carta off the statute book. From there, it was but the shortest of steps ideologically to the Acts of Appeals and Supremacy. Even Chambers concedes that More failed: his 'statesmanship had not compassed the ends he sought'. 'He failed to avert the violence he feared.' He 'opposed a revolution which had behind it Henry VIII, Machiavelli's Prince in action'.[86] From the vantage-point of Roper and Harpsfield in Marian England or that of the Catholic exiles in the Netherlands after 1559, it was better to rewrite history than admit to failure.

Nor is a final issue addressed by the legend. Did More really suppose that he could resign with impunity? Such an event cannot be read through the prism of Victorian constitutionalism.

More was sworn as the King's servant. He was politically active in the House of Lords as late as 13 May, three days before the Submission was engrossed on parchment and the Great Seal returned to the King. One simply did not 'resign' in the Renaissance. And certainly not suddenly, whether or not the Duke of Norfolk had interceded on More's behalf as Roper and Harpsfield claimed. As Machiavelli advised in the *Discourses*, to say 'I want to live quietly and without trouble', or 'I desire neither honour nor profit', will not do. There are only two practical courses of action. One must either avoid princes entirely, or else attach oneself closely to them. 'Whoever attempts any other way, even though he be a person of distinction, exposes himself to constant danger.'[87] By fighting for his principles, More exculpated himself from Lord Acton's charge that he had evaded his moral and political responsibilities as Lord Chancellor. But, as Machiavelli predicted and Elton later concluded, he also 'made certain that his conscience could not in the end be left private to himself'.[88]

Notes

1 Stapleton, pp. 76–7.
2 Stapleton, p. 77.
3 Stapleton, p. 78.
4 Stapleton, p. 78.
5 Roper, pp. 214–18, 224–6; Harpsfield, pp. 44–9, 56–62, 143.
6 Roper, p. 224.
7 Roper, pp. 224–5.
8 Roper, pp. 210, 225.
9 Roper, pp. 224–5.
10 Harpsfield, pp. 59–60.
11 Harpsfield, pp. 58–60.
12 Roper, p. 225.
13 Rogers, ed., *Selected Letters*, pp. 172–7.
14 Rogers, ed., *Correspondence*, pp. 491–501; Rogers, ed., *Selected Letters*, pp. 205–15.
15 PRO, OBS 1419.
16 Rogers, ed., *Selected Letters*, p. 207.
17 J.J. Scarisbrick, *Henry VIII* (London, 1968), pp. 163–97.
18 V.M. Murphy, 'The Literature and Propaganda of Henry VIII's First Divorce', in D. MacCulloch, ed., *The Reign of Henry VIII: Politics, Policy and Piety* (London, 1995), pp. 135–58.
19 Rogers, ed., *Selected Letters*, pp. 207–8.
20 Rogers, ed., *Selected Letters*, p. 208.
21 Rogers, ed., *Selected Letters*, pp. 208–9.

22 Rogers, ed., *Correspondence*, p. 495; Rogers, ed., *Selected Letters*, p. 209.
23 John Guy, 'Thomas Cromwell and the Intellectual Origins of the Henrician Revolution', in Guy, ed., *The Tudor Monarchy* (London, 1997), pp. 213–33.
24 Murphy, 'The Literature and Propaganda of Henry VIII's First Divorce', pp. 146–57; E. Surtz and V.M. Murphy, eds, *The Divorce Tracts of Henry VIII* (Angers, 1988).
25 Rogers, ed., *Selected Letters*, pp. 209–10.
26 Rogers, ed., *Selected Letters*, pp. 210–11.
27 R.W. Chambers, *Thomas More* (London, 1935), p. 354.
28 Chambers, *Thomas More*, p. 354.
29 Harpsfield, p. 222; Chambers, *Thomas More*, p. 236.
30 Chambers, *Thomas More*, p. 236.
31 For the abstracts from Simancas, see *CSPS* IV.i–ii, where the dispatches for More's chancellorship appeared in 1879 and 1883. For the abstracts from Vienna, see *LP* V ff. More's chancellorship is not completely covered in the Vienna archives, but the dispatches for 1531–2 were published in 1880. Further abstracts were published in G. Mattingly, ed., *Further Supplement to Letters, Despatches and State Papers Relating to the Negotiations between England and Spain* (London, 1940).
32 *CSPS* IV.i, p. 727.
33 *CSPS* IV.i, p. 727.
34 G.R. Elton, *Studies in Tudor and Stuart Politics and Government* (4 vols, Cambridge, 1974–92) 1, p. 166.
35 Elton, *Studies* 1, pp. 155–72.
36 G.R. Elton, *Reform and Reformation* (London, 1977), pp. 126–56.
37 John Guy, *The Public Career of Sir Thomas More* (Brighton, 1980), pp. 97–201.
38 G.R. Elton, *England under the Tudors* (London, 1955), pp. 122–6.
39 J.C. Holt, *Magna Carta* (2nd edn., London, 1992), pp. 448–9.
40 Elton, *Reform and Reformation*, pp. 137–8.
41 Elton, *Reform and Reformation*, p. 137.
42 Guy, *Public Career*, pp. 129–30.
43 John Guy, 'Henry VIII and the *Praemunire* Manoeuvres of 1530–1531', *English Historical Review* 97 (1982), pp. 481–503.
44 R. Rex, *The Theology of John Fisher* (Cambridge, 1991), pp. 162–83.
45 Guy, *Public Career*, pp. 136–48, 192–3.
46 Guy, *Public Career*, pp. 142, 198–9, 207–12.
47 Guy, *Public Career*, pp. 142, 150–1, 176.
48 D. MacCulloch, *Thomas Cranmer: A Life* (London, 1996), p. 578.
49 Roper, p. 228.
50 Elton, *Studies* 1, p. 162.
51 *LP* V. no. 171 (p. 84).
52 Charles Whibley, ed., *Henry VIII* [an edition of Hall's Chronicle] (2 vols, London, 1904) 2, p. 185.
53 *LP* V. no. 171 (p. 84).
54 Roper, p. 225.

55 Guy, *Public Career*, pp. 157–8.
56 Roper, p. 225.
57 Guy, *Public Career*, p. 159.
58 Elton, *Studies* 1, p. 171.
59 *LP* V. no. 216.
60 *LP* V. no. 287.
61 *LP* V. no. 120.
62 Guy, *Public Career*, pp. 159–60.
63 *LP* V. no. 171.
64 Guy, *Public Career*, p. 211.
65 S.E. Lehmberg, *The Reformation Parliament, 1529–1536* (Cambridge, 1970), pp. 137–8.
66 *CW* 10, pp. lxviii–xciv.
67 Whibley, ed., *Henry VIII* 2, p. 202.
68 Elton, *Studies* 2, pp. 107–36; Guy, *Public Career*, pp. 186–201.
69 Guy, *Public Career*, pp. 190–1.
70 Lehmberg, *Reformation Parliament*, p. 150.
71 Lehmberg, *Reformation Parliament*, pp. 149–50.
72 Whibley, ed., *Henry VIII* 2, p. 210.
73 M. Kelly, 'The Submission of the Clergy', *Transactions of the Royal Historical Society*, 5th series, 15 (1965), pp. 97–119; Lehmberg, *Reformation Parliament*, pp. 149–53.
74 *LP* V. no. 1013.
75 Lehmberg, *Reformation Parliament*, pp. 151–2.
76 *LP* V. no. 1023 (1).
77 *LP* V. no. 1075.
78 Rogers, ed., *Selected Letters*, p. 202.
79 Rogers, ed., *Selected Letters*, p. 202.
80 *CSPS* IV.i, p. 727.
81 *LP* V. no. 171.
82 G.R. Elton, *The Tudor Revolution in Government* (Cambridge, 1953); John Guy, 'The French King's Council, 1483–1526', in R.A. Griffiths and J.W. Sherborne, eds, *Kings and Nobles in the Middle Ages. A Tribute to Charles Ross* (Gloucester, 1986), pp. 274–94; John Guy, 'The Privy Council: Revolution or Evolution?', in C. Coleman and D.R. Starkey, eds, *Revolution Reassessed: Revisions in the History of Tudor Government and Administration* (Oxford, 1986) pp. 59–85; D.R. Starkey, 'Intimacy and Innovation: the Rise of the Privy Chamber', in Starkey, ed., *The English Court from the Wars of the Roses to the Civil War* (London, 1987), pp. 71–118; D.R. Starkey, 'A Reply. Tudor Government: the Facts?', *Historical Journal* 31 (1988), pp. 921–31.
83 *LP* V. no. 1013.
84 Elton, *Studies* 1, p. 172.
85 Rogers, ed., *Selected Letters*, pp. 209–10.
86 Chambers, *Thomas More*, p. 386.
87 M. Lerner, ed., *The Prince and the Discourses* (New York, 1950), p. 404.
88 Elton, *Studies* 1, p. 172.

|9|

Acquiescence or resistance?

Shortly before his imprisonment in the Tower, More played a trick on his family. He hired one of the King's messengers to visit his house at Chelsea while everyone was at dinner. The messenger knocked at the door, entered, and summoned More on his allegiance to appear next day before the royal commissioners administering the oath of succession. Pandemonium ensued. Some of the family wept or were distraught, while others maintained their composure. The latter More praised, but the former he reprimanded. 'In such ways did he prepare himself and his dependants for future misfortune.'[1] This report of the most macabre of More's practical jokes comes from Stapleton, who relied on Dorothy Colly, Margaret Roper's maid, and her husband John Harris, More's secretary. Even if the story is apocryphal, it contains a grain of truth: it corresponds to a passage in Roper's *Life*, where More told his family that if they would 'encourage him to die in a good cause, it should so comfort him that, for very joy thereof, it would make him run merrily to his death'. This was 'in the time somewhat before his trouble'.[2]

According to the earliest 'Lives', More started to prepare for his ordeal immediately he resigned the chancellorship.[3] His focus was on Christ's death and passion. By prayer and meditation, he sublimated the King's vindictiveness into heavenly visions of the blessings of martyrdom. He did not court martyrdom – that was forbidden by the Church. Throughout his 'trouble', he knew that if he did speak out unguardedly against the King's proceedings he was, in effect, committing suicide. When challenged by Cromwell as to why he did not cross the line, he answered:

I have not been a man of such holy living as I might be bold
to offer myself to death, lest God for my presumption
might suffer me to fall, and therefore I put not myself
forward, but draw back.[4]

While still on earth, he sought consolation in transcendent
glories beyond the reach of reason alone. It was these themes of
'comfort against tribulation' and 'otherworldliness' that he
amplified in his Tower writings, notably in *A Dialogue of
Comfort against Tribulation* (1534) and *The Sadness of Christ*
(1534–5).

More's wife, Alice, acquiesced in the break with Rome. She
took the oath of succession almost without demur. According to
Roper, she found her husband's objections on grounds of
conscience over-scrupulous.[5] Roper characterizes her as a
practical, matter-of-fact woman, who indulged her husband in a
manner similar to a parent gratifying a spoilt child. Whether
Alice was really so compliant, or whether Roper's characterization serves as a foil to that of More, is impossible to judge.
More's favourite daughter, Margaret, also took the oath, but
with the saving clause 'as far as the law of Christ allows', which
neutralized its effect.[6] More knew all along that he would be
denied a similar concession, even though the form of words that
the oath should take had not been prescribed by the Act of
Succession.[7] He told Margaret in the Tower that, before his
arrest, he had counted 'many a restless night, while my wife slept,
and weened that I had slept too, what peril was possible for to
fall to me'.[8]

This has a dramatic purpose. In Stapleton's metaphor of the
Church Militant, More, the 'brave soldier of Christ', prepared
himself 'carefully and religiously' for the 'combat'. 'After laying
down his high office, he betook himself to his home, free at last
from the slavery of the Court and public life'.[9] He 'cut down
rigorously the number of his household'. 'All his gold and silver
plate, which was worth more than £400, he sold.' He moved his
children to their own houses, keeping only Margaret and her
husband with him at Chelsea, but in the farmhouse on the edge
of the estate.[10] The image is of a condemned man settling his
affairs. Nor is it entirely false. The Submission of the Clergy was
the start of a domino effect. When Anne Boleyn became pregnant
in December 1532, the King was persuaded to back the radical
ideas of the *Collectanea satis copiosa*. Cranmer was recalled

from an embassy to Mantua and appointed Archbishop of
Canterbury. Anne and Henry were married in January 1533. And
Cromwell was soon drafting the instrument of schism, the Act in
Restraint of Appeals, which passed in April 1533. It ended
ecclesiastical appeals to Rome, which it ordered to be heard by
the English Church courts and provided that appeals touching
the King were to go directly to Convocation. Catherine of
Aragon's appeal was never mentioned; but it was the one which
the Act envisaged.

As to the Act's political theory, it proclaimed the 'imperial'
monarchy of Henry VIII of which the royal supremacy was an
integral part. The extent to which 'imperial' kingship and the
royal supremacy were interdependent was not yet fully
divulged,[11] but it was obvious to the Act's opponents. Cromwell's
preamble announced that England was 'an empire' governed by
'one Supreme Head and King'. The Kings of England since the
second century AD had enjoyed secular *imperium* (i.e.
sovereignty) and spiritual supremacy over their kingdom and
national Church. At the very least, the Church of England was
outside the Pope's jurisdiction. By way of authority, the Act cited
'divers sundry old authentic histories and chronicles' which
'manifestly declared and expressed' that England was an
'empire'. However, the Act's theory of kingship was modelled on
the prototypes assembled by Foxe and Cranmer in the
Collectanea satis copiosa. Since these were designed to justify the
royal supremacy, it was only a matter of time before Henry's new
title would be proclaimed.[12]

While Parliament debated the Act in Restraint of Appeals, the
bishops ruled Catherine of Aragon's marriage to be invalid. In
May 1533 Cranmer annulled it, and pronounced Anne Boleyn's
marriage valid. Anne was crowned Queen on 1 June in
spectacular celebrations lasting five days, which More refused to
attend. In July, Pope Clement VII threatened to excommunicate
the King, who replied by recalling his envoys from Rome and by
confirming the Act in Conditional Restraint of Annates passed in
1532. Once Anne was anointed Queen, the die, it seems, was
cast.[13] The first blood was shed with the attainder of Elizabeth
Barton, the Nun (or Holy Maid) of Kent, and five of her
associates (February 1534). Barton's prophecies had denounced
the King's divorce, predicting his deposition or death. Henry
insisted on a conviction for treason, even though the judges
advised that under the existing law no offence had been

committed. The only alternative to a trial at common law was an Act of Attainder. Henry next demanded that Fisher and More be included in the bill of attainder as accomplices. He had persuaded himself that both had 'advised' and 'counselled' Barton.[14] He even suspected More as the chief 'deviser' of these prophecies:[15] he therefore required his conformity. If More would not acquiesce to the divorce and Boleyn marriage, his name would remain in the bill: he would be attainted of misprision of treason (i.e. 'bare' knowledge or concealment of treason) for which the penalty was life imprisonment and loss of all property. In the end, More's name was removed from the bill, but only because he petitioned to be allowed to give evidence in the House of Lords. This request was refused, but he was allowed instead to prove his innocence to Cromwell and a committee of the Privy Council preparing the bill for Parliament.[16]

Within a month, the Act of Succession settled the inheritance of the Crown on the King's male heirs by Anne, or failing them, by a subsequent wife. To ensure compliance, a clause was inserted that any subject could be required to swear an oath affirming the 'whole effects and contents' of the Act.[17] It was under this rubric that the royal commissioners who assembled at Lambeth in April 1534 sent for More.[18] The Act made it misprision of treason to refuse the oath, although a legal conviction was still required. When More refused the oath, he was sent to the Tower but not immediately tried or attainted. He was allowed certain privileges in prison, and the King's aim was clearly to persuade him to change his mind.[19] But when More failed to succumb, he was convicted of misprision of treason by an Act of Attainder which claimed that, as well as refusing the oath, he had 'unkindly and ingrately served our sovereign lord by divers and sundry ways' (November 1534).[20] The penalties of the Act of Succession were now exacted, and Alice and the family reduced to penury.

If things had stopped there, More might have died in prison.[21] But the domino effect continued. In the same parliamentary session as his attainder came the Acts of Supremacy and Treason. The Act of Supremacy was declaratory. The King, his heirs and successors 'shall be taken, accepted and reputed the only Supreme Head in earth of the Church of England called *Anglicana Ecclesia*'. They 'shall have and enjoy ... as well the title and style thereof, as all honours, dignities ... profits and commodities, to the said dignity of Supreme Head of the same

Church belonging and appertaining'.[22] To indemnify these rights, the Act of Treason extended the scope of the law to encompass those offenders who had threatened the royal family even by words, or denied their royal titles (notably the King's title as Supreme Head of the English Church), or called the king a heretic, schismatic, tyrant, infidel or usurper.[23] William Rastell wrote: 'the bill was earnestly withstood, and could not be suffered to pass, unless the rigour of it were qualified with this word "maliciously"; and so not every speaking against the Supremacy to be treason, but only maliciously speaking'.[24] It was under this, the most controversial of the Acts of the Reformation Parliament, that the following spring More was interrogated by Cromwell and members of the Privy Council and their legal counsel (30 April–14 June 1535), and tried on 1 July for 'denying' the royal supremacy.

The earliest 'Lives' tell a consistent 'story'. More was a reluctant hero. He kept his opinions to himself. He retired to 'prayer and study' at Chelsea; but, despite being 'the spotless mirror of virtue and fortitude', he was 'attacked by various calumnies'.[25] He was the victim of tyranny. This is first signalled when Roper has More compare Henry VIII to Tiberius, the Roman Emperor who, according to the *Annals* of Tacitus, was corrupted by the flatterers at his Court.[26] More next foretells that the law would be subverted by 'a flexible council' ready to follow the King's 'affections' with the connivance of a 'weak clergy' – the road to tyranny described in the *History of King Richard III*.[27] The slant is strongest in Stapleton's *Life of Thomas More*, where an impious and sacrilegious King put More to death 'by a law which he had violated neither by word or deed'.[28] When imprisoned and 'harassed with a new oath', More 'neither said nor did anything'. He might certainly have spoken, but he did nothing. 'He merely kept silence for conscience' sake'.[29] Stapleton puts the idiom of the Church Militant at centre stage, but this is merely a metaphor for More's spiritual trials – it does not literally imply resistance to Henry VIII. Roper's equivalent is More's pronouncement on shutting the wicket gate at Chelsea for the last time: 'Son Roper, I thank our Lord the field is won'.[30]

Is this 'story' authentic? Or to put it in a more nuanced way, is an alternative possible? When More resigned as Lord Chancellor, he asked to retire to private life. Did he? Or was he still engaged in the public sphere? And once the domino effect began, was his standpoint one of 'silence for conscience' sake'? Did he keep his opinions to himself? Or were his affirmations to almost anyone who would listen that 'in the saving of my body should stand the loss of my soul', and that to swear the oath 'were peril of my damnation', equivalent to a condemnation of the King?[31] Is there any substance in the view that his standpoint amounted to 'obstinacy' as the King maintained?[32]

I argued in my introduction to the Yale Edition of the *Debellation of Salem and Bizance* that More's defence of the Church and clergy's legislative independence did not stop despite the Submission of the Clergy.[33] On the contrary, his literary works took up this cause in his retirement. Roper has no account of the episode, and Harpsfield discusses it only in the context of More's polemical skills.[34] In April 1533, More's *Apology* was published by William Rastell, followed in the autumn by the *Debellation of Salem and Bizance*. At the end of the year, More put the finishing touches to the *Answer to a Poisoned Book*, his confutation of George Joye's *Supper of the Lord*, which Rastell put out in January 1534[35]. More wrote his *Apology* in answer to Christopher St German's *Treatise Concerning the Division between Spiritualty and Temporalty*, a work reprinted at least five times between the end of 1532 and 1537. The *Debellation of Salem and Bizance* was a rebuttal of St German's *Salem and Bizance*, which replied to More's *Apology*. The controversy was ostensibly about the legalities of investigation and prosecution in cases of suspected heresy, but in reality was highly political. St German was the author of *Doctor and Student* (1528–30) and *New Additions* (1531), the first legal and constitutional defences of the supremacy of English parliamentary statute over all other types of ecclesiastical and municipal law and of the King's and Parliament's authority over the English Church and Convocation.[36] Whether or not St German should be counted as a royal propagandist in the period between the fall of Wolsey and the Act of Appeals, his books offered the earliest and most complete defence of the sovereignty of the 'King-in-Parliament'.[37]

More couched his *Apology* and *Debellation* as a critique of Protestant theology and its assumptions, a justification of his own actions against heresy as Lord Chancellor, and a defence of 'the very good old and long-approved laws, both of this realm and of the whole corps of Christendom', which laws the author of the *Division*, as More claimed, 'to the encouraging of heretics and peril of the Catholic faith, with warm words and cold reasons oppugneth'.[38] More denied that there was a conflict between canon law and common law, and upheld the validity of *ex officio* procedure. He was careful not to attack the Submission of the Clergy directly. On the other hand, his claim that the councils and provincial synods of the Catholic Church, of which the Convocation of Canterbury was one, had the power to enact laws which were made with the assistance of the Holy Spirit according to Christ's own promise, repudiated its terms. More insisted that canon law had been the business of councils and synods throughout Christendom since the earliest times: Christians should receive such laws without grudge or argument. So, even if the *Apology* and *Debellation* were not outright attacks on the Submission of the Clergy, they were the next best thing.

More could not have written these books while he remained Lord Chancellor. As a King's councillor and the highest officer of State, he was bound on oath not to resist the King's policy, however much he disagreed with it. Nor did he need to attack St German before he resigned, since St German's proposals for parliamentary legislation were not translated into royal policy before May 1532: this may even testify to More's success behind the scenes.[39] When More resigned, his promise was to withdraw from public life. His personal safety depended on that resolution. Yet, when the *Treatise Concerning the Division* was published, he could not resist a reply. He defended himself and the Catholic cause, but by his action, he returned to the public sphere. He was no longer in 'retirement' from politics. His *Apology* and *Debellation of Salem and Bizance* were politics by other means.

And they were treated politically. In January 1534, Cromwell organized a raid on Rastell's shop to investigate a report that More had written a reply to the *Articles Devised by the Whole Consent of the King's Most Honourable Council*, published in late December 1533 and distributed at Court two days after Christmas.[40] The *Articles* had been drafted by the Privy Council on 2 December. The work was a front-line piece of royal propaganda.[41] It justified the King's divorce and remarriage, denounced Clement VII's threatened excommunication of the King, and claimed that the Pope had no more authority than any other bishop outside his own diocese. It also accused the Pope of heresy, and asserted the right to appeal from him to a General Council of the Church.[42]

More wrote to Cromwell on 1 February to exculpate himself. He had written nothing since the *Articles* were printed. He had read the *Articles* 'once over and never more'.[43] The 'matter pertained unto the King's Highness, and the book professeth openly that it was made by his honourable Council'. It had been 'put in print with his Grace's licence obtained thereunto'. 'I verily trust', said More, that 'yourself will both think and say so much for me, that it were a thing far unlikely, that an answer should be made thereunto by me.' And he gave a clear undertaking: if it should happen that any book should be published under the King's or the Council's authority, even if the book 'seemed such as myself would not have given mine own advice to the making', yet 'I know my bounden duty'. More would neither 'make an answer unto such a book' nor 'counsel and advise any man else to do it'.[44]

The trouble was that by confuting the *Treatise Concerning the Division* and *Salem and Bizance*, More had already subverted the King's policy in the eyes of the regime. Some form of collision was inevitable. And the timing is significant. Within a month of More's letter to Cromwell, the bill for Barton's attainder was under consideration in Parliament. Roper and Harpsfield implied that More's name was inserted into the bill as retribution for his refusal to attend Anne Boleyn's coronation the previous June. But it is just as likely that it was the King's fear of a clandestine Catholic press campaign masterminded by Fisher and More that persuaded him to put both their names into the bill. However More perceived his role when he published his attacks on St German, it is likely that the King believed that his former Lord Chancellor had broken his trust.

As to More's standpoint in the face of the King's main demands, his position was established from the outset. As his letters make clear, to swear to the validity of the King's second marriage and thereby admit to the invalidity of the first, or to admit to the truth of the royal supremacy and thereby abjure the Pope, these 'were peril of my damnation'.[45] More never wavered in his view that acquiescence to either of these demands was impossible. No amount of influence or pressure could induce him to change his mind. When entreated to 'incline to the King's pleasure' by the Duke of Norfolk, he refused;[46] when justifying himself to the privy councillors drafting Barton's attainder, he had replied that he had 'plainly and truly' declared his opinion on the divorce to the King on several previous occasions.[47] The most that he was prepared to offer was to swear to the succession of Anne Boleyn's offspring in a form of the oath which he had personally vetted.[48] Otherwise, he was willing to disclose the scruples that prevented him from taking the oath, provided he received a licence by royal letters patent that discharged him from the penalties of the Act. If 'after the causes disclosed and declared', he would 'find them so answered as my conscience should think itself satisfied', he would then take the oath itself.[49] (More made this offer twice, but the idea fell into abeyance when Cromwell pointed out that a licence would not be sufficient to discharge him from the penalties of the Act.)

More told Nicholas Wilson, who had also been imprisoned for refusing the oath and who sought More's advice, that he had 'determined utterly' to 'discharge my mind of any farther studying or musing of the matter'. He had 'sent home again such books as I had saving that some I burned by the consent of the owner'. He was 'minded . . . no more to meddle of the matter'. As to the causes for which he refused the oath, 'no man wotteth what they be for they be secret in mine own conscience'.[50]

Despite these protestations, More's 'silence for conscience' sake' cannot be taken for granted. In a classic gesture of revisionism, Sir Geoffrey Elton challenged the legend in the final chapter of his *Policy and Police: the Enforcement of the Reformation in the Age of Thomas Cromwell* (1972). He argued that 'it is simply not true that More had consistently offered only silence'.[51] It would be more accurate to say that More had returned answers that were thought insufficient, which were tantamount to saying 'the King and Council both know well that I can never accept the supremacy, but I will certainly not say so now and fall foul of the statute'.[52] More's responses were 'safe', but 'also not really ambiguous or silent'. Again, 'there was never any doubt that More's so-called silence meant total disapproval, and in these statements he stopped short on the very threshold of a condemnation of the act'.[53]

By refusing to conform to Henry VIII's demands, More was accused of 'stubbornness' and 'obstinacy' by the King and (later) Cromwell.[54] As he told Margaret, 'My refusing of this oath is accounted an heinous offence, and my religious fear toward God is called obstinacy toward my Prince'.[55] This was a potentially sinister move, since 'obstinacy' implied malice and perhaps even seditious intent. Identical resonances may be found in More's *Apology* and *Debellation of Salem and Bizance*, where it was not Protestant opinions innocently held that were condemned, but 'obstinate' cases of heresy which were seditious and even treasonable.[56] More denied that he was 'obstinate'.[57] He attributed no fault 'either in the act or any man that made it, or in the oath or any man that sware it'.[58] He would be 'no part taker with no man', but leave 'every other man to their own conscience'.[59] He 'neither will dispute King's titles nor Pope's, but the King's true faithful subject I am'. He had 'fully determined . . . neither to study nor meddle with any matter of this world, but that my whole study should be upon the passion of Christ and mine own passage out of this world'.[60] He was 'the King's true faithful subject'. He prayed daily for the King 'and all his and all the realm'. 'I do nobody harm, I say none harm, I think none harm, but wish everybody good.'[61]

Elton's verdict seems yet another instance of his iconoclasm, since it contradicts the assertions of More's own letters which are, in turn, corroborated by Roper. 'Corroboration' is, however, the wrong word. The later images of Roper's *Life* are so closely modelled on the letters, notably those to Margaret, that they are to all intents and purposes the same source. Roper refers directly to Rastell's transcripts of the letters on two occasions.[62] In particular, he draws on Margaret's 'letter' to Alice Alington, her step-sister, which reports an extended dialogue between More and his daughter in the Tower,[63] but it is likely that this 'letter' was all along written by More. Its authorship has always been disputed.[64] As early as the 1550s, when Rastell first began to collate the sources to be included in his folio edition of the *English Works*, More's own circle were uncertain whether the real author was More or his daughter.[65] Modern scholarship has concluded that the 'letter' is almost certainly by More himself.[66]

More's letters construct the icon of saintliness and 'other-worldly' detachment that is his legacy.[67] But their contents are carefully contrived. They are not false or inaccurate, but they are rhetorically crafted. They are 'works of art', and cannot be taken at face value. More was forced to craft his letters artfully. His study and library had been searched. He knew that every document he wrote might be taken or read by his gaolers, perhaps copied and sent to the King, or used to construct an indictment against him. He asked Wilson to return a letter, once read, to him, 'because, although there is nothing evil in it, yet on account of the servant I would not wish them to discover it'.[68] Still more dangerously, he had written seven or eight times to Fisher, a fact which was used at his trial to support a charge of treasonable conspiracy, even though the letters had been burned.[69]

Despite all these risks, More continued to write to Margaret, justifying his 'silence' and his 'scruple of conscience' even though she had obtained permission to visit her father in the Tower. Surely the very existence of these letters is significant, when More was so careful to have his letters returned or destroyed and when, as in this case, the correspondents spoke face to face? Admittedly the frequency of Margaret's visits to the Tower is unknown. But at least some of the contents of More's letters, and the entire contents of the 'letter' to Alice Alington, repeat what Margaret already knew. From the beginning, these letters had more than one audience. The co-editors of the Yale Edition argue that they are '*art* in every sense of that word, for they show the most artful regard for the presence of two or three or more different audiences'.[70]

In which case we ourselves are an audience. It seems that, when writing to Margaret from the Tower, as previously when writing to Cromwell about his role in the divorce from Chelsea, More was putting his own version of the facts on record. And if further evidence is required, a comparison of the timing of More's letters with the chronology of his refusal of the oath, his belief that new legislation was imminent to punish his 'obstinacy', and his final interrogations, shows an almost exact correlation.[71] In every case, More wrote to Margaret within days of key political developments to set the record straight. Louis Martz, the leading authority on the Tower writings, argues that More is 'taking the occasion to clarify and stake out his position to anyone who might happen to read the letter'.[72] In other words, he is writing for posterity.

'Most artful of all' is the 'letter' to Alice Alington, which Martz believes was planned by More and Margaret, but whose art 'seems to be all More's'.[73] Its purpose is the defence of More's conscience in dramatic or dialogue form. 'Conscience' is the key word, repeated over forty times.[74] The action is scripted as a temptation scene. Margaret plays the part of 'Eve', which enables More to play himself and deliver set-piece speeches on why and how he is equipped to resist temptation. In a virtuoso perform-ance in which the tension is relieved by extracts from Aesop's fables, colloquialisms and laughter, More provides a rigorous analysis of his view of conscience. He gives an interpretation of the conflict of laws in Christendom and the role of the General Council of the Church that is close enough to the wording of his motion in arrest of judgement at his trial as reported by Roper that (retrospectively) it seems to be a critique of the royal supremacy.[75] The drama reaches its climax when More avows:

> But as concerning mine own self, for thy comfort shall I say,
> Daughter, to thee, that mine own conscience in this matter
> (I damn none other man's) is such, as may well stand with
> mine own salvation, thereof am I, Meg, so sure, as that is,
> God is in heaven.[76]

It is impossible at this distance to judge the extent to which More's Tower letters are designed to bolster an image and to what extent they can be read literally. Both forces are at play. Whatever else More intended, he meant to provide a defence against the charge of 'stubbornness' and 'obstinacy' and to shape an interpretation of Catholic 'conscience' which would be preserved as a perpetual memorial. That his mind worked in this way is shown by his conduct immediately after his resignation, when he crafted an image of illness and overwork in letters to Erasmus and John Cochlaeus that justified his 'retirement' to private life. More suffered from angina and regularly consulted his doctors, but his claim that he had 'retired' entirely on their advice stretched licence to its limit.[77] It was a case of what Tacitus or even Cicero in classical literature would have called 'prudence'. It was not deceit, but rather practical wisdom. There is no doubt that on this occasion More followed the advice of the classical rhetoricians to ally 'expediency' with 'honesty' in order to protect the reputation which he believed was rightly his. He sought to insulate himself from the political repercussions of rumours that he had been dismissed after a dispute with the King.[78]

Likewise, in his epitaph, composed within a month of the publication of the *Apology* which marked his return to the public sphere, More created a myth. He claimed that by his resignation, he had achieved what 'always he wished and desired': to have 'some years of his life free, in which he little and little withdrawing himself from the business of this life, might continually remember the immortality of the life to come'.[79] When More had his epitaph cut in stone and its text transcribed in a letter to Erasmus that he knew would be almost immediately published, he was protecting his reputation. Nor is this all. He also informed Erasmus that at the public installation of his successor, Sir Thomas Audley, in the Court of Chancery, the Duke of Norfolk, at the King's request, had confirmed that More's resignation had

been accepted 'unwillingly'. Not satisfied with a single announce-
ment, Henry had insisted that the same message be repeated at
the opening of Parliament in February 1533.[80] Once again, this
was the version of history which More intended for public
consumption.

More had little to learn from Erasmus about the techniques of
public relations. Yet, even from the versions of his letters which
were transcribed by Rastell, the case that he did not consistently
'keep silence' can be sustained. On the contrary, he staked out
three fixed positions between the spring of 1534 and the end of
his interrogations. The first concerned the status of national
legislation as compared to international law. He informed
Cromwell that 'since Christendom is one corps [i.e. body], I
cannot perceive how any member thereof may without the
common assent of the body depart from the common head'. 'We
may', said More, 'not lawfully leave it [i.e. the whole body of
Christendom] by ourself.'[81] The Acts of Appeals and Supremacy
were invalid, since Parliament did not have the power to declare
England's autonomy from Rome unilaterally. The point arose in
the context of a discussion of the papal primacy: More took a
minimalist position, since he held that the Pope's authority was
not superior to that of the General Council of the Church (see
Chapter 10).[82] He said that it would be of no avail to the King's
'cause' if, either by Act of Parliament or by declarations such as
the *Articles Devised by the Whole Consent of the King's Most
Honourable Council*, the Pope's authority or even that of the
General Council itself were repudiated. By this, he meant that
such declarations of autonomy were *ultra vires*: beyond the
power of either Parliament or the King, since the General Council
of the Church was superior to both on a matter of belief. A year
later, he reaffirmed the argument. He said that a man

> is not by a law of one realm [i.e. the Act of Supremacy] so
> bound in his conscience, where there is a law of the whole
> corps of Christendom to the contrary in matter touching
> belief, as he is by a law of the whole corps.[83]

The fact that there happened 'to be made in some place a law
local [i.e. in England] to the contrary' made no difference. Where
there was a conflict of laws between a local or national law and
a law accepted by the whole body of Christendom, the local or
national law, even if correct procedurally, could not bind a man's
conscience.[84]

More's second position concerned the Act of Succession. He was willing to swear a limited oath to the succession of Anne Boleyn's offspring. He could not swear to the remainder 'without the jeoparding of my soul to perpetual damnation'.[85] He could not be bound to change his conscience and 'conform it to the council of one realm, against the General Council of Christendom'.[86] To swear to the oath against the dictates of conscience 'were peril of my damnation'.[87] But this could only be so if the Act of Succession, and therefore the King's divorce and second marriage, were invalid by the law of the 'whole corps of Christendom'. In other words, More was saying that he did not believe Anne Boleyn's marriage to be valid by the law of matrimony which Christendom had enacted and that to affirm the marriage on oath in those circumstances was to commit perjury.

More staked out his third position on the issue of 'stubbornness' and 'obstinacy'. It was this potentially most dangerous charge that led him to offer to disclose his scruples provided he received the safeguard of a licence by royal letters patent.[88] When informed that this would not save him, he answered: 'But yet it thinketh me, lo, that if I may not declare the causes without peril, then to leave them undeclared is no obstinacy'.[89] This was an excellent debating point, but it led More to the edge of an abyss. His punch line was that 'this was one of the cases in which I was bounden that I should not obey my prince, sith that whatsoever other folk thought in the matter ... yet in my conscience the truth seemed on the other side'.[90] This was tantamount to saying that Henry VIII's legislation was sufficiently unlawful to justify civil disobedience. When More later repeated the argument, Cromwell's reaction was to warn that the King's 'displeasure' and 'suspicion' would be so great that he would now believe once again that More had been the chief 'deviser' of the prophecies of Barton.[91] It was this that led More to fear that new legislation was planned to deal with his case. He replied that, even if he died by such a law, 'I should die for that point innocent afore God'.[92] Again, these were not innocuous statements. They cut close to the bone, not least since the King claimed to be God's 'vicar' or deputy on earth after the Act in Restraint of Appeals, and yet More was appealing to God over the head of the King.

By the spring of 1535, the King held that it was More's example that was making men 'stiff' in their opposition to the Act of Supremacy.[93] Overall, the resistance to the Henrician

Reformation was limited before the Dissolution of the Monasteries and the Pilgrimage of Grace, but this was not the King's perspective. Even Cromwell was starting to grow impatient. He could see that Henry's mind was becoming a volcano. When it erupted, it could bring down others as well. Cromwell had hitherto treated More with compassion and fairness. He was quick to warn him that the King's licence by letters patent would not exonerate him from the statutory penalties of the Act of Succession, professional (and political) advice for which More told his daughter he was genuinely grateful.[94]

In June, Henry did explode. He announced that More's example had been 'occasion of much grudge and harm in the realm', and that, as More told Margaret, 'I had an obstinate mind and an evil [will] toward him and that my duty was, being his subject' to give a clear opinion on the Act of Supremacy one way or the other.[95] This was the beginning of the end. More was now commanded 'upon my allegiance' to 'make a plain and [de]terminate answer whether I thought the statute lawful or not'. He was either to '[ac]knowledge and confess it lawful that his Highness should be Supreme Head of the Church of England or else to utter plainly my malignity'.[96]

Yet More was undeterred. 'I answered that I had no malignity and therefore I could none utter.'[97] As to the substance of the Act, 'I could none other answer make than I had before made'. Finally losing patience, Audley and Cromwell replied that the King might 'by his laws compel me to make a plain answer thereto, either the one way or the other'.[98] One would have supposed that More would now fall back unreservedly on his strategy of 'silence'. Instead, he went on to say: 'it were a very hard thing to compel me to say either precisely with it [the Act of Supremacy] against my conscience to the loss of my soul, or precisely against it to the destruction of my body'.[99] His words can only be taken to mean that to accept the Act of Supremacy was to incur damnation, in which case the Act could not be valid, whether for the reason More had already given concerning the power of Parliament and the conflict of laws in Christendom or else for the reason given by Roper when describing More's motion in arrest of judgement at his trial that it was repugnant to God's law and the beliefs of the Catholic Church (see Chapter 10).[100]

The earliest 'Lives' claimed that More withdrew to the private sphere after his resignation. He retired to 'prayer and study' with his family at Chelsea until subjected to unprovoked attacks by a vindictive tyrant. When confronted with the King's demands for conformity, More kept his opinions to himself. In Stapleton's account, 'he neither said nor did anything'. He 'merely kept silence for conscience' sake'.[101] As More told Henry VIII when he returned the Great Seal, he meant 'to bestow the residue of my life in mine age now to come, about the provision for my soul in the service of God';[102] and as he reminded Cromwell, 'I had fully determined with myself neither to study nor meddle with any matter of this world'.[103] His sentiments were the truth, but not the whole truth. Perhaps he did sincerely mean to retire, but when St German's *Treatise Concerning the Division* and *Salem and Bizance* appeared, he could not resist a return to the public sphere. More's *Apology* and *Debellation of Salem and Bizance* were so political, it is hardly surprising that the shop of his publisher was raided. Later, when the domino effect was irreversible, More took up fixed positions that did not cross the line, but made no secret of his views, which were equivalent to a condemnation of Henry VIII. His responses were 'safe', but 'not really ambiguous or silent'. His statements signified 'total disapproval'.[104]

More's earliest biographers tell the 'story' that has become the legend. It is likely that the 'otherworldliness' of More's *Dialogue of Comfort against Tribulation* and *Sadness of Christ* was used to colour their accounts. Their narrative is not fiction, but it is not the whole story. An alternative is possible, one in which More resisted the King within the constraints laid down by the Catholic Church. Of these, the most important was that he should not court martyrdom. Unlike the religious life or the lives of 'civic duty' or moral absolutism that he had debated as a law student and in his Charterhouse years, martyrdom was not a vocation. But after his resignation, it was always an end in view. As he explained in his penultimate letter to Margaret, written a month before his trial, 'Howbeit if God draw me to it himself, then trust I in his great mercy, that he shall not fail to give me grace and strength'.[105]

Until God's purpose was revealed, More continued to play 'safe'. A symbolic incident has, however, been missed by everyone. At More's third interrogation before a committee of the Privy Council on 3 June 1535, Cromwell tried a completely different tack. He offered More 'an oath by which I should be sworn to make true answer to such things as should be asked me on the King's behalf, concerning the King's own person'.[106] More was forced to counter that he 'never purposed to swear any book oath more while I lived'. Cromwell replied that it 'was very obstinate if I would refuse that'. His reason was that 'every man doth it in the Star Chamber'.[107] The move was ingenious, since it now forced More to cross the line. As a former King's councillor, he knew that he could at any point have been put on trial in Star Chamber for contempt of the King. The reason this was not done was that the maximum punishment the Court could impose was a large fine or life imprisonment, penalties irrelevant to anyone already convicted of misprision of treason. But Cromwell had another purpose: in a Star Chamber trial, the accused was forced to answer to the bill of complaint or information of the Attorney-General, and to swear to the truth of his answer. He was then examined on oath upon interrogatories drawn for the Crown or the party.[108] This procedure was obligatory. Compliance was a matter of allegiance: More as Lord Chancellor had himself severely punished defendants who had been in contempt of court. By informing Cromwell that he would refuse an oath couched within this context, More had resisted the King. He did so for a very good reason. As he continued:

> I said that [what Cromwell had replied] was true but I had not so little foresight but that I might well conjecture what should be part of my interrogatory and as good it was to refuse it at the first, as afterward.[109]

The matter was dropped, because the King determined on a treason trial before special commissioners of *oyer et terminer*, who were appointed on 26 June. But Cromwell had made his point. More would have refused an oath in Star Chamber on a scruple of conscience. It was a step for which the monarchy was not prepared until the Court was abolished in 1641. There is no sixteenth-century parallel. In the next *cause célèbre* on a matter of conscience, Thomas Cartwright and the leaders of the Elizabethan presbyterian movement refused the *ex officio* oath in the Court of High Commission, but when hauled into Star Chamber, they took their oaths on their allegiance and swore to tell the truth in their examinations, even if they subsequently defeated the Crown procedurally.[110]

When More denounced Henry VIII outright in his motion in arrest of judgement at his trial, there would be nothing 'radical' about his view of authority and tradition in the Catholic Church. His argument would be as conservative in its dogmatic stance as it could possibly be. And yet, for a former Lord Chancellor to defy the King and claim freedom of conscience against the State was a revolutionary step by the standards of the sixteenth century. More stood at the crossroads of history. It is not for nothing that he became a paragon for those who later sought to emulate his stand even if they abhorred his Catholicism. But whose conscience did More think he was defending? This is the question which has most frequently exercised his biographers, and to it we shall now turn.

Notes

1 Stapleton, p. 159.
2 Roper, pp. 227–8.
3 Roper, pp. 227–8; Stapleton, pp. 158–9.
4 Rogers, ed., *Selected Letters*, p. 253.
5 Roper, p. 243.
6 R.W. Chambers, *Thomas More* (London, 1935), p. 312.
7 The defect was remedied by Parliament in November 1534. S.E. Lehmberg, *The Reformation Parliament, 1529–1536* (Cambridge, 1970), pp. 200, 203.
8 Rogers, ed., *Correspondence*, p. 530.
9 Stapleton, p. 158.
10 Stapleton, pp. 158–9; R. Norrington, *In the Shadow of a Saint: Lady Alice More* (Waddesdon, 1983), pp. 55–6, 76–7.
11 John Guy, ed., *The Tudor Monarchy* (London, 1997).
12 G.D. Nicholson, 'The Act of Appeals and the English Reformation', in C. Cross, D.M. Loades and J.J. Scarisbrick, eds, *Law and Government under the Tudors* (Cambridge, 1988), pp. 19–30.
13 Roper, p. 230; Harpsfield, pp. 158–9.
14 Rogers, ed., *Selected Letters*, p. 193.
15 Rogers, ed., *Selected Letters*, p. 236.
16 Roper, pp. 233–6; Rogers, ed., *Selected Letters*, pp. 193–201; G.R. Elton, *Policy and Police: the Enforcement of the Reformation in the Age of Thomas Cromwell* (Cambridge, 1972), pp. 274–5.
17 Lehmberg, *Reformation Parliament*, pp. 196–9.
18 Rogers, ed., *Selected Letters*, p. 217.
19 Elton, *Policy and Police*, pp. 402–3.
20 Elton, *Policy and Police*, pp. 402–3.
21 Elton, *Policy and Police*, p. 403.
22 26 Henry VIII, c. 1; Lehmberg, *Reformation Parliament*, pp. 202–3.
23 Lehmberg, *Reformation Parliament*, pp. 201–6.
24 Harpsfield, p. 229.
25 Stapleton, p. 152.
26 Roper, pp. 229–30.
27 Roper, p. 240.
28 Stapleton, p. 226.

29 Stapleton, p. 227.
30 Roper, p. 238.
31 Rogers, ed., *Selected Letters*, pp. 228, 237.
32 Rogers, ed., *Selected Letters*, p. 250.
33 *CW* 10, pp. xvii–xxviii; John Guy, 'Thomas More and Christopher St German: the Battle of the Books', in Alistair Fox and John Guy, eds, *Reassessing the Henrician Age: Humanism, Politics, and Reform* (Oxford, 1986), pp. 95–120.
34 Harpsfield, pp. 108–9, 127–30.
35 *CW* 11, pp. xvii–xxxvii.
36 John Guy, *Christopher St German on Chancery and Statute* (London, Selden Society, 1985), pp. 16–55.
37 G.R. Elton, 'Lex terrae victrix: the Triumph of Parliamentary Law in the Sixteenth Century', in D. Dean and N.L. Jones, eds, *The Parliaments of Elizabethan England* (Oxford, 1990), pp. 15–36.
38 *CW* 10, p. 9.
39 Guy, *St German on Chancery and Statute*, pp. 127–35.
40 N. Pocock, ed., *Records of the Reformation: the Divorce, 1527–1533* (2 vols, Oxford, 1870) 2, pp. 524–31.
41 Elton, *Policy and Police*, pp. 180–3, 206–9.
42 *CW* 10, p. xxvi.
43 Rogers, *Selected Letters*, p. 190.
44 Rogers, *Selected Letters*, p. 191.
45 Rogers, ed., *Selected Letters*, pp. 217–18, 227–8, 251–3.
46 Roper, p. 237.
47 Roper, p. 234.
48 Rogers, ed., *Selected Letters*, pp. 217, 222.
49 Rogers, ed., *Selected Letters*, pp. 220, 236.
50 Rogers, ed., *Selected Letters*, pp. 231–2.
51 Elton, *Policy and Police*, p. 415.
52 Elton, *Policy and Police*, p. 416.
53 Elton, *Policy and Police*, p. 416.
54 Rogers, ed., *Selected Letters*, pp. 235–6, 252.
55 Rogers, ed., *Selected Letters*, p. 235.
56 *CW* 9, pp. 135–40, 161–70.
57 Rogers, ed., *Selected Letters*, pp. 206, 236–7.
58 Rogers, ed., *Selected Letters*, p. 217.
59 Rogers, ed., *Selected Letters*, pp. 227–8.
60 Rogers, ed., *Selected Letters*, pp. 246–7.
61 Rogers, ed., *Selected Letters*, pp. 247–8.
62 Roper, pp. 238, 252.
63 Rogers, ed., *Correspondence*, pp. 514–32.
64 Chambers, *Thomas More*, pp. 307–13.
65 *CW* 12, p. lxi.
66 *CW* 12, p. lxi.
67 Rogers, ed., *Selected Letters*, pp. 215–42, 244–53.
68 Rogers, ed., *Selected Letters*, p. 234.
69 J. Duncan M. Derrett, 'The Trial of Sir Thomas More', in R.S. Sylvester and G. Marc'hadour, eds, *Essential Articles for the Study of Thomas More* (Hampden, CT, 1977), pp. 63–4.

70 *CW* 12, p. lix.
71 Rogers, ed., *Correspondence*, pp. 501–7, 540–4, 550–4, 555–9.
72 *CW* 12, p. lix.
73 *CW* 12, p. lxi.
74 *CW* 12, p. lxi.
75 Rogers, ed., *Correspondence*, p. 525.
76 Rogers, ed., *Correspondence*, p. 528.
77 Rogers, ed., *Selected Letters*, pp. 172–7.
78 Rogers, ed., *Selected Letters*, p. 179.
79 Trapp and Herbrüggen, p. 140; Rogers, ed., *Selected Letters*, p. 182.
80 *LP* V, no. 1075; Rogers, ed., *Selected Letters*, p. 180.
81 Rogers, ed., *Selected Letters*, p. 213.
82 Rogers, ed., *Selected Letters*, pp. 213–14.
83 Rogers, ed., *Selected Letters*, p. 252.
84 Rogers, ed., *Selected Letters*, p. 252.
85 Rogers, ed., *Selected Letters*, p. 217.
86 Rogers, ed., *Selected Letters*, p. 222.
87 Rogers, ed., *Selected Letters*, p. 228.
88 Rogers, ed., *Selected Letters*, p. 220.
89 Rogers, ed., *Selected Letters*, p. 220.
90 Rogers, ed., *Selected Letters*, p. 221.
91 Rogers, ed., *Selected Letters*, p. 236.
92 Rogers, ed., *Selected Letters*, p. 237.
93 Rogers, ed., *Selected Letters*, p. 247.
94 Rogers, ed., *Selected Letters*, p. 236.
95 Rogers, ed., *Selected Letters*, pp. 249–50.
96 Rogers, ed., *Selected Letters*, p. 250.
97 Rogers, ed., *Selected Letters*, p. 250.
98 Rogers, ed., *Selected Letters*, p. 251.
99 Rogers, ed., *Selected Letters*, p. 251.
100 Roper, pp. 248–9.
101 Stapleton, p. 227.
102 Rogers, ed., *Selected Letters*, p. 202.
103 Rogers, ed., *Selected Letters*, p. 247.
104 Elton, *Policy and Police*, p. 416.
105 Rogers, ed., *Selected Letters*, p. 253.
106 Rogers, ed., *Selected Letters*, p. 252.
107 Rogers, ed., *Selected Letters*, p. 252.
108 John Guy, *The Cardinal's Court: the Impact of Thomas Wolsey in Star Chamber* (Hassocks, 1977), pp. 72–117.
109 Rogers, ed., *Selected Letters*, p. 252.
110 P. Collinson, *The Elizabethan Puritan Movement* (London, 1967), pp. 417–31.

|10|

Whose conscience?

MORE   ... In matters of conscience, the loyal subject is more bounden to be loyal *to* his conscience than to any other thing.

CROMWELL And so provide a noble motive for his frivolous self-conceit!

MORE   It is not so, Master Cromwell – very and pure necessity for respect of my own soul.

CROMWELL Your own self, you mean!

MORE   Yes, a man's soul is his self![1]

This imaginary encounter from Robert Bolt's *A Man for All Seasons* illustrates the extent to which the trial of Thomas More ranks as one of the most frequently cited, but least understood, events in English history. It exemplifies our preference for the image of conscience that we wish to construct over and above that of the historical More who died for the Catholic faith. In most other respects, Bolt's representation of More's trial accurately reflects the spirit of the Tower letters and Roper's *Life of Sir Thomas More*. But the line, 'Yes, a man's soul is his self!', immortalized by Paul Scofield in the film version directed by Fred Zinnemann, indicates the impossibility of reducing to a sound bite the complexity of More's position as well as the inscrutability of his beliefs to a modern secular audience. Just as esoteric is the position he took on the papal primacy, which is as elusive to Catholics acclimatized to the reforms of the First and Second Vatican Councils as it is to Protestants or agnostics.

More's conscience has always been difficult to encapsulate. The most important stage representation before Bolt's, the

Elizabethan play of *Sir Thomas More*, did not even make the effort. An imperfect and possibly incomplete work, written about 1592 or 1593 by a group of dramatists of whom it is usually thought that Shakespeare was one, it was a play for the edification and entertainment of those predominantly Protestant Londoners who remembered More as 'a special lover and friend in the businesses and causes of this city', and as a friend of the poor.[2] More's trial was completely omitted from the script. The action moves from his (fictional) refusal of the articles for the King's supremacy in the Privy Council to his 'retirement' at Chelsea, and from Chelsea directly to the Tower and thence to the executioner's block. Once More has resigned as Lord Chancellor, the word 'conscience' occurs only twice in the dialogue. More thanks God when he arrives at the Tower that he can sleep with a clear 'conscience', because he cannot be disturbed by the cries of any widows or orphans wronged while he held the highest office in the State.[3] Again, he tells the Lieutenant of the Tower, 'I thank my God, I have peace of conscience, though the world and I, are at a little odds'.[4] As befits a society which had come to stereotype Catholic 'conscience' as treason and Protestant 'conscience' as 'precision-ism' or puritanism, the issue of 'conscientious' objection to the State or royal policy (whatever the moral or philosophical grounds of the scruple) was not one that could be confronted on the public stage except obliquely by means of classical or poetic analogies.

The rationale of More's standpoint cannot be evaluated outside the context of his trial, which must be reconstructed from evidence which is fragmentary, deceptive, and in the case of Roper's *Life* not contemporary with the events it is describing. One of the most important documents to have survived intact is the indictment, which set out the tenor of the Acts of Supremacy and Treason, before alleging that More 'falsely, traitorously and maliciously' imagined and conspired to deprive the King of his title of 'Supreme Head on Earth of the Church of England'. Eight treasonable acts were grouped under four counts.[5] The first count held that at an interrogation on 7 May 1535, More had 'maliciously' refused to accept the King's supremacy. To the questions posed by Cromwell and his legal team, he had replied: 'I will not meddle with any such matters, for I am fully determined to serve God, and to think upon his passion and my passage out of this world'.[6]

The second count claimed that on 12 May, More had written letters to Fisher, a known traitor, who was also attainted and imprisoned in the Tower for offences against the Act of Succession. More had upheld Fisher in his treasonable attitude and acquainted him with his own refusal to give an opinion on the Act of Supremacy. In these letters, More had described the Act in hostile terms. He had said: 'The Act of Parliament is like a sword with two edges, for if a man answer one way it will confound his soul, and if he answer the other way it will confound his body'.[7] On 26 May, More had written again to Fisher, advising him to answer spontaneously at his own interrogations and not to make use of any words or phrases from More's letters in case they became the basis of a charge of conspiracy.[8] Notwithstanding this advice, Fisher on 3 June had refused to answer on the supremacy, and had replied with words taken from More. He had said:

> I will not meddle with that matter, for the statute is like a two-edged sword. And, if I should answer one way, I should offend my conscience. And if I should answer the other way, I should put my life in jeopardy; wherefore I will make no answer to that matter.[9]

The third count charged that on the same day, More, when himself again examined, had 'maliciously' persevered in his silence, and had used the metaphor whereby the Act was likened to a two-edged sword. He had ended by saying: 'Wherefore I will make thereunto none other answer because I will not be occasion of the shorting of my life'. To conceal their treasonable conspiracy, More and Fisher had burned their letters.[10]

The fourth count was the most controversial. On 12 June, More in a long conversation with the Solicitor-General, Sir Richard Rich, was alleged to have admitted that the King might be accepted as Supreme Head of the Church of England, but denied that Parliament had the power so to declare him, thereby 'maliciously' depriving the King of his title. The conversation, according to the indictment, had gone like this. Rich had urged More to comply with the Acts, to which he had replied: 'Your conscience will save you, and my conscience will save me'. Rich then, protesting that he had no commission to examine More officially, put a 'case'. Supposing it were enacted by Parliament that Rich should be King, and that it should be treason to deny the same, what would be More's opinion? More admitted that Parliament had the power to make Rich King and that it would be an offence if he were to deny it. He could be 'bound' by such an Act, because 'he was able to give his consent to it'. But he said that the example was a 'light case'. He then put a 'higher case'. He asked Rich if an Act of Parliament could declare that God were not God. Rich immediately conceded that Parliament could not do this. Rich then proposed a 'case in the middle'. He cited the Act of Supremacy and asked why More should not accept this for the same reason as he had accepted that Parliament could make Rich King. More answered that the cases were not alike: 'because a King can be made by Parliament and deprived by Parliament', to which Act every subject 'may give his assent' in Parliament. On the other hand, a subject 'cannot be bound' to the royal supremacy, 'because he cannot give his consent to that in Parliament'. And he added that although the King was accepted as Supreme Head in England, 'yet many foreign places do not affirm the same'.[11] This is what the indictment claimed was said.

The commissioners of *oyer et terminer* who sat in King's Bench on 1 July 1535 were Lord Chancellor Audley, Cromwell, the Dukes of Norfolk and Suffolk, the Earl of Wiltshire (Anne Boleyn's father) and other privy councillors reinforced by the common-law judges. A fortnight or so before, essentially the same group had sentenced Fisher and a number of the London Carthusians to death for denying the Act of Supremacy.[12] The Attorney-General, Sir Christopher Hales, led for the Crown. He was assisted by Rich as Solicitor-General. This, like Wiltshire's nomination to the bench, was not regarded as improper, even though Rich was the prosecution's principal witness.[13] The prisoner had no copy of the indictment, no witnesses and no legal counsel. This was usual in treason trials. If a prisoner wished to demur to the indictment or raise a point of law, the courts were able to assign counsel, but otherwise the accused had to plead his own cause.[14] The responsibility for ensuring 'fairness' (whatever that meant in the circumstances) lay with the professional judges on the bench and with the jury. In More's case, the lack of counsel was no impediment, since he could equal or outshine the best legal minds. His disadvantage was that the jury appears to have been rigged. Its members included the same City draper and informer, John Parnell, whom Roper knew to have been among the aggrieved Chancery litigants who had 'most grievously' accused More of bribery before the King and Privy Council, and who bore him a grudge.[15]

More heard the charges against him for the first time when his indictment was read out (in Latin) and he was arraigned. The indictment is so long, it would have taken almost an hour just to read out.[16] He was offered the prospect of a pardon if he confessed and recanted, which he refused. He was then required to plead to the indictment. He first tried a professional argument. He maintained that none of the charges constituted an offence under the Act of Treason, since the elements of 'malice' required by the Act had not been specifically disclosed.[17] As Roper (who was not present, but received his information from three eye-witnesses) reported, if only those 'odious terms – "Maliciously, traitorously, and diabolically" – were put out of the indictment, he saw therein nothing justly to charge him'.[18] More's motion was rejected, most likely because the judges ruled that, if the offences cited had taken place, then by the presumption of the law 'malice' was disclosed, in the same way that most criminal offences were presumed to be 'against the King's peace', even if no force or violence was involved. According to Roper, More sought this ruling at a later stage of the trial, but procedurally it was an argument which belonged at the beginning.[19]

More then took a different tack. He argued that the first three counts of the indictment did not amount to a constructive offence under the Act of Treason. He asked the bench to rule that each should be quashed. He accepted the facts as stated in these three counts, but pleaded that even if his silence were construed as an 'act', the legal presumption was that of the civil law maxim, *qui tacet consentire videtur* – 'he who keeps silence seems to consent'. As to his alleged conspiracy in the Tower, Fisher was dead and the letters were burned. Since Fisher could not be called as a witness, the best evidence of the correspondence must come from More. By the rules of treason trials, the prisoner was not allowed to appear as a witness, nor to give testimony on oath. More, however, confirmed with an oath his own account of the letters, which, he said, had an innocent purpose. He conceded that Fisher might have used the metaphor of a 'two-edged sword', but argued that the similarity of their education and outlook might account for this. More did not deny that he himself had used the phrase, but submitted that its import was consistent with an innocent opinion relative to hypothetical legislation.[20]

This was brilliant extempore advocacy. It was as if all of More's rhetorical and legal training had prepared him for this day. It triggered the first of two electric moments, since the professional judges upheld his plea. The result was that three-quarters of the Crown's case suddenly collapsed. To the fourth count of the indictment, More pleaded 'Not Guilty'. This was not from choice. The right to challenge the validity of an indictment by claiming that it was insufficient in law, or that the Act upon which it was based was void, was not available at this stage of the proceedings.[21] More would vigorously challenge both the facts of the fourth count and the validity of the Act at later stages of the trial, but for the moment he had to accept that the fourth count was legally sufficient in the eyes of the bench, since he had already lost the argument that the word 'maliciously' did not require specific instances of 'malice' to be disclosed.

When More's plea was entered, Rich gave his evidence for the Crown. Exactly what happened is uncertain, but there can be no real doubt that the opinion of the Act of Supremacy he attributed to More was true in the sense that it closely corresponded to More's statements under examination in the Tower and in his later letters (see Chapter 9).[22] These were More's views: the difference is that previously he had couched them in ways which were entirely 'safe'. The controversy centres on the nature of the conversation between More and Rich. By a stroke of luck, an original memorandum giving a transcript of it is extant in the version as presented to Cromwell.[23] The document is damaged by damp and vermin and its text can be read only under ultra-violet light. Rich reported that More had said:

'A King [ma]y be made by Parliament and a King deprived by Parliament to which act any [of his] Subjects being of the Parliament may give his consent, but to the case ... [in question] a Subject can not be bound by cause he cannot give his consent ... [in] Parliament Saying further that although the King were accepted in England [as Supreme Head] yet most Utter [i.e. foreign] parts do not affirm the same'. Whereunto the said Rich said, 'Well Sir, God comfort you for I see your mind will not change, which I fear will be very dangerous to you ...'.

The clue is in the last sentence. When Rich left the Tower, he did not believe that More had said anything new. Or to put it

more precisely, the discussion had been privileged. As the indictment itself hinted, the conversation fell within the conventions of
'putting of cases', the protocol at the inns of court which
professional lawyers used to argue hypothetical 'cases' in
readings and moots. Sometimes these cases were very close to
real cases, but they were still treated hypothetically, since
otherwise a case that was still *sub judice* might be prejudiced by
an opinion expressed by a judge or senior barrister in the
audience. More and Rich began their conversation in this mode,
and when Rich proposed a 'case in the middle', he invited More
to continue the protocol. It would appear from his memorandum
that Rich had (at least initially) not attempted to pervert or abuse
the privilege.

Perhaps Cromwell knew better? More's defence relied on
professional privilege, which was subtle, perhaps too subtle for a
jury, especially one that had been rigged. Cromwell may have
thought it possible to secure a conviction on the basis of the
words that More had actually spoken, provided the jury were
directed that if More had spoken the words as alleged in the
indictment, he was guilty of treason under the Act. This is the
interpretation of J. Duncan M. Derrett, the legal expert and
historian who has written the finest account of More's trial.[24]

Or perhaps More slipped somewhere in his dealings with Rich
and crossed the line? This is the verdict of Sir Geoffrey Elton,
whose masterly study of Cromwell and the enforcement of the
Henrician Reformation ends with a reassessment of More's
interrogations and trial.[25] It is obviously possible. The objection
is that the original version of More's words as reported by Rich
in his memorandum does not disagree in the slightest with the
fourth count of the indictment. So, if More crossed the line, what
else did he say, and when?

Perhaps Rich panicked in the electric moment when the judges
quashed the first three counts of the indictment and he was
waiting to take the witness stand? Perhaps to help secure the
conviction that he knew Henry VIII expected, he embellished his
story, or else did not make it completely clear that the context of
his conversation with More was hypothetical? This is the view of
Richard Marius, More's most distinguished modern biographer.[26]

Or perhaps Rich committed perjury? This accusation is the
pivot of Roper's 'story' of the trial. Roper reports Rich as ending
his testimony with More's unqualified denial of the Act of
Supremacy. When Rich admitted that Parliament could not enact

that God is not God, More is said to have immediately retorted: 'No more could the Parliament make the King Supreme Head of the Church'.[27] According to Roper's version of Rich's evidence, the 'case in the middle' was never put.[28] If this was indeed Rich's testimony, it was perjury. As a report of More's actual conversation with Rich, it is completely improbable. It contradicts Rich's own memorandum, and if More had actually said what he is purported to have said, he would have courted martyrdom against the precepts of the Catholic Church. His entire standpoint and the arguments of his Tower letters would be incomprehensible.

Roper's accusation of perjury is reiterated by Harpsfield and Stapleton.[29] It has been disseminated in almost every subsequent biography of Thomas More. It is the one 'fact' about More's trial that everyone knows. It has offered generations of moralists and historians the epitome of the slippery Tudor bureaucrat with 'a soul as black as marble', against whom More's 'virtuous' reputation as a man who would die rather than tell an untruth or take an oath in vain can be indexed. But is it really true? Was this section of the trial genuinely misconstrued by Roper or his informants? Or is a charge of perjury inserted to provide a tabloid image of a Judas figure and of the blatant injustice of More's conviction that would echo down the centuries? The Victorian Catholic T.E. Bridgett was commendably cautious. His *Blessed Thomas More* recited the contemporary accounts and left readers to form their own conclusions.[30] Whereas R.W. Chambers in his classic biography did not even debate the question.[31] He merely quoted Roper's *Life* and chose to suppress the fact that the two contemporary European reports of More's trial do not mention perjury. The Paris Newsletter, which circulated in French on the Continent within a fortnight of More's execution, and which contains an accurate account of the trial as far as it goes, has nothing on the point.[32] Nor is perjury mentioned in the Latin report of the trial, which also circulated in Europe and became one of Stapleton's principal sources, even though the writer's intention was to blacken Henry VIII's name and extol More as the victim of tyranny, impiety and sacrilege.[33] Perjury would have been grist to this author's mill, which makes his silence all the more curious. It is a case of the dog that did not bark in the night.

In the climactic trial scene in *A Man for All Seasons*, Bolt follows Roper almost word for word:

NORFOLK	Repeat the prisoner's words!
RICH	He said 'Parliament has not the competence.' Or words to that effect.
CROMWELL	He denied the title?
RICH	He did.
MORE	In good faith, Rich, I am sorrier for your perjury than my peril.[34]

This image will never be erased from the collective memory of the English-speaking world. With the charge of perjury ringing in his ears, a charge that it is far from certain the historical More had ever levelled, Sir Richard Rich is consigned through the catflap of history.

In Roper's *Life* the clash is followed by More's attack on the character of the witness as a man of 'no commendable fame' and as a 'great dicer'.[35] There is no independent evidence of this speech. It is impossible to judge whether it is real or fictional. It is a remarkable coincidence that Rich is accused of the chief of the 'idle' pastimes that Erasmus claimed More utterly despised and which he proscribed in Book II of *Utopia*.[36] No one has ever disputed that Roper reinforced his 'story' of the trial with material appropriated from More's Tower letters, and Erasmus' letters were also used repeatedly for the *Life*. Nothing is certain. Except that, whether More sought to undermine Rich's credibility, or whether the speech as recorded by Roper is an embellishment, there is still no proof of perjury.

Roper went on to claim that the two assistants to Rich, Sir Richard Southwell and one Palmer, who were present in the Tower, refused to give evidence when called by the Crown as supporting witnesses. (In Bolt's account they are in Ireland on the King's business and unavailable.) During the crucial conversation, they had been 'trussing up' the remainder of More's books, which the Privy Council had ordered should be confiscated. It was presumed that they had heard what was said, but they claimed they had been too preoccupied to listen.[37] Roper's 'story' is repeated by Harpsfield, but omitted by Stapleton.[38] No other report of More's trial mentions this incident. If it occurred, it reinforces the claim that Rich committed perjury. But we simply do not know. The story may have a basis in fact. Or it may have been inserted to highlight the Crown's embarrassment that More's conviction was secured on the basis of testimony from a single witness, contrary to the legal presumption (later made statutory) that two lawful witnesses were required in treason trials.

When the Crown's evidence was concluded, More submitted that there was no case to answer. He maintained first that his conversation with Rich was privileged. He does not seem to have contested that the words as reported in the indictment were spoken. His defence was that the conversation lacked treasonable intent. He argued that the word 'maliciously' had been inserted into the Act of Treason by Parliament to cover such circumstances. As in his earlier motion, he claimed that proof of 'malice' was intrinsic to establishing the nature of the crime alleged. Extraneous events could not be coupled to the allegations in order to create a presumption of 'malice'. Lastly, he argued that the history of his relations with the King was one of mutual trust, and that even if it were alleged that he had withheld his assent to the Act of Succession, he had already been attainted by Parliament for this offence, and it was a principle of English law that 'no man can be punished twice for the same offence'.[39]

Every one of these submissions was overruled. The jury was then sent to consider its verdict. They returned after a quarter of an hour with the verdict of 'Guilty'.[40] It is likely they were directed that the case turned on a simple issue of fact. Did More speak the words as alleged with Rich? If so, the context of the conversation was irrelevant.[41] What followed was the second electric moment of the trial. When a 'Guilty' verdict was received, it was open to the prisoner to attack the indictment on the grounds that it was insufficient in law or because the Act upon which it was based was void. This had not been possible earlier, but now the moment had arrived. And this is exactly what More did. He now spoke out unequivocally.[42]

Audley fumbled with the procedure. He began to pass sentence, but More interposed and began his motion in arrest of judgement. He argued that his indictment was invalid because the Act of Supremacy was repugnant to God's law and the beliefs of the Catholic Church: ' "Forasmuch as, my lord," quoth he, "this indictment is grounded upon an act of Parliament directly repugnant to the laws of God and His Holy Church . . . it is therefore in law, amongst Christian men, insufficient to charge any Christian man." '[43] The King cannot be Supreme Head of the Church. Human positive law, which included common law and parliamentary statutes, had to be consistent with God's law and the law of reason. The law of reason conformed to God's law and the law of nature, and was recognized by jurists as moral or fundamental law. The theory had been comprehensively expounded in the works of St Thomas Aquinas. When human law went against reason, it was void, and an unreasonable Act of Parliament was void.

When Audley interjected that the Act of Supremacy had been approved by the bishops, universities and 'best learned of this realm', More addressed the issue of competence. He answered that Parliament's competence was to be judged by God's law and the law of reason as determined by a competent majority. And a competent majority was framed not by reference merely to the 'well-learned bishops' and 'virtuous men' who happened to be alive at any one time in any particular State. It was framed by reference to Catholic tradition since the time of the Apostles: both those who were alive and those who were dead, 'of whom many be now holy saints in heaven', who had kept the faith while they lived.[44]

According to the European reports of the trial, More cited some contemporary parallels. He argued that, despite threats to establish national churches on the Continent, no actual steps had resulted. He named several countries, notably France, which had failed to break with Rome despite Henry VIII's encouragement. The inference must be that moral or fundamental law had dissuaded these countries from schism.[45] Hearing this, the Duke of Norfolk, who had recently returned from just such a fruitless embassy to France, interrupted to claim that More was showing his resolve to frustrate the King's policy, thereby demonstrating the 'malice' established by the verdict.[46] More denied that his intentions were malicious. His words were necessary if he was to 'discharge' his conscience.[47]

More next addressed the conflict of laws. He held that 'this realm, being but one member and small part of the Church' could not legislate in a manner 'disagreeable with the general law of Christ's universal Catholic Church'.[48] A local or national law could not override the general law of Christendom in a matter of belief. The fact that there happened 'to be made in some place a law local to the contrary' made no difference. 'No more than the City of London, being but one poor member in respect of the whole realm, might make a law against an act of Parliament to bind the whole realm'.[49] This was the point More had made in his penultimate letter to Margaret Roper, where he argued that a man is not by a law of one realm so bound in his conscience, where there is a law of the whole corps of Christendom to the contrary in matter touching belief, as he is by a law of the whole corps.[50]

More's motion did not mince its words. In both Roper's and the European version, it alluded to the King's coronation oath, and implied that Henry VIII had committed perjury by enacting the Submission of the Clergy and the Reformation statutes when he was sworn to defend the Church and uphold the legislative independence of the Church and clergy as guaranteed by chapter 1 of Magna Carta.[51]

But the crux was 'conscience': the point of intersection for the issues of competence and the conflict of laws. More asserted that neither individuals nor national States were competent to determine what someone should believe in 'conscience'. Individuals or national assemblies had no status in the matter. Otherwise, there would be anarchy. 'Conscience' should conform to Catholic tradition as this had evolved since the time of the Apostles. The General Council of the Church was the primary point of reference. All the reports are sketchy at this point, but More had explained his rationale in the 'letter' sent by his daughter to Alice Alington.[52] In a doubtful case such as the Act of Supremacy, no one could be compelled to swear on oath that the 'local' law of a 'particular' part of Christendom was lawfully made 'standing his own conscience to the contrary', nor could they be bound to change their conscience to conform to that law, except in cases where the General Council of the Church reached a decision in favour of that law. The only alternative was in cases where 'a general faith grown by the working of God universally through all Christian nations' reached a consensus that was equivalent to a decision of the General Council.[53] More's anti-Lutheran writings had considered the 'general faith' of Christendom as the correlative or equivalent of the decrees of the General Council of the Church. He meant that the 'explicit' and 'implicit' consensus of the General Council and of the faithful was the only infallible sign of the authenticity of a dogmatic position. The Act of Supremacy lacked this 'consensus'. And so, More's motion concluded, 'therefore am I not bound, my lord, to conform my conscience to the council of one realm against the General Council of Christendom'.[54]

Audley seems to have been dumbfounded. At any rate, he stumbled. There was no precedent in living memory for such a plea. Not only was More's motion a virtuoso legal performance, it raised moral and philosophical issues of the highest order. Finally, Audley turned to the Lord Chief Justice, Sir John Fitzjames, and asked whether the indictment was sufficient in law or not. According to Roper, he answered, ' "My lords all, by St Julian" (that was ever his oath), "I must needs confess that if the act of Parliament be not unlawful, then is not the indictment in my conscience insufficient." '[55] More's motion was rebutted with a double negative; what alternative was there as King's Bench was the King's court? The presumption was that Acts of Parliament were both reasonable and lawful. More's adversary in 1533, Christopher St German, when discussing 'the power of the Parliament' in *New Additions*, had made the same presumption. He had given a similar answer to the equivalent of More's motion:

> I hold it not best to reason or to make arguments whether they [i.e. Parliament] had authority to do that they did or not. For I suppose that no man would think, that they would do any thing, that they had not power to do.[56]

When More's motion was rejected, sentence was passed. A prisoner on a charge of treason was entitled to the court's protection, and was allowed to appeal for clemency. Such a plea was unlikely to succeed. But More never missed an opportunity to speak:

> More have I not to say, my lords, but like as the blessed apostle Saint Paul, as we read in the Acts of the Apostles, was present and consented to the death of Saint Stephen, and kept their clothes that stoned him to death, and yet be they now both twain holy saints in heaven, and shall continue there friends forever, so I verily trust, and shall therefore right heartily pray, that though your lordships have now here in earth been judges to my condemnation, we may yet hereafter in heaven merrily all meet together, to our everlasting salvation.[57]

For almost the last time, More laid down a marker for posterity. He built on the imagery of the *Dialogue of Comfort against Tribulation*, which he had written in the Tower. At his trial before the high priest, St Stephen had witnessed the heavens open and seen Jesus at God's right hand. When he pointed upwards, the people covered their ears at his blasphemy and led him outside the gates of the city to be stoned. St Paul, before his conversion to Christianity on the road to Damascus, was a persecutor. He was present and consented to St Stephen's death. In the *Dialogue of Comfort*, More argued that the 'faithful wise man' should not dread the prospect of a shameful death, since how could it not be 'but glorious to die for the faith of Christ'?[58] God had beheld St Stephen's martyrdom and 'verily looked on'.[59] More's prayer for his judges must have made them feel uncomfortable, but the sting was in the tail. As well as hinting at his own martyrdom and offering them the prospect of meeting him 'merrily' in heaven, the prayer implied that, like St Paul before his conversion, the judges were themselves persecutors. They had been 'present and consented', but like St Paul would eventually have the scales lifted from their eyes.

No one who attended More's trial could possibly have forgotten it. And yet, what exactly was it that people remembered? The author of the Paris Newsletter depicts More's motion in arrest of judgement as delivered 'for the declaration of my conscience and satisfaction of my soul'.[60] The Newsletter upholds the tradition that More was taking a stand against Henry VIII's tyranny. Whereas Sir John Spelman, one of the professional judges of King's Bench, who annotated the trial in his notebook, reinforces Roper's impression that More's speech was a legal plea addressed to the insufficiency of the indictment and the lack of competence of the Act of Supremacy. He wrote: '[More was] found guilty, and the said Chancellor gave judgment. And the said More stood firmly upon the statute of 26 Hen. 8, for he said that the Parliament could not make the king Supreme Head, etc.'[61] Spelman may perhaps have found it reassuring that More in the end spoke out unequivocally, thereby removing any residual doubt in the minds of the judges that he had denied the royal supremacy. By contrast, More's definition of 'conscience' did not seem to interest him.

In the twentieth century, Bolt's *A Man for All Seasons* has created the myth that More's motion in arrest of judgement was a defence of individual conscience against the State. Plainly it was not. It was a defence of an individual's right to frame his or her own 'conscience', but the operative framework was not that of individual opinion. Quite the reverse. The Church was never to be judged by such opinions. The view that individuals could read the Bible and make judgements about religious doctrine and the

Church was a Protestant position. Catholic 'conscience' was to be anchored to the 'consensus' or 'common faith' of Christendom, whether this was 'explicit' in the decrees of the General Council of the Church or 'implicit' in the 'general faith grown by the working of God universally through all Christian nations'.[62]

More's agenda was rooted in his view of authority and tradition. The key was the Catholic oral tradition which had been handed down from the Apostles and safeguarded by the Church. His anti-Lutheran writings taught him that Catholic tradition not expressly warranted by Scripture was as valid as if documented in Scripture, providing it was authenticated by the Church. The judge of what was authenticated by the Church was 'consensus'. The Church was not to be judged by the opinions of individuals, even if their beliefs were rooted in what they held to be Scripture. Only the 'consensus' of the Church could canonize Scripture. And in any case, the oral tradition was equally valid.[63] God had revealed himself to his Church 'partly by writing, partly without, and that in those two manners the revelations of God still abide and continue in his church'.[64] The Holy Spirit inspires consent, whereupon 'we believe as well the church concerning God's words taught us by the church and by God [en]graved in men's hearts without scripture, as his holy words written in his holy scripture'.[65]

The effect of More's view of 'conscience' is demonstrated by his verbal tussle with Audley and Cromwell in the Tower on 3 June 1535. They told him that in the last resort, the King might compel him 'by his laws' to make a 'plain answer' to the royal supremacy 'either the one way or the other'.[66] More said he would not 'dispute the King's authority', but 'it seemed to me somewhat hard'.[67] The implication in a professional context was that a new Act which compelled him to state his true opinion might be judged contrary to the law of reason by the courts and therefore void. It might be considered as an abuse of Parliament. It might trigger a *cause célèbre* couched exactly in the terms of More's motion in arrest of judgement.

Cromwell retorted that this scruple had not weighed in More's judgement when he and the bishops had examined suspected heretics while he was Lord Chancellor. The bishops deployed the *ex officio* oath to compel suspects to answer, for instance, 'whether they believed the Pope to be head of the Church'. An oath was 'used to compel them to make a precise answer'. Where

was the difference? Why could the King, now that the Act of
Supremacy was passed, not 'compel men to answer precisely to
the law here as they did then concerning the Pope'?[68]
More had his rejoinder ready. The two cases were not alike.
The *ex officio* oath could only be used in conformity with the
received doctrines of the Catholic Church. 'I said there was a
difference between those two cases because that at that time as
well here as elsewhere through the corps of Christendom the
Pope's power was recognized for an undoubted thing.' It was not
'a thing agreed in this realm and the contrary taken for truth in
other realms'.[69] In the absence of an 'explicit' or 'implicit'
Catholic 'consensus', there could be no requirement for a man to
be 'bound' in conscience.

Cromwell's riposte was devastating. 'They were as well burned
for the denying of that as they be beheaded for denying of this,
and therefore as good reason to compel them to make precise
answer to the one as to the other.'[70] But More could not see the
point. He thought the cases were morally different. 'Obstinate'
heretics were 'well burned'.[71] He had repeatedly said this. They
were not allowed consciences, since they had deviated from the
authority and tradition of the Catholic Church. Individual
opinions of conscience were not admissible. They were not
protected by the law of reason. As More concluded:

> the reasonableness or the unreasonableness in binding a
> man to precise answer standeth not in the respect or differ-
> ence between beheading or burning, *but because of the
> difference in charge of conscience*, the difference standeth
> between beheading and hell.[72]

Yet, if More repudiated the King's supremacy, neither would
he affirm the Pope's. He had always doubted that the papacy was
ordained by Christ to govern Christendom absolutely. The
superior authority he recognized in the Church was the General
Council. More was a papal minimalist; it was Fisher who was the
maximalist. This was already true when the *Defence of the Seven
Sacraments* was compiled. In his sermon at the first public
condemnation of Luther at St Paul's in 1521, Fisher held that the
Pope was the head of Christ's universal Church *jure divino* ('by
the law of God'). In his *Refutation of Martin Luther*, he argued
that the Pope, like Christ, possessed the plenitude of power.
While not expressly committing himself to papal infallibility
(which was not decided until the First Vatican Council in 1870),

Fisher exalted the Pope's role in the Church in extravagant language.[73] The Pope was above the General Council; he had 'supreme authority' within the Church – no one on earth was superior.[74]

More's position was different. He avoided identifying authority in the Church with any one individual.[75] The Pope was not above the General Council, which could depose an unworthy Pope.[76] This is not to say that More's conciliarism was unqualified. He insisted that the General Council should be 'lawfully' assembled and held that the Pope could only be deposed for reasons of 'incorrigible mind and lack of amendment'.[77] His position was nuanced. Although the Pope was not above the General Council, the Council was not itself above the Pope, unless the Pope had sinned and failed to acknowledge correction. In the last resort, More saw the General Council and the Pope as interdependent.[78] And there was scarcely a practical alternative, since the Council met infrequently. Whether a valid Council had been held since the fourth Lateran Council of 1215 was itself an inflammatory issue in the Church, since the papacy refused to recognize the Councils convoked during the Great Schism (1378–1415), and the fifth Lateran Council of 1512–17 was poorly attended.

Six weeks before More refused the oath of succession, he was approached by Cromwell about the papal primacy.[79] After their discussion, More put his response on record in his usual way. 'As touching ... the primacy of the Pope', he wrote, 'I nothing meddle in the matter.' The idiom signalled jeopardy, but not 'silence'. (As yet, the Act of Supremacy was eight months away.)

> Truth it is ... I was myself some time not of the mind that the primacy of that see should be begun by the institution of God, until that I read in that matter those things that the King's Highness had written in his most famous book against the heresies of Martin Luther.[80]

More's argument that the King had taught him the divine origins of the papacy was a palpable hit. As he explained, the case was addressed by the Greek and Latin Church Fathers, and by the decrees of General Councils. He had studied the evidence for a decade after assisting Henry with the *Defence*. Was the papacy ordained by God? On this, the authorities disagreed. In the end, More had reasoned that the case in favour was inconclusive, but the case on the other side was too weak for the dogma to be denied. Or, at any rate, denied in 'conscience'. To deny the divine origins of the papal primacy as a matter of 'conscience', as opposed merely to debating the subject as an academic question, would put him 'in right peril'.[81] But, More innocently asked, why did it matter? At the very least the papal primacy was 'instituted by the corps of Christendom and for a great urgent cause in avoiding of schisms'.[82] That the primacy existed for reasons of human convenience was unquestionable. It had been corroborated 'by continual succession more than the space of a thousand year at the least'.[83]

Allowance has to be made for More's justifiable caution. This was a dangerous issue. Without a doubt, he had upheld the divine origins of the papacy but his standpoint was always that of the 'primacy', and not the 'supremacy', of the Pope. It is a fine, but critical, distinction. According to More, the Pope's role was to provide the pastoral direction of the Church and ensure the right operation of its representative institutions, of which the General Council was the chief. In theory, the General Council was superior. As it was so rarely convoked, the Pope was the legitimate authority in the Church. But More denied the Pope the plenitude of power: the 'supreme authority' under God which ensured that nothing and no one else on earth was superior. He assured Cromwell that he had never placed the Pope above the General Council.[84] He also offered his support for Henry VIII's appeal to the General Council in his divorce suit, which he wished all 'comfortable speed' – this despite the fact that the King's appeal flew in the teeth of the papal bull *Execrabilis*, which Pope Pius II had promulgated in 1460, and which insisted under pain of excommunication that no litigant was allowed to appeal from the Pope to a future General Council of the Church.[85]

More's rejection of the Act of Supremacy must have pushed him closer towards Rome. By the time of his trial, he may have reached a position that was closer to that of Fisher, but there is no firm evidence that he did. His final views on the papacy are unknown. The topic is a complete blank. He did not mention the Pope's authority in his later letters to his daughter, and there is no reference to his opinion of the papal supremacy at his trial beyond what Roper reports. According to the *Life*, he claimed that the 'supreme government' of the Church belonged 'rightfully . . . to the See of Rome, a spiritual pre-eminence by the mouth of Our Saviour himself, personally present upon the earth, only to Saint Peter and his successors ... by special prerogative granted'.[86] Roper attributed to More an uncompromising belief in the papal 'supremacy'. This is almost bizarre when one takes into account the fact that no one else noticed it. He conflated More's views with Fisher's. He was not present at More's trial. He wrote in Mary's reign, when the royal supremacy had been abrogated and the Pope's authority restored. His version of this section of More's motion in arrest of judgement is uncorroborated. It is striking that the two contemporary European reports do not discuss this, the topic which would have been of the greatest interest on the Continent.[87] Roper's attributed speech is almost certainly a fiction. It is not what More said, it is what he ought to have said.

But it was enough. The Spanish sailors on board the Armada of 1588 were promised the aid of the saints and martyrs of England, including Thomas More.[88] Even as they sailed up the Channel, Stapleton reaffirmed that More was martyred in the cause of the Pope's 'supremacy'.[89] The legend was already entrenched. It will never be dispelled. In the Tower, More's commitment to the Pope probably hardened. There was nowhere else to go. By extrapolation, we might affirm that he died for the Pope; but he was a lukewarm papalist. To ignore these nuances is to obliterate the significance of his view of the authority of the General Council of the Church, the cornerstone of his theory of 'consensus', which is, in turn, the key to his definition of 'conscience'.

In the Preface to *A Man for All Seasons*, Bolt imagines More as a man who possesses 'an adamantine sense of his own self'. He knows exactly how far he will bend; he becomes unyielding when asked 'to retreat from that final area where he located his self'. Thereafter, this 'supple, humorous, unassuming and sophisticated person set like metal'. He could 'no more be budged than a cliff'.[90] All this makes for thrilling drama, but entirely misrepresents the way that the historical More understood his 'conscience'. At one point, Bolt has More say to the Duke of Norfolk: 'what matters to me is not whether it's true or not but that I believe it to be true, or rather not that I *believe* it, but that *I* believe it'.[91]

This definition of conscience is not More's. It is the one which the authors of the *Collectanea satis copiosa* created for Henry VIII in the later stages of his divorce suit, and which the King was soon citing vigorously against the Pope.[92] Henry argued that the Pope could be lawfully resisted when a man was guided by 'conscience' or 'private law' as written in his heart by the Holy Spirit. In the public sphere, the moral law was 'established and confirmed' by the agreement of all nations and was perpetual.[93] It was the foundation of 'public law'. This element of Henry's argument is not so far from More's. But Henry also maintained that the Holy Spirit could inscribe the moral law on the hearts of individuals. The result was 'private law', which 'is of more dignity than the public law'.[94] It was 'private law' which moved an individual's 'conscience'. And when a man was 'moved by the private law of his conscience', there was 'no reason' why 'he should be bound to the public law'.[95] 'Conscience' set a man free. Its dictates must be obeyed, especially when a man discovered that his marriage was against God's law! A man whose 'private conscience' told him that his marriage was unlawful was 'bound to make a divorce with her'. As the logic was encapsulated, 'we must obey our conscience: and in other things the church'.[96]

That it was Henry VIII, not Thomas More, who believed that 'Yes, a man's soul is his self!' and that 'what matters to me is . . . that *I* believe it' is perhaps the ultimate irony. Roles are reversed and 'history' is seemingly rewritten. The trouble with any discussion of More's stand against Henry VIII is that we always seem to be standing in a hall of mirrors.

Notes

1 R. Bolt, *A Man for All Seasons* (London, 1960), pp. 92–3.
2 W.W. Greg, ed., *The Book of Sir Thomas More* (rev. edn., Oxford, 1961), pp. 1–93; R.W. Chambers, *Thomas More* (London, 1935), pp. 45–7.
3 Greg, ed., *Book of Sir Thomas More*, p. 55.
4 Greg, ed., *Book of Sir Thomas More*, p. 57.
5 Harpsfield, pp. 269–76; LP VIII. no. 974; J. Duncan M. Derrett, 'The Trial of Sir Thomas More', in R.S. Sylvester and G. Marc'hadour, eds, *Essential Articles for the Study of Thomas More* (Hampden, CT, 1977), pp. 58–9. On all procedural and legal matters concerning More's trial, I have followed Derrett, whose article is considered definitive.
6 Harpsfield, p. 271.
7 Harpsfield, p. 272; Derrett, 'The Trial of Sir Thomas More', in Sylvester and Marc'hadour, eds, *Essential Articles*, p. 59.
8 Harpsfield, pp. 272–3; Derrett, 'The Trial of Sir Thomas More', in Sylvester and Marc'hadour, eds, *Essential Articles*, p. 59.
9 Harpsfield, p. 273; Derrett, 'The Trial of Sir Thomas More', in Sylvester and Marc'hadour, eds, *Essential Articles*, p. 59.

10 Harpsfield, pp. 273–4; Derrett, 'The Trial of Sir Thomas More', in Sylvester and Marc'hadour, eds, *Essential Articles*, p. 59.

11 Harpsfield, pp. 274–6; *LP* VIII. no. 974; Derrett, 'The Trial of Sir Thomas More', in Sylvester and Marc'hadour, eds, *Essential Articles*, p. 59.

12 Derrett, 'The Trial of Sir Thomas More', in Sylvester and Marc'hadour, eds, *Essential Articles*, pp. 59–60.

13 Derrett, 'The Trial of Sir Thomas More', in Sylvester and Marc'hadour, eds, *Essential Articles*, p. 60.

14 Derrett, 'The Trial of Sir Thomas More', in Sylvester and Marc'hadour, eds, *Essential Articles*, p. 60.

15 Harpsfield, pp. 349–50; Roper, p. 231; John Guy, *The Public Career of Sir Thomas More* (Brighton, 1980), pp. 75–7.

16 The text is transcribed in Appendix III to Harpsfield, pp. 269–76.

17 Derrett, 'The Trial of Sir Thomas More', in Sylvester and Marc'hadour, eds, *Essential Articles*, pp. 60–5.

18 Roper, p. 245.

19 Roper, pp. 246–7. I disagree with Sir Geoffrey Elton that this plea came later in More's trial; G.R. Elton, *Policy and Police: the Enforcement of the Reformation in the Age of Thomas Cromwell* (London, 1972), p. 412 n. 2.

20 Derrett, 'The Trial of Sir Thomas More', in Sylvester and Marc'hadour, eds, *Essential Articles*, pp. 61–5.

21 Derrett, 'The Trial of Sir Thomas More', in Sylvester and Marc'hadour, eds, *Essential Articles*, p. 62.

22 Derrett, 'The Trial of Sir Thomas More', in Sylvester and Marc'hadour, eds, *Essential Articles*, p. 66.

23 PRO, SP 2/R, fos. 24–5.

24 Derrett, 'The Trial of Sir Thomas More', in Sylvester and Marc'hadour, eds, *Essential Articles*, pp. 66–8.

25 Elton, *Policy and Police*, p. 415.

26 R. Marius, *Thomas More* (New York, 1984), pp. 506–8.

27 Roper, pp. 244–5.

28 There was, however, a 'case' put by Rich (according to Roper) as to whether an Act of Parliament could make Rich Pope, which More deflected with his 'case' whether the Parliament could enact that God were not God. Roper, p. 244. Roper's account is probably confused here, since it does not tally with the indictment.

29 Harpsfield, pp. 188–90; Stapleton, pp. 175–6.

30 T.E. Bridgett, *Life and Writings of Blessed Thomas More* (London, 1924), pp. 415–29.

31 Chambers, *Thomas More*, pp. 337–8.

32 Harpsfield, pp. 258–66.

33 Derrett, 'The Trial of Sir Thomas More', in Sylvester and Marc'hadour, eds, *Essential Articles*, pp. 56, 65–70.

34 Bolt, *A Man for All Seasons*, p. 94.

35 Roper, pp. 245–6.

36 *CWE* 7, p. 18; Logan, Adams and Miller, pp. 67, 129, 171.

37 Roper, pp. 244, 247–8.

38 Harpsfield, p. 192.

39 Derrett, 'The Trial of Sir Thomas More', in Sylvester and Marc'hadour, eds, *Essential Articles*, pp. 68–70.
40 Derrett, 'The Trial of Sir Thomas More', in Sylvester and Marc'hadour, eds, *Essential Articles*, pp. 60, 70–2.
41 Derrett, 'The Trial of Sir Thomas More', in Sylvester and Marc'hadour, eds, *Essential Articles*, p. 70.
42 Elton, *Policy and Police*, pp. 409–10; Derrett, 'The Trial of Sir Thomas More', in Sylvester and Marc'hadour, eds, *Essential Articles*, pp. 70–5.
43 Roper, p. 248.
44 Roper, pp. 248–50.
45 Derrett, 'The Trial of Sir Thomas More', in Sylvester and Marc'hadour, eds, *Essential Articles*, p. 73.
46 Stapleton, pp. 196–7; Derrett, 'The Trial of Sir Thomas More', in Sylvester and Marc'hadour, eds, *Essential Articles*, p. 73.
47 Stapleton, p. 196; Harpsfield, p. 263; Derrett, 'The Trial of Sir Thomas More', in Sylvester and Marc'hadour, eds, *Essential Articles*, p. 73.
48 Roper, p. 248.
49 Roper, p. 248.
50 Rogers, ed., *Selected Letters*, p. 252.
51 Roper, p. 249; Stapleton, p. 197.
52 Rogers, ed., *Correspondence*, pp. 514–32.
53 Rogers, ed., *Correspondence*, p. 525.
54 Roper, pp. 249–50.
55 Roper, p. 250.
56 T.F.T. Plucknett and J.L. Barton, eds, *Doctor and Student* (London, Selden Society, 1974), pp. 317–18.
57 Roper, p. 250.
58 *CW* 12, pp. 288–9.
59 *CW* 12, p. 289.
60 Harpsfield, p. 264.
61 J.H. Baker, ed., *The Reports of Sir John Spelman* (2 vols, Selden Society, London, 1976–7) 1, p. 58.
62 Rogers, ed., *Correspondence*, p. 525.
63 *CW* 5, pp. 733–9.
64 *CW* 8, Pt. 2, p. 996.
65 *CW* 6, Pt. 1, p. 254.
66 Rogers, ed., *Selected Letters*, p. 251.
67 Rogers, ed., *Selected Letters*, p. 251.
68 Rogers, ed., *Selected Letters*, p. 251.
69 Rogers, ed., *Selected Letters*, p. 251.
70 Rogers, ed., *Selected Letters*, pp. 251–2.
71 *CW* 8, Pt. 1, pp. 3–40.
72 Rogers, ed., *Selected Letters*, p. 252 (my italics).
73 B. Gogan, *The Common Corps of Christendom: Ecclesiological Themes in the Writings of Sir Thomas More* (Leiden, 1982), pp. 340–1.
74 R. Rex, *The Theology of John Fisher* (Cambridge, 1991), pp. 102–9.
75 *CW* 8, Pt. 3, pp. 1294–1315.

76 Rogers, ed., *Selected Letters*, pp. 213–14.
77 *CW* 8, Pt. 2, p. 590.
78 Gogan, *Common Corps of Christendom*, pp. 341–70.
79 Rogers, ed., *Selected Letters*, p. 212.
80 Rogers, ed., *Selected Letters*, p. 212.
81 Rogers, ed., *Selected Letters*, p. 212.
82 Rogers, ed., *Selected Letters*, pp. 212–13.
83 Rogers, ed., *Selected Letters*, p. 213.
84 Rogers, ed., *Selected Letters*, p. 214.
85 Rogers, ed., *Selected Letters*, p. 213; *CW* 8, Pt. 3, p. 1299.
86 Roper, p. 248.
87 Harpsfield, pp. 263–4; Derrett, 'The Trial of Sir Thomas More', in Sylvester and Marc'hadour, eds, *Essential Articles*, pp. 70–5.
88 J. Wormald, *Mary Queen of Scots* (London, 1988), p. 14.
89 Stapleton, pp. 205–6, 211–12.
90 Bolt, *A Man for All Seasons*, p. xii.
91 Bolt, *A Man for All Seasons*, p. 53.
92 E. Surtz and V. Murphy, eds, *The Divorce Tracts of Henry VIII* (Angers, 1988).
93 Surtz and Murphy, eds, *Divorce Tracts*, pp. 167–85.
94 Surtz and Murphy, eds, *Divorce Tracts*, p. 267.
95 Surtz and Murphy, eds, *Divorce Tracts*, pp. 267–9.
96 Surtz and Murphy, eds, *Divorce Tracts*, pp. 267–9.

|11|

Conclusion

More mounted the scaffold on 6 July 1535. What happened is
encrusted in legend. No one in England was allowed to publish
an independent account during the lifetime of Henry VIII. The
'story' was first told by the Paris Newsletter, which circulated in
France within a fortnight of More's death. Early in Edward VI's
reign, the first account in English was published by the chronicler,
Edward Hall. It offered many examples of the 'mocks' with
which he believed More ended his life, but most seem to have
been derived from the 'sayings' of More and were most likely
apocryphal. There were few eyewitnesses. The only member of
More's own household present was Margaret Clement (née
Gigs): his adopted daughter who had married John Clement, the
former tutor to his children. She was there to ensure that the
decapitated body was handed over to the family as the King had
promised, so that it could be buried in the Chapel of St Peter ad
Vincula in the Tower. More's head was put on a pole on London
Bridge, where it remained for a month until it was taken down to
make room for other heads. The head was recovered by
Margaret Roper, who kept track of its position on the bridge,
identifying it by a missing tooth. According to Stapleton, she was
summoned by the Privy Council, and charged with attempting to
propagate a cult. She persuaded the Council that she meant only
to bury the head. When allowed to keep it, she preserved it with
spices until she herself died in 1544.[1] The head was then placed
in the Roper family vault in St Dunstan's Church, Canterbury,
where it is still said to remain.

What do we know about the execution? Early in the morning,
according to Roper's version, Cromwell's agent, Thomas Pope,

came to More's cell with a message from the King and Privy Council: 'he should before nine of the clock the same morning suffer death'.[2] When the appointed hour came, he was led out of the Tower to the scaffold on Tower Hill, where he knelt to say the words of the Psalm: 'Have mercy upon me, O God, after thy great goodness; according to the multitude of thy mercies do away mine offences'.[3] He rose. The executioner knelt and asked for the customary pardon. More embraced him. The executioner asked if he should bind More's eyes, but More had brought his own linen cloth and bound them himself. Before doing so, he made a short speech. He had already been instructed 'that at your execution you shall not use many words'.[4] Judging by Roper's account, More had negotiated (probably through Pope, who later rose to be Treasurer of the Court of Augmentations) what today would be called a 'trade-off'. He undertook to say very few words in exchange for permission for his family to take his body away for burial.

> 'Master Pope', quoth he, 'you do well to give me warning of his grace's pleasure, for otherwise I had purposed at that time somewhat to have spoken, but of no matter wherewith his grace, or any other, should have had cause to be offended. Nevertheless, whatsoever I intended, I am ready obediently to conform myself to his grace's command-ments. And I beseech you, good Master Pope, to be a mean unto his highness that my daughter Margaret may be at my burial.'[5]

In reply, Pope confirmed that the King had conceded that More's family could be present to receive his body for burial.

Scaffold speeches were extremely sensitive. The ritual was that the victim acknowledged his guilt and showed respect for the King and the law. Decorum and the social order were thought to be at peril if a victim challenged the validity of the sentence or his guilt. We do not know what More really said in his speech. The 'story' of the Paris Newsletter is this:

> He spoke little before his execution. Only he asked the bystanders to pray for him in this world, and he would pray for them elsewhere. He then begged them earnestly to pray for the King, that it might please God to give him good counsel, protesting that he died the King's good servant but God's first.[6]

All but the last resounding phrase makes perfect sense. In particular, that More urged the bystanders to pray for the King that it might please God to send him 'good' (i.e. 'better') counsel conforms exactly to his sentiments to Cromwell in the Tower and to Chapuys and Sir George Throckmorton while he was still Lord Chancellor. But the final 'protest' must be questioned. Despite the legendary status of these words as represented in the 'Lives' of More and the later literature, did he really say: 'he died the King's good servant but God's first'? Even R.W. Chambers expressed his astonishment. He noted that 'More's words are in striking contrast to the usual speech from the scaffold in Tudor times'. He compared the words to those of Cromwell at his own execution in 1540: 'I am by the law condemned to die; I have offended my Prince, for the which I ask him heartily forgiveness'.[7] As Chambers eulogized, 'More's words are the most weighty and the most haughty ever spoken on the scaffold.'[8]

I do not believe More said these words. The threat of reprisals against his family was too great. Almost certainly, he said something which conveyed the same meaning but was 'safe' and unimpeachable. I think that More, with all due modesty and respect for the King's authority, but with scorifying irony, threw back in Henry's face the words which he had spoken to More at his 'first coming' into royal service. The King had then told More that he should 'first look unto God and after God unto him'.[9] As soon as we look back at this quotation, which comes from More's letter to Cromwell of 5 March 1534, it becomes obvious. Knowing how More's mind worked under pressure, what else could he have said? His speech completed, he turned, knelt on the block, and prayed. The axe almost immediately fell.

Do we know Thomas More? Can we know him? I think that few of his contemporaries, if any, knew the inner man. Only his daughter, Margaret, fully understood what made him tick and the precise rationale of his scruple of conscience. I think that Erasmus 'knew' More, but did not know him well. Grocyn, Colet and Linacre knew him as a young man. Roper knew him after 1518, but not so well that he could write his 'Life' without reference to William Rastell's transcripts of his letters, to which he found it necessary to refer constantly. More knew Henry VIII, but not vice versa. Cranmer caught glimpses of More. He opposed his execution, and was troubled in his conscience afterwards. Cromwell knew More. He liked and probably understood him, but could not agree with his opinions. Whether Jane Colt or

Alice Middleton knew More will never be known. Almost certainly, More kept his distance even in his own household. He was not well known because he did not wish to be known. As soon as his family moved to Chelsea, he built the New Building so that he could study and pray undisturbed. Margaret is the exception. That she and her father were on the same wavelength, and that More loved her more than anyone except God, is obvious from the Tower letters and especially the 'letter' of Margaret (or More!) to Alice Alington. And yet, More turned his daughter into an intellectual clone. His educational methods in his 'school', notably the way the curriculum was regulated so that the texts to be studied by each member of the family were prescribed by More, suggest that there was no room for individuality or intellectual dissent. The Victorian T.E. Bridgett, perhaps the most distinguished of More's biographers before 1970, despite his confessional bias, never said a truer word than when he wrote: 'It is clear that Sir Thomas had a little Utopia of his own in his family.'[10]

What can we say about Thomas More? He was the most avant-garde humanist north of the Alps. *Utopia* is a work of genius, whichever modern interpretation is adopted. He was a brilliant classical scholar. He was a connoisseur of the arts. If Holbein had not been commissioned by More to paint the family group portrait in 1527, Henry VIII would not have encountered the artist, in which case the most potent images of the King and the 'imperial' Tudor monarchy would be unknown. More trained professionally as a lawyer. His career as Lord Chancellor created myths in its own right. His legal skills were so finely honed that his trial, supposedly a foregone conclusion to the point where the Crown had prepared circular letters describing his 'conviction' a week in advance, was electric.[11] His irony, jokes and 'merry tales' annoyed some people. He saw life as a series of comic interludes. Even as a page in Cardinal Morton's household, he had loved to 'step' in and out of plays and entertainments, delivering extempore speeches in fictional and real-life guises. He saw humour as a correlative of the Holy Spirit. He used it to cut people down to size, especially himself. The sin of pride was top of his list of pet hates. Humour or 'teasing' kept people in their places. This was quintessential More, but it was not a recipe for popularity among his contemporaries. And we shall never know what his own family thought about his jokes at their expense.

More was a master of public relations; Erasmus had taught him the skills. Philosophy is a different matter. Erasmus focused on the evangelical brand of Christian piety which he and his circle called *philosophia Christi*: a 'simple' philosophy of Christ. Erasmus was the most scintillating classical scholar in Europe, but his humanism is less complex than More's. His *Praise of Folly* and the *Education of a Christian Prince* are outstanding, but the paradigm is relatively simple. More's *Utopia* is more intense and far more ironical. It is more closely linked to Plato's ideal of social justice and the perfection of the commonwealth, and to Cicero's notion that the highest 'duty' of the active citizen was to enter public life. The difference between Erasmus and More is that Erasmus was a scholar and More wanted to put his humanism into practice. Whether the two were personally close, whether in the last analysis their brands of humanism were intellectually compatible, are questions that will always be debated. More was Erasmus' 'friend', reflecting his easy social manner and capacity for banter. But More's best 'friendships' (other than with his daughter, Margaret) were always literary ones. It was much easier to have 'friends' on paper than to deal with people in real life. We are told that one of More's best 'friends' was Antonio Bonvisi, the merchant of Lucca, who had purchased the lease of Crosby Place from More. They spent hours together, and Harpsfield, who alludes to their friendship but then proceeds to tell us nothing about it, deserved his sentence of 15 years in the Fleet prison if only for this omission!

More failed in politics. It has been argued that he was 'too straightforward, too free from self-deception, too conscious of the contingencies of human existence ever to commit himself totally to a policy or programme no matter how apparently good or glorious'.[12] It was his tragedy to become embroiled in events which are often read as the beginning of the rise of the national sovereign State.[13] He was temperamentally unsuited to this transition. He respected authority and tradition too much. He began his career by trying to understand the proper relationship between philosophy and public life and ended up as a moral absolutist. A pattern was increasingly established. No one has ever noticed that he threw back the King's words in his face almost as a habit. I think he did it on the scaffold. He did it when he told Cromwell that it was only when he read the initial draft of the King's *Defence of the Seven Sacraments* that he learned of the divine origins of the papal primacy.[14] He also did it when he reminded Cromwell (whom he knew would tell the King) that on the occasion he had been asked about the divorce shortly after he was appointed Lord Chancellor, the King had said: 'that I should first look unto God and after God unto him, which most gracious words were the first lesson also that ever his Grace gave me at my first coming into his noble service'.[15] More always liked to set the record straight, but in the process he sorely tempted the gods.

His 'scruple of conscience' is iconic. He took 'legalistic' stances in political contexts that stretched the patience of others. No criticism is intended. Although his definitions of 'conscience' and of the conflict of laws in Christendom were deeply legalistic, one can understand exactly why More had to do what he did. He had his principles. Whether he pursued them in ways wholly consistent with a standpoint of moral absolutism is another matter. His methods were too political. He conveyed what he really thought to almost anyone who would listen in coded but 'safe' language, while pretending to 'keep silence'. To speak unequivocally was to court martyrdom, which was tantamount to suicide and forbidden by the Church. But More always wanted people to know why he could not accept Henry VIII's proceedings. There were occasions when his desire to 'score points' must have deeply irritated his friends and ex-colleagues. When sent an invitation to Anne Boleyn's coronation with the gift of £20 to buy a new gown, he told his benefactors that he was happy to oblige them for the money, but the other he would have to deny them. He was the 'bolder' to deny them one request because he had 'granted' them the other.[16] He then told his friends a fable from Tacitus that made it look as if they were colluding in tyranny by attending the coronation themselves.[17]

This is not a unique instance. When More's name was put into the bill for Barton's attainder as an accomplice for prophesying the King's deposition or death, he immediately petitioned to be allowed to give evidence in the House of Lords when the bill was brought before Parliament.[18] It was a legal *coup*, which exploited the right of private individuals to petition Parliament on prospective legislation in which they had an interest. It worked: his attainder on this occasion was pre-empted. His guilt was investigated by a committee of the Privy Council outside of Parliament and his name removed from the bill, but his request caused ructions in the Privy Council and cannot have won him friends. Cromwell and Audley had to grovel to the King to obtain permission to interview More privately. They foresaw the political danger of a petition in Parliament, but Henry was never easy to dissuade. It is a tribute to Cromwell that he treated More fairly and honourably in the Tower. The King's mind was a volcano: Cromwell feared More would destroy others as well as himself. No one was safe when the King was in this mood.

When Cromwell (bullied by the King) started to lose patience and asked More in the Tower to give a plain answer to the Act of Supremacy once and for all, or else 'to utter plainly my malignity', More could not resist a repartee: 'I had no malignity and therefore I could none utter'.[19] Lastly, when Cromwell put to More the King's accusation of 'obstinacy', he answered: 'if I may not declare the causes without peril, then to leave them un-declared is no obstinacy'.[20] It was a brilliant reply, but More went on to say: 'this was one of the cases in which I was bounden that I should not obey my prince'.[21] Did he really think he could get away with this? One can have nothing but admiration for his willingness to stand up for his principles, but far from 'keeping silence', he talked incessantly to Cromwell (and perhaps to Henry) as if the relationship between him and his sovereign was one of equality. We know from Erasmus that More admired intensely the classical ideal of 'equality', and the communism of Book II of *Utopia* is predicated on it, but Parliament and Convocation alike had declared Henry VIII to be Supreme Head of the Church of England. The King was God's representative on earth. And yet More insisted on appealing to God over the head of the King: not 'silently' but as audibly as he could possibly manage in safety.

Cromwell came to dislike More's standpoint less because he himself was open to Protestant opinions (if indeed he was: he professed in 1540 that he died a Catholic) than because More refused to share his 'equality' with others. More's 'equality' is like that which existed in the kitchens of Utopia or among the pigs in George Orwell's *Animal Farm*: some are 'more equal than others'. More as Lord Chancellor had demanded that the eye-witnesses to Bilney's burning attend in Star Chamber, where he put them on oath and questioned them on interrogatories of his own devising. His action was not illegal. It was irregular, but that is not the issue. He required that they swear the oath, and answer whatever he asked. Yet when Cromwell, his patience exhausted, offered More a similar oath, he countered that he 'never purposed to swear any book oath more while I lived'.[22] It was one thing for More to demand that the eyewitnesses to Bilney's death take an oath. It was different when it applied to him. Cromwell retorted that this scruple of 'conscience' had not weighed in More's judgement when he had examined suspected heretics as Lord Chancellor. More replied that the two cases were not alike. Oaths could be demanded only in conformity with the doctrines of the Catholic Church.[23] The cases were morally distinct. Heretics were not allowed consciences: they had deviated from the authority of the Church. Individual opinions were not admissible.[24]

Can the other shibboleths discussed in this book be resolved? The answer is, hardly ever. There will always be uncertainty about More's Charterhouse years: the evidence is defective and deceptive. The same applies to his entry into royal service and attitude to Court life. We cannot settle the provenance of his 'letter' to Fisher as 'transcribed' in Stapleton's *Life of Thomas More*. There is no manuscript or other text. Is it genuine? It makes all the difference. The greatest riddle of all is More's family and domestic life. The topic is emblazoned with mythology. It can never be analysed objectively because the requisite sources do not exist. Those which do are too reliant on Erasmus' vignette to Hutten. That is not a factual description, but an idealized depiction of a Christian humanist life, which seeks to create a model of decorum in which the clashes between Christian and classical values are harmonized. And Erasmus never set foot in Chelsea.

More will always be renowned for his *Utopia*. The significance of this jewel of political thought has been obfuscated by the translations of Robinson and Burnet, which dominated received opinion until the Yale Edition appeared in 1965. Burnet's reading of Book II was particularly perverse. By subordinating More's social radicalism to his religious 'radicalism', *Utopia* was turned upside down. The readings of Hexter, Skinner and Bradshaw mark a watershed. The view that *Utopia* is a quest for the Holy Grail of humanist philosophy – the reconciliation of 'moral absolutism' or the 'contemplative' values of Plato's *Republic* with the 'civil philosophy' of the 'active' or 'politick life' as set forth by Cicero in *De officiis* – is highly persuasive. More made the realization of Plato's ideal the mission of the Ciceronian politician, and thereby issued a challenge to his humanist contemporaries. Whether he sought the 'only possible solution' (Skinner) or the 'best possible solution' (Bradshaw) to the problems of social justice and the perfection of the common-wealth, More meant what he said. Yet a cardinal doubt remains: did he believe that communism was the 'only possible solution' to the issue of the 'best state of a commonwealth' in practice? As to More's role as an inquisitor, historians will increasingly separate the 'facts' from the 'stories'. No responsible scholar would now recite the litany of accusation of John Foxe's *Acts and Monuments* without reference to More's *Apology* or the work of the co-editors of the Yale Edition. We can see exactly how More came to do what he did. Henry VIII had 'set' him to the anti-Lutheran agenda in 1521. His ideological assumptions were defined by his role as the King's surrogate, and by his attachment to Wolsey's censorship commissioners. When he raided the German Steelyard as Chancellor of the Duchy of Lancaster, his 'career' as an inquisitor had begun. It should not be overlooked that when he returned to the Steelyard, the Hanse merchants had to swear that they would destroy any heretical books in their possession. This was, I believe, the first occasion on which More required a suspected heretic to take an oath: it set a pattern for his later responses as Lord Chancellor.

More's actions in heresy cases can be explained. To defend the Catholic Church was not only a religious obligation, it was a secular one before the Reformation. The Act *De Heretico Comburendo* is quite clear, and the Act of 1414 amended the oaths of the King's secular officials to incorporate these obligations. More had his duty to perform. But he laid down hostages to fortune. His confession to Erasmus that 'I find that breed of men absolutely loathsome . . . I want to be as hateful to them as anyone can possibly be', is his undoing.[25] In his epitaph, More declared that he had been 'grievous' to 'thieves, murderers and heretics'.[26] This is too extreme. There is too much passion, even satisfaction. The schizophrenia in the minds of historians between the acclaim of More's heroism and the excoriation of his inquisitorial actions on moral and humanitarian grounds will never be dispelled. Erasmus praised More for the fact that no heretic was burned while he was Lord Chancellor. Little did he know! But the comment is highly instructive: it was a mark of approbation and shows what he would have liked More's policy to be. Erasmus was willing to burn heretical books, but he had qualms about killing men. It was a fundamental change of out-look that was central to the transition between the Middle Ages and the modern world.

As Lord Chancellor, More was in his element in the Courts of Star Chamber and Chancery. He stood up for Wolsey's principles of 'equal' and 'impartial' justice, and vindicated his predecessor's standpoint on the question of equitable injunctions. Whereas Wolsey had been hubristic and relaxed about justice, More tightened up the practical procedures. If he had remained within the legal profession and ended up as Chief Justice of King's Bench or Commons Pleas, he might have gone down in history as a legal reformer. But the lure of politics was too great. One cannot become too excited over More's legal work. His emphasis on justice was no more than the Lord Chancellor was bound to do by virtue of his oath of office. Whether he might have become a Utopian reformer under the right conditions can never be resolved. As it was, he became deeply involved in politics, where he fought for his beliefs. Shortly after he became Lord Chancellor, he reached what was tantamount to a concordat with the King whereby he would be excused involvement in the divorce suit. On 'other matters', his hands were not tied and he fought his corner. Lord Acton was right to query whether he had evaded his moral and political responsibilities, but the fact that he was in trouble with the King for defending the independent legislative authority of the Church speaks for itself. More had almost overstepped the mark, since the price of an understanding with the King was that More respect the *quid pro quo*. The issue of the Church's immunity was implicitly linked to the divorce: it was only when Convocation was subordinated to the Crown that the divorce plan in the *Collectanea satis copiosa* could be implemented.

In his 'retirement' More deployed all his rhetorical skills to assume the mask of a sick man who meant 'to bestow the residue of my life in mine age now to come, about the provision for my soul in the service of God'.[27] Perhaps he did sincerely mean to retire, but when St German's *Treatise Concerning the Division* and *Salem and Bizance* appeared, he returned to the public sphere. His *Apology* and *Debellation of Salem and Bizance* were so political, the shop of his publisher was raided and he was forced to exculpate himself. When the domino effect was irreversible, he took up fixed positions that did not cross the line, but made no secret of his views, which were equivalent to a condemnation of Henry VIII. His responses were 'safe', but 'not really ambiguous or silent'. Nowhere was Sir Geoffrey Elton's revisionism more compelling than in disentangling the extent to which More's statements in the Tower signified 'total dis-approval'.[28]

More struggled to avoid courting martyrdom, but never doubted the end that lay in sight. His trial deployed the full panoply of his legal and rhetorical skills: even his unrivalled Latin comprehension was essential if he were to understand the long indictment which he heard for the first time in court. His demurrer to the first three counts of the indictment, and his motion in arrest of judgement, were brilliant extempore advocacy. More's trial makes the trial of Charles I or the impeach-ment of President Clinton look tawdry in comparison. Nor has posterity paid much attention to the 'facts'. Whether Richard Rich committed perjury, and whether More expressed an uncom-promising belief in the papal 'supremacy' when he finally spoke unequivocally, as Roper claimed, are dubious propositions. There is no corroboration. Roper was telling a 'story'. He was writing 20 years later and had not even been present at More's trial. He relied on three 'credible' reports, but how credible are these witnesses? The question arises when it becomes obvious that Roper's 'story' is underpinned at key points by More's Tower letters and (I would argue) even Erasmus' vignette or Book II of *Utopia* in its character assassination of Rich. Roper's account of More's trial is in the style of a *Sun* journalist writing for *The Times*, describing an event that happened 20 years ago, which the writer has only heard about from his friends. And yet, it is the most important record we have apart from the original indictment. Nor can we lightly snipe at Roper, since his account of the case of the Pope's ship, which the revisionists so disparaged, turned out to be true in almost every detail.

Were there 'two' Thomas Mores? Was there a Utopian reformer of 1516 and a persecutor of heretics? A Soft Man and a Hard Man? This is effectively what Burnet, Warner, Froude and many others since have thought. Or was More consistently virtuous and gentle: a man whose 'patience and courtesy towards heretics' is 'revealed only to the careful student of his private life'?[29] One of the most distinguished scholars of the humanist-classical tradition believes that there were two Mores. In the *London Review of Books* in 1983, J.B. Trapp wrote:

I cannot see the transition from failed monk, via Humanist lawyer, to religious controversialist and examiner, not to say hunter, of heretics, as anything other than a change in

degree so great as to be almost a change in character. In the
later More, there is a hardness, a ferocity, which is the
direct result of the drawing of the lines with Luther about
1521. More could never have been thought of as the Soft
Man, but his transformation into the hardest of Hard Men
is profound and far-reaching. When salvation and
damnation were the issue, as they were now, and not
scholastic obscurantism or silly superstition, More, so far
from being a man for all seasons, is a man of deepest midwinter.[30]

Is this correct (always supposing that More was a 'failed
monk')? Responsibility for the question lies at the door of
Burnet. By representing More as a Protestant reformer *avant la
lettre*, he made an indelible imprint on the historiography. More's
religious 'radicalism' in 1516 must be stripped out. Utopian
religion is not at all 'radical'. King Utopus required conformity to
two theological beliefs: one is the immortality of the soul, the
other that the universe is ruled by divine providence.[31] If the soul
were not immortal, and if life on earth were purely random, there
would be no 'moral probity' (to cite the phrase More used to
Gonell about the purpose of education in his 'school'). No one
would feel inhibited from pursuing hedonism rather than a life of
virtue. Any Utopian who denies the two prescribed beliefs is
'offered no honours, entrusted with no offices, and given no
public responsibility'.[32] He or she is universally ostracized. There
is no religious persecution in Utopia, but that is only because
Utopus was confident that 'reason' will prevail. Those who
dissent may not discuss their opinions with anyone, except
privately to priests and other 'important' persons. Such discussions are encouraged, since the Utopians 'are confident that in the
end ... madness will yield to reason'. All of this is modelled on
what the Catholic Church called 'admonishing' heretics when
their heterodoxy first became known. Dissidents were given the
opportunity to learn the 'truth' before legal proceedings in the
Church courts were initiated or 'penitential pains' imposed. It
was only 'obstinate' heretics who were punished. And in 1516,
when More wrote *Utopia*, there were few heretics and only a
handful of burnings. There is nothing in *Utopia* that contradicts
the ideals of Catholicism at that time.
    It is also clear that the truly 'radical' provisions in Book II such
as divorce, women priests or euthanasia are exceptionally rare in

practice. Furthermore, they are possible only because Utopia is a heathen society. The limitations of the moral code of the Utopians mislead them into supposing that actions which are mortal sins are actually pious and honourable. The conversion of Utopia to Christianity is integral to the structure of Book II. It is intrinsic to More's purpose. The 'reason' of the Utopians is complemented by the 'revelation' of Christianity, without which their heathen society cannot be considered as exemplary. The Utopians need not just Christian baptism, but also those Catholic sacraments such as confirmation and the Eucharist which require the office of a priest.[33] The argument shifts from a focus on 'reason' to a focus on 'revelation'. This is why the interpretations of Kautsky and the Marxist historians are so anachronistic, and why Hexter's notion of Utopia as a parallel society for Christian Europe is unsustainable.

As to the social institutions of the Utopians, these are certainly 'radical', but there is nothing liberal about them. No society is more strictly regulated or predicated upon Plato's educational ideals or (in a Christian context) upon monastic principles of collectivism and austerity. As a philosophical model, Utopian society is the most avant-garde critique of humanist values written by a humanist. But who would want to live there? It is not More's original editions, but Robinson's translation, which is responsible for the impression that there is colour, a degree of consumerism and social freedom – what today would be called a 'social life' – in Utopia. The trouble with interpreting the social milieu of *Utopia* is that the work can only be properly appreciated in the language in which it was composed.

At the other end of the scale, More's ideological perspective as Lord Chancellor was directly indexed to the officially-approved doctrines and mind-set of the Catholic Church. His commitment to Catholic tradition was more vehement than that shown by his English contemporaries, but this merely reflected his prescience and appreciation of the danger posed to the Church by Luther and the reformers. It is less that something in More changed between 1529 and 1532 than that the Catholic Church hardened its own outlook: already the shift was towards Counter-Reformation. Luther posed a fundamental threat to the notions of tradition and authority in the Church. He argued in the *Babylonian Captivity* that the Word of God was the authority for salvation, and that the Bible set the standards by which the Church and clergy should be judged. It was a revolutionary claim. The most subversive heresy that More could imagine was the notion that Scripture stood in opposition to the teaching and practice of the Catholic Church. From his perspective, the division between the 'known Church' and the 'Word of God' which the reformers had constructed was the crux of the Reformation divide. I have already argued that this explains why the notion of 'consensus' or the 'common faith' of Christendom became More's most important ecclesiological concept, culminating in his refusal to accept the Act of Supremacy. The tragedy is that More's concern for this argument was first stimulated, if not originally derived, from his role as Henry VIII's surrogate against Luther. It is as if More was told to stake his life on a doctrinal position, only to find the rug pulled out from under his feet by the King.

At both ends of the spectrum – in 1516 and 1529–32 – the argument that there were 'two' Thomas Mores depends on elements of misunderstanding and hyperbole. This is not to say that the question is irrelevant. It is not: when anachronism is stripped out, it cuts to the quick. Trapp is correct that in the later More, there is a 'hardness, a ferocity, which is the direct result of the drawing of the lines with Luther'. But it needs to be stressed that More's outlook was always authoritarian. He was always a Hard Man: once more the difference is only one of degree. This does not mean that he was an ardent monarchist or papalist. The most important article of his political and theological creeds is his refusal to attribute absolute authority or supremacy to any one individual in Church or State. His Latin poems, most of which were written between 1510 and 1518, contain a number of verses with quasi-republican overtones.[34] As to the papal primacy, the crux of his position was his assurance to Cromwell that he had never placed the Pope above the General Council.[35] His rejection of the Act of Supremacy must have pushed him closer towards Rome. When he mounted the scaffold, he may have reached a position that was closer to that of Fisher, who ascribed the plenitude of power to the Pope from the outset – but there is no evidence that he did. I have already argued that his final views on the papacy are unknown. It is virtually certain that the words attributed by Roper to More at his trial on this subject are not what he said, but what he ought to have said (see Chapter 10).

Thomas More died for the right to 'frame' his own conscience, but not for the right to 'authenticate' it independently of the beliefs of the Roman Catholic Church. There is no more freedom for the rights of individual conscience in More's philosophy than there is in Utopia. That is why it was possible in 1886 for the Catholic Church to beatify him and in 1935 to canonize him as a saint. Robert Bolt's 'story' in *A Man for All Seasons* is sumptuous drama but appalling history. Very few people will ever care. What matters is what Congressman Hyde told the United States' Senate in January 1999 (see Chapter 1). From the beginning, many of the sources for More's life and career were contrived or manipulated for rhetorical or polemical effect. The earliest 'Lives' are less 'primary sources' than layered interpretations. They blur the lines between 'history' and 'story', interlacing truth, half-truth and fiction in intricate ways. But their 'story' is now everyone's 'story': More is the paragon of the family man who, when pushed to make choices, became the *refusenik*. He sacrificed his life to defend 'moral probity' against the totalitarian State. It is no coincidence that 1935 was the date of his canonization. It was the 400th anniversary of his execution. Hitler was in power in Germany; Mussolini in Italy; Stalin in Russia. Henry VIII had become the surrogate for Fascism and Stalinism.

Everyone who has seen the film of *A Man for All Seasons* wants to know about More, but not to know too much. Their illusions might be shattered, their ideals infringed, their delight in a moral tale defaced. The world will need More as much as ever in the third millennium, but not in an historical guise. We need him as the epitome of the 'man of singular virtue', 'the King's good servant but God's first'. There is an historical Thomas More, but no one really knows where he can be found. He is an enigma. He defies objective analysis. 'History' defines him up to a point, but there is a boundary that can never be crossed. We need More in the same way that he himself needed *Utopia*: as a Platonic Form or Idea, as the moral 'standard' against which the values of our own society can be judged. In this re-evaluation, a revolution has occurred since the sixteenth century. In 1556, when Cranmer was burned at Oxford, it was held that Fisher's death was worth four times as much as More's. It was to redress this imbalance that Roper began writing his biography. Between 1600 and the Revolution of 1688, More sank into obscurity. He was virtually unknown except to those who read Foxe's *Acts and Monuments* or Robinson's translation of *Utopia*. By 1800, his 'rehabilitation' was well advanced. After Catholic Emancipation, his beatification was simply a matter of time. By 1935, Chesterton could acclaim him as 'the greatest Englishman, or, at least, the greatest historical character in English history'.[36] Now the imbalance with Fisher is reversed. When a commemoration of the 450th anniversary of the death of Fisher was held in 1985, the keynote speaker lamented the disproportionate level of interest in More that 'has served to obscure the . . . significance of Fisher's career, and has contributed to [his] continuing marginalisation'.[37] Nor is this view hyperbole. Who in the United States' Senate ever heard of Fisher? After *A Man for All Seasons*, there are no limitations. More's reputation is unassailable, but the 'story' will only be historical in a minority of cases. Posterity now insists that we are told the 'story' that matches the man to the legend.

Notes

1 Stapleton, pp. 213–5.
2 Roper, p. 252.
3 R.W. Chambers, *Thomas More* (London, 1935), p. 348.
4 Roper, p. 253.
5 Roper, p. 253.
6 Harpsfield, p. 266; Chambers, *Thomas More*, p. 349.
7 Chambers, *Thomas More*, p. 350.
8 Chambers, *Thomas More*, p. 350.
9 Rogers, ed., *Correspondence*, p. 495.
10 T.E. Bridgett, *Life and Writings of Blessed Thomas More* (London, 1924), p. 138.
11 *LP* VIII, no. 921.
12 J.M. Headley, 'The New Debate on More's Political Career', *Thought* 52 (1977), p. 274.
13 G.R. Elton, *The Tudor Constitution* (2nd edn., Cambridge, 1982), pp. 233–40, 338–45.
14 Rogers, ed., *Selected Letters*, p. 212.
15 Rogers, ed., *Selected Letters*, p. 209.
16 Roper, p. 229.
17 Roper, pp. 229–30.
18 Roper, pp. 233–4.
19 Rogers, ed., *Selected Letters*, p. 250.
20 Rogers, ed., *Selected Letters*, p. 220.
21 Rogers, ed., *Selected Letters*, p. 221.
22 Rogers, ed., *Selected Letters*, p. 252.
23 Rogers, ed., *Selected Letters*, p. 251.
24 Rogers, ed., *Selected Letters*, p. 252.
25 Rogers, ed., *Selected Letters*, p. 180.
26 Trapp and Herbrüggen, p. 139; Harpsfield, p. 280.

27 Rogers, ed., *Selected Letters*, p. 202.
28 G.R. Elton, *Policy and Police: the Enforcement of the Reformation in the Age of Thomas Cromwell* (Cambridge, 1972), p. 416.
29 Chambers, *Thomas More*, p. 86.
30 J.B. Trapp, 'Midwinter', *London Review of Books* (17–30 November 1983), p. 16.
31 Logan, Adams and Miller, pp. 222–5.
32 Logan, Adams and Miller, p. 225.
33 Logan, Adams and Miller, p. 221.
34 *CW* 3, Pt. 2, pp. 145, 165, 179, 205, 229–31.
35 Rogers, ed., *Selected Letters*, p. 214.
36 J. Ridley, *The Statesman and the Fanatic: Thomas Wolsey and Thomas More* (London, 1982), p. 290.
37 B. Bradshaw, 'Bishop John Fisher, 1469–1535: the Man and His Work', in B. Bradshaw and E. Duffy, eds, *Humanism, Reform and the Reformation: the Career of Bishop John Fisher* (Cambridge, 1989), p. 1.

Chronology

1478
6 February   Most likely birth date of Thomas More
                     (other possible dates: 6/7 February 1477, or
                     7 February 1478).

1485
22 August   Battle of Bosworth. Henry VII defeats
                     Richard III and founds the Tudor dynasty.

c. **1490**   More is a page in the household of Cardinal
                     Morton, Lord Chancellor.

1491
28 June   Birth of Henry VIII.

c. **1492**   More studies at Oxford University.

c. **1494**   More is a law student at New Inn.

1496   More admitted to Lincoln's Inn.

1499   Linacre returns from Padua and Venice.
                     More and Erasmus meet Prince Henry at
                     Eltham.

c. **1499–1503**   More is lecturing to law students at
                     Furnivall's Inn and living in or about the
                     London Charterhouse.

c. **1501**   More lectures on St Augustine's *City of
                     God*.

1503

18 February | Prince Henry is created Prince of Wales after the death of his elder brother, Arthur.
25 June | Betrothal of Prince Henry and Catherine of Aragon.
26 December | Pope Julius II grants a dispensation for their marriage.

1504 | More sits in the House of Commons. His constituency is unknown.

1505

January | More marries Jane Colt. Lives at the Old Barge, Bucklersbury, London.
October | Margaret, More's eldest daughter, born.

1505–6 | Erasmus stays with More at Bucklersbury.

1506 | Birth of Elizabeth, More's second daughter.

1507 | Birth of Cicely, More's third daughter.

1509 | Birth of John, More's son.
March | Admitted to the freedom of the Mercers' Company.
21 April | Henry VII dies at 11 p.m. His death is kept secret until the afternoon of the 23rd, when it is revealed to the main body of councillors.
23 April | Henry VIII's accession is proclaimed.
11 June | Henry VIII marries Catherine of Aragon.
October | Erasmus begins the *Praise of Folly* at More's house at Bucklersbury.

1510

January | More sits in the House of Commons as MP for London.
3 September | More is appointed an undersheriff of London.

c. **1510** | More's *Life of John Picus* is printed by John Rastell.

1511 | Jane More dies. More marries Dame Alice Middleton within a month.

1513–19	More writes the *History of King Richard III*.
1514	More is Lent Reader at Lincoln's Inn.
1515	
May	Sent on the embassy to Bruges which produces *Utopia*.
December	Cardinal Wolsey appointed Lord Chancellor.
1516	Completes *Utopia* in London. The first edition is published at Louvain in *c.* December.
1517	
1 May	Evil May Day.
August	More goes on a second commercial embassy to Calais.
1518	
March	More enters royal service. He has entered the King's Council by 26 March.
21 June	More granted a King's councillor's annuity of £100.
23 July	More resigns as undersheriff of London.
1519	
23 July	Erasmus writes his vignette of More to Ulrich von Hutten.
1520	
May–June	More is with Wolsey and Henry VIII at the Field of Cloth of Gold.
July–August	More is at Bruges, negotiating on behalf of Henry VIII with the Hanseatic League.
1521	
2 May	More appointed Under-Treasurer of the Exchequer and knighted.
spring	More is appointed to edit Henry VIII's *Defence of the Seven Sacraments* with the 'consent' of the King's panel of advisers.
2 July	More's daughter Margaret marries William Roper.
August–October	With Wolsey on an embassy to Calais and Bruges.

1523	More writes the *Answer to Luther*.
15 April	More elected Speaker of the House of Commons.
1 June	More buys lease of Crosby Place, St Helen's, Bishopsgate.
1524	More buys his estate at Chelsea.
20 January	The lease of Crosby Place is sold to Antonio Bonvisi.
1525	
summer	More helps to negotiate an Anglo-French *entente* leading to the treaty of the More.
29 September	More appointed Chancellor of the Duchy of Lancaster. On the same day, his daughter Elizabeth marries William Dauncey, and his daughter Cicely marries Giles Heron.
December	Between December 1525 and February 1526, More writes the *Letter to Bugenhagen*.
1526	
January	More raids the German Steelyard in search of Lutheran books and Bible translations.
autumn	Holbein arrives at More's house in Chelsea from Basel on the recommendation of Erasmus and is given commissions, including the family group portrait.
autumn	More assists Henry VIII in composing the *Letter in Reply to Martin Luther*, published in December.
1527	
spring	Henry VIII first expresses his doubts to Wolsey about the validity of his marriage to Catherine of Aragon.
8 July	More present when the King's Council devises a censorship order against heretical books and preaching.
July–September	More with Wolsey at Amiens to ratify the peace treaty with France.
12–17 October	More first consulted by Henry VIII about the divorce at Hampton Court.

1528

7 March — More commissioned by Bishop Tunstal to refute Lutheran and other heretical books, and is sent a bundle of books which he is licensed to read.

1529

    More's son, John, marries Anne Cresacre.

June — More's *Dialogue concerning Heresies* is published by his nephew, William Rastell.

July–August — More at Cambrai for the negotiations leading to a peace treaty between France, Spain, the Holy Roman Empire and England.

October — More completes the *Supplication of Souls*.

8 October — Wolsey accused of *praemunire* in the Court of King's Bench.

17 October — Wolsey surrenders the Great Seal to Henry VIII.

25 October — More appointed Lord Chancellor.

3 November — More opens the Reformation Parliament.

1530

25 May — Henry VIII and More at a meeting of the King's Council in Star Chamber which condemns heretical books.

22 June — The first of More's proclamations against heretical books issued.

December — Death of More's father, John More.

1531

February — Henry VIII requires the Convocation of Canterbury to grant him the title of 'Supreme Head of the English Church', which Convocation grants only with the addition of the words 'as far as the law of Christ allows'.

11 March — Charles V writes a letter of thanks to More.

30 March — More required to present to Parliament the opinions on the divorce which Henry VIII has obtained from a number of European universities.

1532

January — The first part of More's *Confutation of Tyndale's Answer* published.

March	Act in Conditional Restraint of Annates.
15 May	The Submission of the Clergy.
16 May	More resigns as Lord Chancellor.
December	Anne Boleyn becomes pregnant.

1533

early	More's *Letter to John Frith* and the second part of his *Confutation of Tyndale's Answer* published.
January	Henry VIII marries Anne Boleyn.
April	More's *Apology* published. Act in Restraint of Appeals passed by Parliament.
May	Catherine of Aragon's marriage annulled by Cranmer.
1 June	More refuses to attend Anne Boleyn's coronation.
November	More's *Debellation of Salem and Bizance* published.

1534

January	More's *Answer to a Poisoned Book* published. William Rastell's shop is raided to investigate a report that More had written a reply to the *Articles Devised by the Whole Consent of the King's Most Honourable Council*.
February	Attainder for high treason of Elizabeth Barton, the Nun (or Holy Maid) of Kent. The names of Fisher and More are inserted in the bill as accomplices to be attainted of misprision of treason. More's name is removed after he successfully defends himself before a committee of the Privy Council.
March	Act of Succession.
13 April	More refuses the oath of succession before the royal commissioners at Lambeth. He is kept in custody.
17 April	More is sent to the Tower. Between his first imprisonment and the spring of 1535, he writes the *Treatise on the Passion*, *Treatise on the Blessed Body*, *Dialogue of Comfort against Tribulation*, and *On the Sadness of Christ*.

November	More is attainted of misprision of treason. Acts of Supremacy and Treason.

1535

30 April	More is interrogated by Cromwell and the legal counsel of the Privy Council in the Tower.
4 May	More and his daughter Margaret watch four Carthusian monks on the final journey to Tyburn for execution.
7 May	More's second interrogation by Cromwell.
20 May	Fisher is created a cardinal by Pope Paul III.
3 June	More's third interrogation before Cromwell and a committee of the Privy Council.
11 June	More's fourth interrogation.
12 June	Richard Rich and More 'discuss' the power of Popes and Parliaments in the Tower. More's remaining books and writing materials are confiscated by the Privy Council.
14 June	More's final interrogation.
17 June	Fisher and three Carthusian monks tried for 'denying' the Act of Supremacy.
19 June	Execution of the Carthusians.
22 June	Execution of Fisher.
26 June	Special commissioners of *oyer et terminer* are appointed to try More.
1 July	More's trial at Westminster Hall for 'denying' the Act of Supremacy.
6 July	More is executed on Tower Hill.
1551	Ralph Robinson's translation of *Utopia* is dedicated to Sir William Cecil.
1557	William Rastell publishes the folio edition of More's *English Works*.
*c.*1557	Roper writes his *Life of Sir Thomas More*. Harpsfield is commissioned to write the *Life and Death of Sir Thomas More*, completed by 1558 or the beginning of 1559 and presented to Roper as a New Year's gift.

1579	Fisher and More recognized as martyrs by Pope Gregory XIII.
1584	More is included in the *Ecclesiae Anglicanae Trophaea*, published at Rome.
1588	Stapleton's *Life of Thomas More* is published at Douai.
c. **1599**	Ro. Ba. writes the *Life of Sir Thomas More*.
1626	Roper's *Life* is published at St Omer as the *Life, Arraignment and Death of that Mirror of All True Honour and Virtue, Sir Thomas More*.
c. **1631**	Cresacre More's *Life of Sir Thomas More* is published at Douai.
1684	Burnet's *Utopia Translated into English* is published.
1886 29 December	Beatification of Fisher and More by Pope Leo XIII.
1918	Obelisk including More's name is sculptured on Lenin's orders and unveiled in Moscow's Alexandrovsky Gardens.
1935 19 May	Canonization of Fisher and More by Pope Pius XI.
1977/1978	The 500th anniversary of More's birth is celebrated by exhibitions and conferences in London, Dublin, Angers, New York, and Washington DC.

Further reading

The starting-point is always the earliest 'Lives' of Thomas More. The most accessible edition of William Roper's 'Life' is *Two Early Tudor Lives: the Life and Death of Cardinal Wolsey by George Cavendish; The Life of Sir Thomas More by William Roper* ed. R.S. Sylvester and D.P. Harding (New Haven, CT, 1962). The other earliest 'Lives' are: Nicholas Harpsfield, *The life and death of Sir Thomas Moore, knight, sometymes Lord high Chancellor of England, written in the tyme of Queene Marie* ed. E.V. Hitchcock (Early English Text Society, Original Series no. 186, London, 1932); Thomas Stapleton, *Tres Thomae, seu de S. Thomae Apostoli rebus gestis, de S. Thoma Archiepiscopo Cantuariensi et Martyre, D. Thomae Mori Angliae quondam Cancellarii Vita* (Douai, 1588), which is translated by P.E. Hallett as *The Life and Illustrious Martyrdom of Sir Thomas More* (London, 1928). The later generation of recusant 'Lives' comprises: Ro. Ba., *The lyfe of Syr Thomas More, sometymes Lord Chancellor of England* ed. E.V. Hitchcock and P.E. Hallett (Early English Text Society, Original Series no. 222, London, 1950); Cresacre More, *The Life of Sir Thomas More* ed. J. Hunter (London, 1828).

Modern biographies of Thomas More begin with T.E. Bridgett, *Life and Writings of Blessed Thomas More* (London, 1924), an outstanding work of scholarship first published in 1891 to mark More's beatification in 1886. Its confessional bias is not unduly obtrusive. The most influential 'Life' is R.W. Chambers, *Thomas More* (London, 1935), but the work is dated, patronizing and not averse to misrepresentation despite its apparent cosiness. The most distinguished modern biography is Richard Marius,

Thomas More (New York, 1984). Marius is the leading revisionist of Thomas More. He can be severe in his judgement, and the biography has psychobiographical elements. These also appear in Alistair Fox, *Thomas More: History and Providence* (Oxford, 1983). A study of More's literary works, the book has important biographical themes linked to the work of the revisionists. Although not a biographer, G.R. Elton laid down the lines of the revisionist argument in a series of articles. See especially, 'Thomas More, Councillor', 'Thomas More and the Opposition to Henry VIII', 'The Real Thomas More', and 'Thomas More and Thomas Cromwell' in G.R. Elton, *Studies in Tudor and Stuart Politics and Government* (4 vols, Cambridge, 1974–92) 1, pp. 129–54, 155–72; 3, pp. 344–55; 4, pp. 144–60. Elton's *Policy and Police: the Enforcement of the Reformation in the Age of Thomas Cromwell* (Cambridge, 1972) is also essential for More's interrogations and trial. More's professional career is discussed by John Guy, *The Public Career of Sir Thomas More* (Brighton and New Haven, CT, 1980). An attempt to reverse the revisionist tide is L.L. Martz, *Thomas More: the Search for the Inner Man* (New Haven, CT, 1990). The latest and most accessible biography is P. Ackroyd, *The Life of Thomas More* (London, 1998). Other accessible works with a Catholic confessional bias are E.E. Reynolds, *The Life and Death of St Thomas More* (London, 1978); Reynolds, *Saint Thomas More* (London, 1953); Reynolds, *The Field is Won* (London, 1968); *The Trial of St Thomas More* (London, 1964); *Thomas More and Erasmus* (London, 1965).

There are several outstanding introductory studies of the reign of Henry VIII. G.R. Elton, *Reform and Reformation: England, 1509–1558* (London, 1977) is a lively summary of Elton's revisionist views and a standard textbook. John Guy, *Tudor England* (Oxford, 1990) is a comprehensive standard textbook on the Tudors. Guy, ed., *The Tudor Monarchy* (London, 1997) is a collection of seminal essays by distinguished historians on Tudor politics, the monarchy, and the break with Rome. John Guy, *The Tudors: A Very Short Introduction* (Oxford, 2000) is the simplest and most accessible introduction to the Tudors. Guy, *Cardinal Wolsey* (Oxford, Headstart History Papers, 1998) is the most concise survey of Wolsey's career and relationship with Henry VIII. P. Gwyn, *The King's Cardinal: the Rise and Fall of Thomas Wolsey* (London, 1990) is a useful survey of the latest academic research, but at indiscriminate length. C. Haigh,

English Reformations: Religion, Politics, and Society under the Tudors (Oxford, 1993) is the leading current textbook on the Henrician and later Reformations. E.W. Ives, *Anne Boleyn* (Oxford, 1986) is not merely a life of Anne, but a highly readable survey of the politics of the reign. D. Knowles, *The Religious Orders in England, Volume III, The Tudor Age* (Cambridge, 1959) is a classic account of Henry VIII's 'domino effect' at its climax. D. MacCulloch, ed., *The Reign of Henry VIII: Politics, Policy and Piety* (London, 1995) is a collection of essays summarizing the latest research aimed at students, especially strong on politics and the Church. MacCulloch's *Thomas Cranmer: A Life* (London, 1996) is a distinguished history of the period from a viewpoint different to More's. R. Rex, *Henry VIII and the English Reformation* (London, 1993) is a valuable survey for students, illuminating the anti-Lutheran campaign and the aims of Henry VIII's policy on the Church. The most distinguished and readable biography of the King is still J.J. Scarisbrick, *Henry VIII* (London, 1968). D.R. Starkey, *The Reign of Henry VIII: Personalities and Politics* (London, 1985) is a lively and accessible account of Court politics and faction.

For modern critical editions of More's own writings, scholars are indebted to the Yale Edition of the Complete Works of St Thomas More (New Haven, CT, 1963–). More's writings fall into four groups: (1) humanistic; (2) controversial; (3) devotional; (4) letters. The humanistic writings (1) comprise: *Translations of Lucian* (Yale Edition, Vol. 3, Pt. 1, ed. C.R. Thompson); *Latin Poems* (Yale Edition, Vol. 3, Pt. 2, ed. C.H. Miller *et al.*); *Utopia* (Yale Edition, Vol. 4, ed. E. Surtz and J.H. Hexter); *Historia Richardi Tertii* and *History of King Richard III* (Latin and English versions: Yale Edition, Vol. 2, ed. R.S. Sylvester; Vol. 15, ed. D. Kinney); *Letter to Martin Dorp, Letter to the University of Oxford, Letter to Edward Lee, Letter to a Monk* (Yale Edition, Vol. 15, ed. D. Kinney). The controversial works (2) comprise: *Responsio ad Lutherum* (Yale Edition, Vol. 5, ed. J.M. Headley); *Dialogue Concerning Heresies* (Yale Edition, Vol. 6, ed. T. Lawler *et al.*); *Confutation of Tyndale's Answer* (Yale Edition, Vol. 8, ed. L.A. Schuster *et al.*); *Apology* (Yale Edition, Vol. 9, ed. J.B. Trapp); *Debellation of Salem and Bizance* (Yale Edition, Vol. 10, ed. John Guy *et al.*); *Answer to a Poisoned Book* (Yale Edition, Vol. 11, ed. S.M. Foley *et al.*). The devotional writings (3) comprise: *English Poems, Life of Pico, Four Last Things* (Yale Edition, Vol 1, ed. C.H. Miller *et al.*); *Dialogue of Comfort against Tribulation* (Yale Edition, Vol. 12, ed. L.L. Martz *et al.*); *Treatise on the Passion, Treatise on the Blessed Body, Instructions and Prayers* (Yale Edition, Vol. 13, ed. G.E. Haupt); *De Tristitia Christi* (Yale Edition, Vol. 14, ed. C.H. Miller). More's letters (4) are published in *The Correspondence of Sir Thomas More* ed. E.F. Rogers (Princeton, NJ, 1947); *St Thomas More: Selected Letters* ed. E.F. Rogers (New Haven, CT, 1961); *Sir Thomas More: Neue Briefe* ed. H. Schulte Herbrüggen (Münster, 1966); C.H. Miller, ed., 'Thomas More's Letters to Frans van Cranevelt', *Moreana* 31 (1994), pp. 3–66.

The best critical edition of *Utopia* and translation is *More: Utopia. Latin Text and English Translation* ed. G.M. Logan, R.M. Adams and C.H. Miller (Cambridge, 1995). Ralph Robinson's 1551 translation is available in *Utopia and the Dialogue of Comfort*, ed. J. Warrington (London, 1910, repr. 1962). For the context of *Utopia* in Renaissance political thought, see Q. Skinner, *The Foundations of Modern Political Thought* (2 vols, Cambridge, 1978), and Skinner's chapter in *The Cambridge History of Renaissance Philosophy* ed. C.B. Schmitt *et al.* (Cambridge, 1988), pp. 387–452. A full bibliography of editions of *Utopia* and works of modern critical scholarship is provided by Logan, Adams and Miller, pp. xlii–xlvi. The crucial modern interpretations are: Q. Skinner, 'More's *Utopia*', *Past and Present* 38 (1967), pp. 153–68; Skinner, 'Sir Thomas More's *Utopia* and the Language of Renaissance Humanism', in A. Pagden, ed., *The Languages of Political Theory in Early Modern Europe* (Cambridge, 1987), pp. 123–57; B. Bradshaw, 'More on Utopia', *Historical Journal* 24 (1981), pp. 1–27; J.H. Hexter, *More's 'Utopia': the Biography of an Idea* (Princeton, 1952); Hexter, '*Utopia* and its Historical Milieu', in *CW* 4, pp. xxiii–cxxiv; E. Surtz, '*Utopia* as a Work of Literary Art' and 'Sources, Parallels and Influences', in *CW* 4, pp. cxxv–cliii, cliii–clxxxi; Surtz, *The Praise of Wisdom: A Commentary of the Religious and Moral Problems and Backgrounds of St Thomas More's 'Utopia'* (Chicago, 1957); D.B. Fenlon, 'England and Europe: Utopia and its Aftermath', *Transactions of the Royal Historical Society, 5th Series* 25 (1975), pp. 115–36. A Marxist interpretation is K. Kautsky, *Thomas More and his Utopia with a Historical Introduction* trans. H.J. Stenning (London, 1927). A more sophisticated version of the same paradigm is R. Ames, *Citizen Thomas More and his Utopia* (Oxford, 1949). For a literalist reading, see

M. Eliav-Feldon, *Realistic Utopias: the Ideal Imaginary Societies of the Renaissance 1516–1630* (Oxford, 1982). G.M. Logan, *The Meaning of More's 'Utopia'* (Princeton, 1983) is useful for the classical and Renaissance contexts.

Other invaluable specialist works include: D. Baker-Smith, ' "A Fool Among Knaves": the Humanist Dilemma of Counsel', *Bulletin of the Society for Renaissance Studies* 1:1 (1983), pp. 1–9; Baker-Smith, *More's Utopia* (London, 1991); P.W.M. Blayney, 'The Booke of Sir Thomas Moore Re-examined', *Studies in Philology*, 69 (1972), pp. 167–91; B. Bradshaw, 'The Controversial Sir Thomas More', *Journal of Ecclesiastical History* 36 (1985), pp. 535–69; J. Bruce, ed., 'Inedited Documents Relating to the Imprisonment and Condemnation of Sir Thomas More', *Archaeologia* 27 (1838), pp. 361–74; B. Byron, *Loyalty in the Spirituality of St Thomas More*, Bibliotheca Humanistica et Reformatorica, no. 4 (Nieuwkoop, 1972); J. Duncan M. Derrett, 'Sir Thomas More as a Martyr', *Downside Review* 101 (1983), pp. 187–93; Derrett, 'The Trial of Sir Thomas More', *English Historical Review* 79 (1964), pp. 449–77; Derrett, 'The "New" Document on Thomas More's Trial', *Moreana*, 3 (1964), pp. 5–19; Derrett, 'Neglected Versions of the Contemporary Account of the Trial of Sir Thomas More', *Bulletin of the Institute of Historical Research* 33 (1960), pp. 202–23; D. Fenlon, 'Thomas More and Tyranny', *Journal of Ecclesiastical History* 32 (1981), pp. 453–76; M. Fleisher, *Radical Reform and Political Persuasion in the Life and Writings of Thomas More* (Geneva, 1973); Alistair Fox and John Guy, *Reassessing the Henrician Age: Humanism, Politics and Reform 1500–1550* (Oxford, 1986); R.W. Gibson and J.M. Patrick, *St Thomas More: A Preliminary Bibliography of His Works and of Moreana to the Year 1750* (New Haven, 1961); D. Ginsberg, 'Ploughboys versus Prelates: Tyndale and More and the Politics of Biblical Translation', *Sixteenth Century Journal* 19 (1988), pp. 45–61; B. Gogan, *The Common Corps of Christendom: Ecclesiological Themes in the Writings of Sir Thomas More* (Leiden, 1982); John Guy, 'Sir Thomas More and the Heretics', *History Today* 30:2 (1980), pp. 11–15; John Guy, 'Thomas More as Successor to Wolsey', *Thought* 52 (1977), pp. 275–92; D. Hay, 'A Note on More and the General Council', *Moreana* 15 (1967), pp. 249–51; J.M. Headley, 'More against Luther: On Laws and the Magistrate', *Moreana* 15 (1967), pp. 211–23; S.B. House, 'Sir Thomas More as Church Patron', *Journal of Ecclesiastical*

History 40 (1989), pp. 208–18; A. Kenny, *Thomas More* (Oxford, 1983); G. Marc'hadour, *L'Univers de Thomas More* (Paris, 1963); G. Marc'hadour, *The Bible in the Works of St Thomas More* (5 vols, Nieuwkoop, 1969–71); G. Marc'hadour, *Thomas More et la Bible. La place des livres saints dans son apologétique et sa spiritualité* (Paris, 1969); R. Marius, 'Henry VIII, Thomas More, and the Bishop of Rome', in M.J. Moore, ed., *Quincentennial Essays on St Thomas More* (Boone, 1978), pp. 89–107; R. Marius, 'Thomas More and the Early Church Fathers', *Traditio* 24 (1968), pp. 379–407; L.L. Martz, 'Thomas More: the Sacramental Life', *Thought* 52 (1977), pp. 300–18; J.K. McConica, *English Humanists and Reformation Politics under Henry VIII and Edward VI* (Oxford, 1965); C.H. Miller, 'The Heart of the Final Struggle: More's Commentary on the Agony in the Garden', in Moore, ed., *Quincentennial Essays on St Thomas More*, pp. 108–23; S. Morison, *The Likeness of Thomas More: an Iconographical Survey of Three Centuries* supplemented by N. Barker (London, 1963); R. Norrington, *In the Shadow of a Saint: Lady Alice More* (Waddesdon, 1983); F. Oakley, 'Headley, Marius and Conciliarism', *Moreana* 64 (1980), pp. 82–88; R. Pineas, *Thomas More and Tudor Polemics* (Bloomington, 1968); G.D. Ramsay, 'A Saint in the City: Thomas More at Mercers' Hall, London', *English Historical Review* 97 (1982), pp. 269–88; J. Ridley, *The Statesman and the Fanatic: Thomas Wolsey and Thomas More* (London, 1982); E.M.G. Routh, *Sir Thomas More and His Friends 1477–1535* (London, 1934); J.J. Scarisbrick, 'Thomas More: the King's Good Servant', *Thought* 52 (1977), pp. 249–68; R.J. Schoeck, 'The Place of Sir Thomas More in Legal History and Tradition', *Moreana* 51 (1976), pp. 83–94; R.J. Schoeck, *The Achievement of Thomas More: Aspects of His Life and Works* (Victoria, 1976); P. Sheldrake, 'Authority and Consensus in Thomas More's Doctrine of the Church', *Heythrop Journal* 20 (1979), pp. 146–72; C. Smith, 'An Updating of R.W. Gibson's *St Thomas More: A Preliminary Bibliography*', *Sixteenth Century Bibliography* 20 (1981), pp. i–iii, 1–46; R.S. Sylvester, 'Thomas More: Humanist in Action', in O.B. Hardison Jr., ed., *Medieval and Renaissance Studies* (Chapel Hill, 1966), pp. 125–37; R.S. Sylvester and G. Marc'hadour, eds, *Essential Articles for the Study of Thomas More* (Hamden, CT, 1977); R.S. Sylvester, ed., *St Thomas More: Action and Contemplation. Proceedings of the Symposium held at St John's University, October 9–10, 1970*

(New Haven, CT, 1972); J.B. Trapp and H. Schulte Herbrüggen, *'The King's Good Servant': Sir Thomas More 1477/8–1535* (London, 1977); H. Trevor-Roper, 'The Intellectual World of Sir Thomas More', *American Scholar* 48 (1978–9), pp. 19–32; H. de Vocht, *Acta Thomae Mori. History of the Reports of his Trial and Death with an Unedited Contemporary Narrative* (Louvain, 1947); R.M. Warnicke, 'The Harpy in More's Household: Was It Lady Alice?', *Moreana* 22 (1985), pp. 5–13; K. Wells, 'The Iconography of Saint Thomas More', *Studies (Ireland)* 70 (1981), pp. 55–71.

Web Sites

Institute of Historical Research, University of London: http://www.ihr.sas.ac.uk

Author: http://www.tudors.org

Index

Levellers 95
Leycester, Johanna 22
Leycester, John 22
Ligham, Peter 154
Lily, William 27
Linacre, Thomas 24, 25, 27, 28, 52, 57, 211
Lincoln, Abraham (President of the United States) 2
Lincoln's Inn 23, 26, 28, 43
loans 2
localities 131
Lollardy 127
  see also heresy; heretics
London 2, 22–4, 28, 29, 35, 38, 43–6, 51, 54, 57, 58, 62, 63, 84, 94, 110, 112, 118, 119, 121, 128, 136, 138, 151, 157, 189, 196, 209
Longland, John (Bishop of Lincoln) 127, 156
Lords, House of 127, 129, 141–3, 155, 158, 160, 161, 163, 169, 214
Louvain 9, 10, 35, 44, 90, 92, 94
Lucca 62, 213
Lucian of Samosata 68
Lupset, Thomas 74, 91
Luther, Martin 111, 114–19, 122, 201, 202, 220–2
  Babylonian Captivity of the Church 115, 116, 221

Machiavelli, Niccolò 162, 163
  Discourses 163
Mackintosh, Sir James 130
Magna Carta 153, 162, 197
Manne, Catherine 34
Manning, Anne 78
Manning, Henry Edward (Cardinal) 10
Mantua 168
Mao Tse-tung 101
Marc'hadour, Germain 50
Marius, Richard 15, 30, 31, 33–5, 49, 50, 73, 74, 79, 113, 114, 116, 120, 122, 192
martyrdom 4, 8, 166, 181, 193, 199, 214, 219, 223
Martz, Louis 176
Marx, Karl 95, 96, 101
Mary I (Queen of England) 7, 11, 22, 42, 53, 108, 147, 154, 204
Mary II (Queen of England) 12
mercantile litigation 132, 133
Mercers' Company 44

Middlesex 46, 120
Milk Street, Cripplegate 22, 28
Mirandola, Pico della 37, 38
misprision of treason 169, 182
More, Alice 2, 5, 34, 44, 63–5, 69–73, 78, 167, 169, 212
  and oath of succession 167
More, Cicely 63
More, Cresacre
  Life of Sir Thomas More 11, 30, 37
More, Elizabeth 63
More, John (father of Thomas More) 22, 23, 27, 43, 78
More, John (son of Thomas More) 63, 75, 78
More, Sir Thomas 1–3, 6–8, 10, 11, 13, 15–17, 21–3, 30, 31, 33, 42, 49, 58, 62, 68, 71, 78, 84, 85, 94, 110, 111, 112, 113, 126, 128, 139, 146, 147, 152, 170, 186, 187, 193, 204, 205, 211, 212, 216, 222, 223
  anti-Lutheran campaign 37, 113, 114, 116, 119, 122, 154
  and art 67
  attainder 169, 173, 214
  and authority and tradition 36, 115, 116, 117, 182, 196, 197, 200, 201, 213, 221
  his barge 63, 78
  and Elizabeth Barton 169, 179, 214
  his beatification and canonization 4, 9, 10, 30, 68, 91, 223
  and blood sports 66, 87
  and case of the Pope's ship 7, 44, 54, 56, 58, 219
  and censorship 119, 121, 217
  confiscation of his books 194
  and conflict of laws 196
  and consensus of Christendom 12, 90, 114, 117, 118, 154, 171, 178, 179, 197, 200, 201, 203, 204, 222
  conversation with Rich 189, 191, 193, 195
  and coronation of Anne Boleyn 168, 214
  diet 66
  dress 66
  entry into royal service 7, 47–9, 50, 52, 53, 56, 102, 162, 211, 216
  epitaph 6, 11, 79, 106, 120, 177, 217
  and equality 89, 97, 215
  his execution 1, 45, 75, 193, 209
  family and domestic life 1, 2, 5, 31,